A Theory of the Firm

Michael C. Jensen

A THEORY OF THE FIRM

Governance, Residual Claims, and Organizational Forms

Harvard University Press

Cambridge, Massachusetts

London, England

First Harvard University Press paperback edition, 2003

Second printing, 2003

Library of Congress Cataloging-in-Publication Data

Jensen, Michael C.
    A theory of the firm : governance, residual claims, and organizational forms /
Michael C. Jensen.
    p. cm.
Includes bibliographical references and index.
ISBN 0-674-00295-4 (cloth)
ISBN 0-674-01229-1 (paper)
1. Corporate governance. 2. Industrial management. 3. Stockholders. I. Title.
HD2741 .J46 2000
658.4—dc21   00-040908

To my daughters,
Natalie and Stephanie

Contents

Preface

In preparing a collection such as this every author has to resolve the temptation to update everything to the present, and to correct whatever ambiguities and mistakes might have crept into the original documents. Without admitting to such ambiguities, much less mistakes, I have resisted the temptation to engage in wholesale changes. Where possible and necessary I have taken the liberty of updating the text to reflect historical events. Therefore, where the original text may have noted that a legislative act was pending, I have updated the text to show that it has passed. However, I have been careful not to rework the text to prove my point. Nor have I reworked the language to make myself look prescient—despite the temptation. Rather I have tried to make it easy for a reader to use this text without having to remember when the original article was published and what was front page news at the time. Please note that articles were abridged when there was significant overlap in content. The original, unabridged publications are cited at the beginning of each chapter.

Many people deserve recognition for their contribution to this work, including first my coauthors, who are noted at the beginning of each chapter. Second are the many colleagues at both Harvard and the University of Rochester and elsewhere in the profession who have given selflessly of their time and ideas to improve this work. Many of them are noted in the acknowledgements section at the end of the book. This work has been supported by the Harvard Business School Division of Research, The Monitor Company, and the University of Rochester Simon School of Business. I have been aided by the devoted efforts of Margaret Oliveira, my assistant at Harvard, and Nancy Nichols, at Monitor. In her role as editor, Nancy contributed enormously to the organization, integration, and updating of this manuscript. Margie has handled the production of the manuscript, finding and updating material and creating the index with her usual incredible competence and care. Without these two people this book would not exist.

Michael C. Jensen

May 2000

A Theory of the Firm

Introduction

This book contains eight articles written over the past thirty years in which my coauthors (noted in the chapters) and I address various aspects of the theory of the firm. These articles emanated from our desire to understand more thoroughly the forces pushing firms to operate efficiently and create value, thereby improving human living standards. Only a thorough understanding of such forces can lead to better organizational and management practices and to more effective legal and political rules of the game. To accomplish these goals it is necessary to understand the nature of the corporation in a very fundamental way. After all, the corporation is only one of many ways of organizing productive activities, and the existence of other organizational forms (such as partnerships, mutuals, and nonprofits) indicates that it is not always the best way.

The public corporation is the nexus for a complex set of voluntary contracts among customers, workers, managers, and the suppliers of materials, capital, and risk bearing. This means the parties contract, not between themselves bilaterally, but unilaterally with the legal fiction called the "corporation," thus greatly simplifying the contracting process. The rights of the interacting parties are determined by law, the corporation's charter, and the implicit and explicit contracts with each individual.

Corporations, like all organizations, vest control rights in the constituency bearing the residual risk, which is the risk associated with the difference between the random cash inflows and outflows of the organization. In partnerships and privately held companies, for example, these residual claims and the organizational control rights are restricted to major decision agents (directors and managers); in mutuals and consumer cooperatives, to customers; and in supplier cooperatives, to suppliers.

Corporations are unique organizations because they make no restrictions on who can own their residual claims, thus making it possible for customers, managers, labor, and suppliers to avoid bearing any of the corporate residual risk. Because stockholders guarantee the contracts of all constituents, they bear the corporation's residual risk. The absence of restrictions on who can own corporate residual claims allows specialization in risk bearing by those investors who are most adept at carrying out that function. As a result, the corporation realizes great efficiencies in risk bearing that reduce cost substantially and allow it to meet market demand more efficiently than other organizations.

Although the identities of the bearers of residual risk may differ, all business organizations vest organizational control rights in them. For control to rest in any other group would be equivalent to allowing the group to play poker with someone else's money and would create inefficiencies that lead to the possibility of failure. The implicit denial of this basic proposition is the fallacy lying behind the so-called stakeholder theory of the corporation. According to this theory, the directors and managers of the corporation are to run it in the interests of all stakeholders, not just the residual claimants.

Unfortunately, proponents of stakeholder theory offer no explanation of how conflicts between different stakeholders are to be resolved. This leaves managers with no principle on which to base decisions, making them accountable to no one but their own preferences—ironically, the very opposite result from that stakeholder theorists hope to achieve. Rather, maximizing the total market value of the organization's claims makes the largest contribution to society as a whole (as long as there are no externalities or single-price monopolies). Moreover, this criterion gives managers a decision rule for making trade-offs among conflicting stakeholders: invest an additional dollar in increasing product quality, in improving working conditions for employees, or in serving suppliers up to the point at which such expenditures increase the value of the firm by at least a dollar. This condition will generally hold as long as consumers, employees, and suppliers value the output of the additional expenditures by at least a dollar. This makes it clear why the value-maximizing criterion is the corporate objective that maximizes the size of the social pie. Stockholders, as the bearers of residual risk, hold the right to control the corporation and have incentives to maximize corporate value, although they delegate much of this control to a board of directors who hire, fire, and set the compensation of at least the chief executive officer (CEO).

Proof of the efficiency of the corporate organizational form shows dramatically in market performance. In principle, any organizational form can supply goods and services. All organizational forms compete for consumers, managers, labor, and supplies of capital and other goods. Those that supply the goods demanded by customers at the lowest price win out. The dominance of the corporate form of organization in large-scale, nonfinancial activities indicates that it is winning in this competition. Yet in spite of this relative success it is clear from the evidence of the last twenty-five years that the corporation has failed in many ways as an organizing device.

When control of the agency costs in the relationship between the board and the stockholders broke down in the 1960s, the solution that arose in the 1970s and 1980s was hostile takeovers and other highly controversial activities in the market for corporate control. By my estimates the frenzy of activity in the corporate control market that began in the early 1970s and led to a major restructuring of corporate America came about when the value destruction inherent in the typical U.S. corporation began to approach 30% of its total value.

Consider the following: during the height of the frenzy of activity in the corporate control market premiums routinely averaged 50%. Assuming a company was valued at $10 per share, the price offered to take the company over would then have averaged around $15. Using that logic we can see that the pre-takeover managers had destroyed roughly 30% of that company's value. The sources of that destruction and various remedies imposed are covered in the first part of this book. The takeover movement generated increases in corporate efficiency that exceeded a trillion and a half dollars in value at the time and laid the foundation for the even greater gains from the booming economy enjoyed in the 1990s.

The three chapters in Part I deal with the effects of internal governance systems and the market for corporate control on the behavior and value of corporations. They were motivated by the vast controversy and changes in the structure of corporate America brought about by hostile takeovers, leveraged buyouts (LBOs), and the market for corporate control in the 1970s and 1980s. The first chapter summarizes the lessons from the 1980s. The second chapter discusses in detail the effects that the major political and technological revolutions of the past twenty-five years are having on corporate control systems, corporate efficiency, and the necessity for major corporate restructuring worldwide. The final chapter of this part of the book discusses the important innovations in management, organizational, and financial practices during this period that are bringing about substantial increases in efficiency and productivity.

I think it is useful to revisit the debate surrounding takeovers because it is a cautionary tale. It reminds us that what we were most afraid of—the massive restructuring that most politicians, journalists, and managers believed was making America weak—was actually making us strong; that those who looked strong and stable (the Japanese) were actually stagnating; and that what appeared virtuous—investing in our future through research and development (R&D)—was actually wasteful. Perhaps more important, the debate over takeovers highlights a very important truth about business: assets in the hands of one set of managers (the leveraged buyout specialists, for example) can be much more productive and worth much more than assets in the hands of another group (those we used to call "entrenched" management). And the interesting thing about this difference is that it seems to be due to the systems rather than to the particular people involved. By systems I mean to include such factors as ownership, governance, and financial policies, decentralized management, and better and higher powered incentives.

The success of these massive real-time experiments in new management and governance techniques over the last two decades is a testament to the power of aligning the interests of principals and agents. And it is the reason that we must think hard about the topics in the rest of the book—including, but not limited to, the conflict between principals and agents, and how we organize our work. All of this takes on more importance in light of the fact that we are in the midst of an unusually powerful shift in the worldwide economy, one strong enough to be labeled the "Third Industrial Revolution."

The chapters in Part I have an external focus. They are concerned with major changes in the external rules of the game within which businesses operate, including the financial and control markets, the political and regulatory systems, and the vast changes and challenges brought about by the worldwide political and technological revolutions that are increasing efficiency and capacity in almost every corner of economic activity. As such the reader will connect with many familiar themes on the political and media landscape in the 1970s and 1980s.

Part II on the other hand offers a detailed analysis of various aspects of the internal organizational rules of the game. It deals with how the game is played inside the organization. These chapters have a much more scholarly, analytical tone. They deal with the deep and inherent conflicts of interest between individuals as managers, owners, creditors, employees, and suppliers, and how alternative ways of organizing and managing can exacerbate or ameliorate these conflicts and the resulting inefficiencies and wealth destruction. Eliminating such inefficiencies provides huge opportunities for wealth creation.

Chapter 4, whose title echoes that of this book, deals with the fundamental principles of agency theory, but centered on the conflicts of interest between managers, common stockholders, and debtholders. Because of its centrality to the topic of this volume I have included it here even though the chapter also appears in my earlier collection *Foundations of Organizational Strategy* (Harvard University Press, 1998). My coauthor, Bill Meckling, and I derive the general principles of agency theory, based on the proposition that all individuals are rational beings who choose among alternatives in an effort to better themselves. This means that ultimately people are self-interested, which is frequently misinterpreted to mean they have no altruistic desires and preferences for the well-being of others. In fact, it means only that people are not perfect agents for others; in other words, people will not act in the interests of others (their principals or partners) to the exclusion of their own preferences. (See Jensen 1994.) Even the late Mother Teresa, devoted as she was to the welfare of the poor of Calcutta, would probably have refused an invitation to devote her time to raising funds for the Boston Symphony Orchestra. She would likely have chosen to exercise her own preferences over the allocation of her time, not ours. Even more obvious, perhaps, is the fact that while I care deeply about the welfare of my daughters, that does not mean that I am willing to do their bidding independently of my own desires—as any parent surely will agree. This no-perfect-agent proposition is true for everyone, and it leads inevitably to conflicts of interest anytime human beings attempt to engage in cooperative behavior. Indeed, it was these agency costs that led to the takeover movement discussed in Part I when the costs of the conflicts of interest between managers and shareholders became excessively large.

Agency theory as Bill and I derived it is founded on the self-interest of all individuals and leads to the conclusion that it pays individuals to create structures and incentives that minimize the costs due to conflicts of interest between themselves. They do so because they can benefit by reducing the waste that otherwise results from these conflicts. The principles of agency theory apply to all cooperative endeavors by human beings, including social relationships as well as commercial ones. Agency costs are just as real as the costs of the iron ore and labor hours that go into the manufacture of automobiles or any other product. They are the costs associated with cooperation of virtually any type.

We concentrate in Chapter 4 on the contributions that agency theory can make to helping us understand the role of incentive compensation, auditing, bonding, strip financing, the structure of LBOs, and other interesting phenomena on the worldwide business scene. Those who wish a more detailed discussion of these matters, including the development of a more complete theory of organizations and management, will find the material in my *Foundations of Organizational Strategy* (Harvard University Press, 1998) of interest. Chapter 5 pursues this agency analysis in more depth and with a wider range of conflicts of interest between managers and shareholders and between shareholders and creditors.

Chapter 6 deals with the efficiency effects of alternative ways of organizing the claims on a firm, including organizational structures that do not allow common stock residual claims to be held by anyone other than the corporations' employees—what has commonly been called the "labor-managed" or "codetermined" firm. It has much relevance to the failure of former Soviet, Eastern bloc, and Asian firms that have been organized in ways like this. Chapter 7 deals with the effects of alternative forms of residual claims that range all the way from the common stock of the publicly held corporation, to the privately held partnership, to the nonprofit organization. Chapter 8 surveys the scientific work on the distribution of power among corporate managers, shareholders, and directors. The chapter summarizes empirical evidence on the effects of insider and outsider stock ownership on managerial behavior, corporate performance, and stockholder voting in proxy contests; corporate leverage, managerial stock ownership, and the control market; the effects of departures from one share, one vote on firm value and efficiency; and the increased turnover of top managers when corporate performance is poor.

PART I   Corporate Governance and the Market for Corporate Control

1 | U.S. Corporate Governance: Lessons from the 1980s

Corporate governance is an issue of great concern to owners of common stocks because stockholder wealth depends in large part upon the goals of people who set the strategy of the corporation. Who is the boss, and whose interests come first?

The objectives of corporate managers often conflict with those of the shareholders who own the company. Laws and regulations enacted since the 1930s have effectively put most of the power in the hands of management, frequently at the expense of the interests of the owners of the corporation. At the same time, boards of directors have tended to go along with management and to ignore the interests of the very party they were created to protect.

The takeover boom of the 1980s brought the subject of corporate governance to the front pages of newspapers as a revolution was mounted against the power complexes at corporate headquarters. The mergers, acquisitions, leveraged buyouts (LBOs), and other leveraged restructurings of the 1980s constituted an assault on entrenched authority that was long overdue. Control of the corporation was transformed from a means of perpetuating established arrangements into a marketplace where the highest bidder made certain that the owners' interests would prevail. In many cases, the result was a convergence of interests between management and owners. New methods of finance meant that even large companies were vulnerable to attack; the steady increase in the size of the deals culminated in the $25 billion buyout of RJR-Nabisco in 1989 by Kohlberg, Kravis, and Roberts (KKR), a leveraged buyout firm organized as a partnership with fewer than sixty employees.

The effect of such transactions was to transfer control over vast cor-

By Michael C. Jensen with Donald H. Chew; originally published in *The Portable MBA in Investment,* ed. Peter Bernstein (New York: John Wiley and Sons, 1995), pp. 377–406. Reprinted by permission of John Wiley and Sons, Inc.

porate resources—often trapped in mature industries or uneconomic conglomerates—to those prepared to pay large premiums to use those resources more efficiently. In some cases, the acquirers functioned as agents rather than principals, selling part or all of the assets they acquired to others. In many cases, the acquirers were unaffiliated individual investors (branded as "corporate raiders" by those opposed to the transfer of control) rather than other large public corporations. The increased asset sales, enlarged payouts, and heavy use of debt to finance such takeovers led to a large-scale return of equity capital to shareholders.

The consequence of this control activity has been a pronounced trend toward smaller, more focused, more efficient—and in many cases private—corporations. While capital and resources were being forced out of our largest companies throughout the 1980s, the small- to medium-sized U.S. corporate sector experienced vigorous growth in employment and capital spending. And, at the same time our capital markets were bringing about this massive transfer of corporate resources, the U.S. economy experienced a ninety-two-month expansion and record-high percentages of people employed.

The resulting transfer of control from corporate managers to increasingly active investors aroused enormous controversy. The strongest opposition came from groups whose power and influence were being challenged by corporate restructuring, notably the Business Roundtable (the voice of managers of large corporations), organized labor, and politicians whose ties to wealth and power were being weakened. The media, always responsive to popular opinion even as they help shape it, succeeded in reinvigorating the American populist tradition of hostility to Wall Street financiers. The controversy pitting Main Street against Wall Street was wrought to a pitch that recalled the intensity of the 1930s. Newspapers, books, and magazines obliged the public's desire for villains by furnishing unflattering detailed accounts of the private behavior of corporate raiders.

Barbarians at the Gate, for example, the best-selling account of the RJR-Nabisco transaction, is perhaps best described as an attempt to expose the greed and chicanery that went into the making of some Wall Street deals.[1] And, on that score, the book is effective (although it is worth noting that, amid the general destruction of reputations, the principals of KKR and most of the Drexel team come across as professional and principled). But what also emerges from the more than 500 pages—although the authors seem to have failed to grasp its import—is clear evidence of corporate-wide inefficiencies at RJR-Nabisco, including massive waste of corporate "free cash flow." It was the prospect of eliminating this waste that allowed KKR to pay existing stockholders $12 billion over the previous market value for the right to bring about change.

Since this control change, KKR defied skeptics by managing the company's huge debt load without losses, extracted some $6 billion in capital through asset sales, and brought the company public again in two separate offerings in March and April of 1991. KKR ended its investment in the RJR-Nabisco LBO in March 1995—exchanging much of its stake in RJR for 100% ownership of Borden in an LBO of that company. KKR's remaining shares of RJR were subsequently transferred to Borden to help improve the firm's balance sheet. As of April 1995, the consequences of the RJR buyout for pre-buyout shareholders, the banks, and junk bond investors were a remarkable $15 billion in added value over what an investment in the S&P 500 would have earned (Kaplan 1995). The deal was much less successful, however, for KKR's original equity investors in the RJR buyout. The return on their investment amounted to only 0.5% annually compounded,[2] substantially less than the S&P 500 earned during the same period, and dramatically below the 30% annual returns earned by its other investments.[3]

For economists and management scientists concerned about corporate efficiency, the RJR story is deeply disturbing. What troubles us is not so much the millions of dollars spent on sports celebrities and airplanes—or the greed and unprofessional behavior of several leading investment bankers—but rather the waste prior to the KKR buyout of billions in unproductive capital expenditures and organizational inefficiencies.[4] Viewed in this light—although, here again, the authors do not seem aware of the significance of their findings—*Barbarians* is testimony to the massive failure of the internal control system under the lead of RJR's board of directors. As former head of the Securities and Exchange Commission (SEC) Joseph Grundfest has put it, the real "barbarians" in this book were *inside* the gates (Grundfest 1990a).

Moreover, the fact that RJR's chief executive officer (CEO) Ross Johnson was held up by *Fortune* as a model corporate leader only months before the buyout (Saporito 1988) attests to the difficulty of detecting even such gross inefficiencies and thus suggests that organizational problems of this magnitude may extend well beyond RJR. Although parts of Corporate America may be guilty of underinvesting—as the media continually assert—there is little doubt that many of the largest U.S. companies have grossly overinvested, whether in desperate attempts to maintain sales and earnings in mature or declining businesses or by diversifying outside of their core businesses.

This is what we mean by waste of corporate free cash flow. Many of the best-known companies—GE, IBM, and Kodak come to mind most readily—have wasted vast amounts of resources by chronically overinvesting and overstaffing—a fact that reflects the widespread failure of corporate internal control systems. It is this fundamental control problem over free cash flow that gave rise to a large part of the corporate restructuring movement of the 1980s.

1.1 The Media and the Academy

The role of takeovers and LBOs in curbing corporate inefficiency was not, for the most part, the story being told by our mass media. The journalistic method of inquiry is based on the investigation of individual cases, a process highly prone to "selection bias." The typical journalistic product is a series of anecdotes—stories that almost invariably carry with them a strong emotive appeal for the "victims" of control changes, but with little or no attention paid to long-run efficiency effects. So when media accounts do manage to raise their focus above the "morality play" craved by the public to consider broader issues of economic efficiency and competitiveness, the message is invariably the same: leveraged restructurings are eroding the competitive strength of U.S. corporations by forcing cutbacks in employment, research and development (R&D), and capital investment.

Using very different methods and language than journalists, academic economists have subjected corporate control activity to intensive study. Their results are in stark contrast to the popular rhetoric. Indeed, we know of no area in economics today where the divergence between popular belief and the evidence from scholarly research is so great.

The most careful academic research strongly suggests that takeovers—along with leveraged restructurings prompted by the threat of takeover—have generated large gains for shareholders and for the economy as a whole. Our estimates indicate that from 1976 to 1994 over 45,000 control transactions occurred—including mergers, tender offers, divestitures, and LBOs, totaling $3.3 trillion (in 1994 dollars). The premiums paid to selling firms and their shareholders in these transactions totaled $959 billion (1994 dollars) (*Mergerstat Review* 1994). And this estimate includes neither the gains to the buyers in such transactions nor the value of efficiency improvements by companies pressured by control market activity into reforming *without* a visible control transaction.

To be sure, some part of the shareholder gains in highly leveraged transactions (HLTs) came at the expense of bondholders, banks, and other creditors who financed the deals. But total creditor losses probably did not exceed $25 billion through 1990 and, accrued through 1994, were probably less than $50 billion in 1994 dollars.[5] (To put this number into perspective, IBM alone saw its equity value fall by $25 billion in a six-month period during 1991.) Thus far there is no reliable evidence that any appreciable part of the remaining $900 billion or so of net gains to stockholders came at the expense of other corporate stakeholders such as employees, suppliers, and the IRS.[6]

These well-documented increases in shareholder value were largely dismissed by journalists and other critics of restructuring as "paper gains" having little bearing on the long-term vitality and competitiveness of American business. For such observers, these gains were interpreted as evidence of the "short-term" investor mentality that was said to be destroying American business.

For financial economists, however, theory and evidence suggest that as long as such value increases do not arise from transfers from other parties to the corporate "contract," they should be viewed as reliable predictors of increases in corporate operating efficiency. And, as discussed later, research on LBOs has indeed produced direct evidence of such efficiencies. Moreover, macroeconomic data suggest a dramatic improvement in the health and productivity of American industry during the 1980s.

1.2 The Political Reaction

Widespread misunderstanding of the nature of these transactions brought both increased scrutiny and additional regulation to HLTs. As a result, toward the end of 1989 and in the first two years of the 1990s restructuring transactions came to a virtual standstill. For example, total merger and acquisition transactions fell from a peak of $247 billion in 1988 to $108 billion in 1990 and to $71 billion in 1992. Although there have been a handful of hostile takeover attempts in recent years (principally by large companies for smaller ones), these acquisitions tended to be the value-destroying "strategic"-type acquisition that we saw in the mid- to late 1960s. They tended to be stock-for-stock deals (where overpayment caused no financial distress) or cash acquisitions funded by free cash flow.

Widespread savings and loan (S&L) failures and a number of highly publicized cases of troubled HLTs have combined with the criminalization of securities law disclosure violations and high-profile RICO and insider trading prosecutions to create a highly charged political climate.[7] Such political forces produced a major reregulation of our financial markets. The political origin of such regulatory initiatives was made clear by the fact that bad real estate loans dwarfed junk bond losses and troubled HLT loans as contributors to the weakness of S&Ls and other financial institutions at the time.

With the eclipse of the new issue market for junk bonds, the application of HLT rules to commercial bank lending, and new restrictions on insurance companies, funding for large HLTs all but disappeared. Even when financing was available, moreover, court decisions (including those authorizing the use of poison pills and defensive employee stock ownership plans) and state antitakeover and control shareholder amendments greatly increased the difficulty of making a successful hostile offer.

1.3 Contracting Problems Compounded by Politics

So what went wrong with the leveraged deals of the 1980s? The story in brief is as follows. As prices were bid up to more competitive levels in the second half of the 1980s, the markets "overshot." Contracting problems between the promoters of HLTs and the suppliers of capital—most important, too little equity capital put up by deal makers and participating managements and front-loaded fees for promoters that paid them for doing deals—led to too many overpriced deals. In this sense, the financial press was right in attributing *part* of the current constraints on debt and takeover markets to unsound transactions. Such transactions, especially those completed after 1985, were overpriced by their promoters and also overleveraged. The transactions, however, would have resulted in significant losses to the new owners regardless of how they were financed; high debt converted the losses into financial distress in some cases.

It is also clear that intense political pressures to curb the corporate control market greatly compounded the problems caused by this "contracting failure." However genuine and justified the concern about our deposit insurance funds, the reactions of Congress, the courts, and regulators to losses (which, again, were predominantly the result of real estate, not HLT loans) had several unfortunate side effects. They sharply restricted the availability of capital to non–investment-grade companies, thereby increasing the rate of corporate defaults. They also limited the ability of financially troubled companies to reorganize outside of court, thus ensuring that most defaulted companies wound up in bankruptcy. All these factors, in our view, contributed greatly to the weakness of the U.S. economy in the early 1990s.

However, it is also clear that the restructuring movement of the 1980s addressed a fundamental problem that still faces many large, mature public companies both in the United States and abroad: namely, excess capacity and, more generally, the conflict between management and shareholders over control of corporate free cash flow. Technological and other developments that began in the mid-twentieth century have led over the past two decades to rapid improvements in productivity, the creation of massive overcapacity, and, consequently, the requirement for exit. The discussion in the chapters that follow considers in some detail worldwide changes driving the demand for exit in today's economy. Also described are the barriers to efficient exit in the U.S. economy and the role of the market for corporate control—takeovers, LBOs, and other leveraged restructurings—in surmounting those barriers.

2 | The Modern Industrial Revolution, Exit, and the Failure of Internal Control Systems

2.1   Introduction

Parallels between the Modern and Historical Industrial Revolutions

Fundamental technological, political, regulatory, and economic forces are radically changing the worldwide competitive environment. We have not seen such a metamorphosis of the economic landscape since the Industrial Revolution of the nineteenth century. The scope and pace of the changes over the past two decades qualify this period as a modern industrial revolution, and I predict it will take decades for these forces to be fully worked out in the worldwide economy.

Although more than a century separates the current and historical economic transformations, the parallels between the two are strikingly similar: most notably the widespread technological and organizational change leading to declining costs, increasing average but decreasing marginal productivity of labor, reduced growth rates in labor income, excess capacity, and—ultimately—downsizing and exit.

The capital markets played a major role in eliminating excess capacity both in the nineteenth century and in the 1980s. The merger boom of the 1890s brought about a massive consolidation of independent firms and the closure of marginal facilities. In the 1980s the capital markets helped eliminate excess capacity through leveraged acquisitions, stock buybacks, hostile takeovers, leveraged buyouts (LBOs), and divisional sales. Just as the takeover specialists of the 1980s were disparaged by managers, policy makers, and the press, the so-called

By Michael C. Jensen; presidential address to the American Finance Association, originally published in *Journal of Finance* (July 1993), pp. 831–880.

Robber Barons were criticized in the nineteenth century. In both cases the criticism was followed by public policy changes that restricted the capital markets: in the nineteenth century the passage of antitrust laws restricting combinations, and in the late 1980s the renewed regulation of the credit markets, antitakeover legislation, and court decisions that restricted the market for corporate control.

Although the vast increases in productivity associated with the nineteenth-century Industrial Revolution increased aggregate welfare, the large costs associated with the obsolescence of human and physical capital generated substantial hardship, misunderstanding, and bitterness. Technological and other developments that began in the mid-twentieth century have culminated in the past two decades in a similar situation: rapidly improving productivity, the creation of overcapacity, and, consequently, the requirement for exit and its attendant displacement of workers. Although efficient exit—because of the ramifications it has on productivity and human welfare—remains an issue of great importance, research on the topic has been relatively sparse since the 1942 publication of Schumpeter's insights on creative destruction.[1] These insights will almost certainly receive renewed attention in the coming decade:

> Every piece of business strategy acquires its true significance only against the background of that process and within the situation created by it. It must be seen in its role in the perennial gale of creative destruction; it cannot be understood irrespective of it or, in fact, on the hypothesis that there is a perennial lull . . . The usual theorist's paper and the usual government commission's report practically never try to see that behavior, on the one hand, as a result of a piece of past history and, on the other hand, as an attempt to deal with a situation that is sure to change presently—as an attempt by those firms to keep on their feet, on ground that is slipping away from under them. In other words, the problem that is usually being visualized is how capitalism administers existing structures, whereas the relevant problem is how it creates and destroys them. (Schumpeter 1976, p. 83)

Current technological and political changes are bringing this issue to the forefront. It is important for managers, policy makers, and researchers to understand the magnitude and generality of the implications of these forces.

Outline of the Chapter

In this chapter, I review the First and Second Industrial Revolutions of the nineteenth century and draw on these experiences to enlighten our understanding of current economic trends. Drawing parallels to the 1800s, I discuss in some detail the changes that mandate exit in today's economy. I address those factors that hinder efficient exit and outline the control forces acting on the corporation to eventually overcome these barriers. Specifically, I describe the role of the market for corporate control in affecting efficient exit and how the shutdown of the capital markets has, to a great extent, transferred this challenge to corporate internal control mechanisms. I summarize evidence, however, indicating that internal control systems have largely failed in bringing about timely exit and downsizing, leaving only the product market or legal/political/regulatory system to resolve excess capacity. Although overcapacity will in the end be eliminated by product market forces, this solution generates large, unnecessary costs. I discuss the forces that render internal control mechanisms ineffective and offer suggestions for their reform. Lastly I address the challenge this modern industrial revolution poses for finance professionals, namely, the changes that we too must undergo to aid in the learning and adjustments that must occur over the next several decades.

2.2   The First and Second Industrial Revolutions

The First Industrial Revolution was distinguished by a shift to capital-intensive production, rapid growth in productivity and living standards, the formation of large corporate hierarchies, overcapacity, and, eventually, closure of facilities. (See the excellent discussions of the period by Chandler 1977, 1990, 1992; Lamoreaux 1985; and McCraw 1981, 1992.) Originating in Britain in the late eighteenth century, the First Industrial Revolution—as Chandler (1990, p. 250) labels it—witnessed the application of new energy sources to methods of production. The mid-nineteenth century witnessed another wave of massive change with the birth of modern transportation and communication facilities, including the railroad, telegraph, steamship, and cable systems. Coupled with the development of high-speed consumer packaging technology, these innovations gave rise to the mass production and distribution systems of the late nineteenth and early twentieth centuries—the Second Industrial Revolution (Chandler 1990, p. 62).

The dramatic changes that occurred from the middle to the end of the century clearly warranted the term "revolution." The invention of the McCormick reaper (1830s), the sewing machine (1844), and high-volume canning and packaging devices (mid-1880s) exemplified a worldwide surge in productivity that "substituted machine tools for human craftsmen, interchangeable parts for hand-tooled components, and the energy of coal for that of wood, water, and animals" (McCraw 1981, p. 3). New technology in the paper industry allowed wood pulp to replace rags as the primary input material (Lamoreaux 1985, p. 41). Continuous rod rolling transformed the wire industry: within a decade, wire nails replaced cut nails as the main source of supply (Lamoreaux 1985, p. 64). Worsted textiles resulting from advances in combing technology changed the woolen textile industry (Lamoreaux 1985, p. 98). Between 1869 and 1899, the capital invested per American manufacturer grew from about $700 to $2,000; in the period 1889 to 1919, the annual growth of total factor productivity was almost six times higher than that which had occurred for most of the nineteenth century (McCraw 1981, p. 3).

As productivity climbed steadily, production costs and prices fell dramatically. The 1882 formation of the Standard Oil Trust, which concentrated nearly 25% of the world's kerosene production into three refineries, reduced the average cost of a gallon of kerosene by 70% between 1882 and 1885. In tobacco, the invention of the Bonsack machine in the early 1880s reduced the labor costs of cigarette production 98.5% (Chandler 1992, p. 5). The Bessemer process reduced the cost of steel rails by 88% from the early 1870s to the late 1890s, and the electrolytic refining process invented in the 1880s reduced the price of a kilo of aluminum by 96% between 1888 and 1895 (Chandler 1992, pp. 4–6). In chemicals, the mass production of synthetic dyes, alkalis, nitrates, fibers, plastics, and film occurred rapidly after 1880. Production costs of synthetic blue dye, for example, fell by 95% from the 1870s to 1886 (Chandler 1992, p. 5). New low-cost sources of superphosphate rock and the manufacture of superphosphates changed the fertilizer industry. In sugar refining, technological changes dramatically lowered the costs of sugar production and changed the industry (Lamoreaux 1985, p. 99).

Lamoreaux (1985) discusses other cases where various stimuli led to major increases in demand and, in turn, expansion that led to excess capacity. This growth occurred in cereals (when "Schumacher broke down the American prejudice against eating oats," p. 98), whisky (when crop failures in Europe created a sudden large demand for U.S. producers, p. 99), and tin plate (when the McKinley tariff raised domestic demand and prices, p. 97).

The surplus capacity developed during the period was exacerbated by the fall in demand brought about by the recession and panic of 1893. Although attempts were made to eliminate overcapacity through pools, associations, and cartels (Lamoreaux 1985, p. 100), not until the capital markets motivated exit in the 1890s' mergers and acquisitions (M&A) boom was the problem substantially resolved. Capacity was reduced through the consolidation and closure of marginal facilities in the merged entities (p. i).

2.3 The Third Industrial Revolution

The major restructuring of the American business community that began in the 1970s and continues at the beginning of the twenty-first century is being brought about by a variety of factors, including changes in physical and management technology, global competition, regulation, taxes, and the conversion of formerly closed, centrally planned socialist and communist economies to capitalism, along with open participation in international trade. These changes are significant in scope and effect; indeed, they are bringing about the Third Industrial Revolution. To understand fully the challenges that current control systems face in light of this change, we must understand more about these general forces sweeping the world economy and why they are generating excess capacity and thus the requirement for exit.

What has generally been referred to as the "decade of the '80s" in the United States actually began in the early 1970s with the tenfold increase in energy prices from 1973 to 1979, and the emergence of the modern market for corporate control and high-yield nonrated bonds in the mid-1970s. These events, among others, were associated with the beginnings of the Third Industrial Revolution, which—if I were to pinpoint a particular date—started at the time of the oil price increases beginning in 1973.

The Decade of the 1980s: Capital Markets Provided an Early Response to the Modern Industrial Revolution

The macroeconomic data for the 1980s shows major productivity gains (Jensen 1991). In fact, 1981 was a watershed year: total factor productivity growth in the manufacturing sector more than doubled after 1981 from 1.4% per year in the period from 1950 to 1981 to 3.3% in the period from 1981 to 1990.[2] Nominal unit labor costs stopped their seventeen-year rise, and real unit labor costs declined by 25%. These lower labor costs came not from reduced wages or employment, but from increased productivity: nominal and real hourly compensation increased by a total of 4.2% and 0.3% per year respectively over the 1981–1989 period.[3] Manufacturing employment reached a low in 1983 but by 1989 had experienced a small cumulative increase of 5.5% (U.S. Department of Labor 1991). Meanwhile, the annual growth in labor productivity increased from 2.3% between 1950 and 1981 to 3.8% between 1981 and 1990, while a thirty-year decline in capital productivity was reversed when the annual change in the productivity of capital increased from −1.03% between 1950 and 1981 to 2.03% between 1981 and 1990.[4]

During the 1980s, the real value of public firms' equity more than doubled from $1.4 to $3 trillion.[5] In addition, real median income increased at the rate of 1.8% per year between 1982 and 1989, reversing the 1.0% per year decrease that occurred from 1973 to 1982 (U.S. Bureau of the Census 1991). Contrary to generally held beliefs, real research and development (R&D) expenditures set record levels every year from 1975 to 1990, growing at an average annual rate of 5.8% *(Business Week). Economist* (1990), in one of the media's few accurate portrayals of this period, noted that from 1980 to 1985, "American industry went on an R&D spending spree, with few big successes to show for it."

Regardless of the gains in productivity, efficiency, and welfare, the 1980s are generally portrayed by politicians, the media, and others as a "decade of greed and excess." In particular, criticism centered on M&A transactions, 35,000 of which occurred from 1976 to 1990, with a total value of $2.6 trillion (1992 dollars). Contrary to common beliefs, only 364 of these offers were contested, and of those only 172 resulted in successful hostile takeovers (*Mergerstat Review* 1991). Indeed, Marty Lipton, prominent defender of American chief executive officers (CEOs), expresses a common, but incorrect, view of the 1980s when he states that "the takeover activity in the United States has imposed short-term profit maximization strategies on American Business at the expense of research, development and capital investment. This is minimizing our ability to compete in world markets and still maintain a growing standard of living at home" (Lipton 1989, p. 2).

On average, selling-firm shareholders in all M&A transactions in the period 1976–1990 were paid premiums over market value of 41%,[6] and total M&A transactions generated $750 billion in gains to target firms' shareholders (measured in 1992 dollars).[7] This value change represents the minimum forecast value change by the buyer (the amount the buyer is willing to pay the seller) and does not include further gains (or losses) reaped by the buyer after execution of the transaction.[8] It includes synergy gains from combining the assets of two or more organizations and the gains from replacing inefficient governance systems, as well as possible wealth transfers from employees, communities, and bondholders.[9] As Shleifer and Summers (1988) point out, if the value gains are merely transfers of wealth from creditors, employees, suppliers, or communities, they do not represent efficiency improvements. Thus far, however, little evidence has been found to support substantial wealth transfers from any group,[10] and it appears that most of these gains represent increases in efficiency.

Part of the attack on M&A transactions centered on the high-yield (or so-called junk) bond market, which eliminated mere size as an effective deterrent against takeover. This opened the management of America's largest corporations to monitoring and discipline from the capital markets. It also helped provide capital for newcomers to compete with existing firms in the product markets.

High-yield bonds opened the public capital markets to small, risky, and unrated firms across the country and made it possible for some of the country's largest firms to be taken over. The sentiment of J. Richard Munro (1989, p. 472), chairman and CEO of Time Inc., exemplifies the critical appraisal of their role: "Notwithstanding television ads to the contrary, junk bonds are designed as the currency of 'casino economics' . . . [T]hey've been used not to create new plants or jobs or products but to do the opposite: to dismantle existing companies so the players can make their profit . . . This isn't the Seventh Cavalry coming to the rescue. It's a scalping party."

The high leverage incurred in the eighties contributed to an increase in the bankruptcy rate of large firms in the early 1990s. That increase was also encouraged by the recession (which in turn was at least partly caused by the restriction in the credit markets implemented in late 1989 and 1990 to offset the trend toward higher leverage) and the revisions in bankruptcy procedures and the tax code (which made it much more difficult to restructure financially distressed firms outside the courts; see

Wruck 1990). The unwise public policy and court decisions that contributed significantly to hampering private adjustment to this financial distress seemed to be at least partially motivated by the general antagonism toward the control market at the time. Even given the difficulties, the general effects of financial distress in the high-yield markets were greatly overemphasized. While precise numbers are difficult to come by, I estimate the total bankruptcy losses to junk bond and bank highly leveraged transaction (HLT) loans from inception of the market in the mid-1970s through 1990 amounted to less than $50 billion (Jensen 1991, n. 9). In comparison, IBM alone lost $51 billion (almost 65% of the total market value of its equity) from its 1991 high to its 1992 close.[11]

Mistakes were made in the takeover activity of the 1980s; indeed, given the far-reaching nature of the restructuring, it would be surprising if none occurred. However, the negative character of general opinion is inconsistent with both the empirical evidence and the almost universal opinion of finance scholars who have studied the phenomenon. In fact, takeover activities were addressing an important set of problems in Corporate America, and doing it before the companies faced serious trouble in the product markets. They were, in effect, providing an early warning system that motivated healthy adjustments to the excess capacity that began to proliferate in the worldwide economy.

Causes of Excess Capacity

Excess capacity can arise in at least four ways, the most obvious of which occurs when market demand falls below the level required to yield returns that will support the currently installed production capacity. This *demand-reduction* scenario is most familiarly associated with recession episodes in the business cycle.

Excess capacity can also arise from two types of technological change. The first type, *capacity-expanding* technological change, increases the output of a given capital stock and organization. An example is the Reduced Instruction Set CPU (RISC) processor innovation in the computer workstation market. RISC processors bring about a tenfold increase in power, but they can be produced by adapting the current production technology. With no increase in the quantity demanded, this change implies that production capacity must fall by 90%. Price declines increase the quantity demanded in these situations and therefore reduce the capacity adjustment that would otherwise be required. If demand is elastic, output of the higher-powered units will grow as it did for much of the computing industry's history; now, however, the new workstation technology is reducing the demand for mainframe computers.

The second type is *obsolescence-creating* change—that is, one that obsoletes the current capital stock and organization. Wal-Mart and the wholesale clubs that are revolutionizing retailing are examples of such change. These new, focused, large-scale, low-cost retailers are dominating old-line department stores, which can no longer compete. Building these new low-cost stores means much current retail capacity becomes obsolete: when Wal-Mart enters a new market total retail capacity expands, and it is common for some of the existing high-cost retail capacity to go out of business.[12] More intensive use of information and other technologies, direct dealing with manufacturers, and the replacement of high-cost, restrictive work-rule union labor are several sources of the competitive advantage of these new organizations.

Finally, excess capacity also results when many competitors simultaneously rush to implement new, highly productive technologies without considering whether the aggregate effects of all such investment will be greater capacity than can be supported by demand in the final product market. Sahlman and Stevenson's (1985) analysis of the Winchester disk drive industry provides an example of this phenomenon. Between 1977 and 1984, venture capitalists invested over $400 million in forty-three different manufacturers of Winchester disk drives; initial public offerings of common stock infused additional capital in excess of $800 million. In mid-1983, the capital markets assigned a value of $5.4 billion to twelve publicly traded, venture-capital-backed hard disk drive manufacturers—yet by the end of 1984, the value assigned to those companies had plummeted to $1.4 billion. Christensen (1993) finds that over 138 firms entered the industry in the period from its creation in 1956 to 1990, and of these 103 subsequently failed and 6 were acquired. Sahlman and Stevenson (1985, p. 7) emphasize the lack of foresight in the industry: "The investment mania visited on the hard disk industry contained inherent assumptions about the long-run industry size and profitability and about future growth, profitability and access to capital for each individual company. These assumptions, had they been stated explicitly, would not have been acceptable to the rational investor." There are clues in the history of the nineteenth century that similar overshooting occurred then as well. Elsewhere (Jensen 1991), I analyze the incentive, information, and contracting problems that cause this overshooting and argue that these problems of boom–bust cycles are general in venture markets—but that they can be corrected by reforming contracts that currently pay promoters for doing deals, rather than for doing successful deals.

Current Forces Leading to Excess Capacity and Exit

The tenfold increase in crude oil prices between 1973 and 1979 had ubiquitous effects, forcing contraction in oil, chemicals, steel, aluminum, and international shipping, among other industries. In addition, the sharp crude oil price increases that motivated major changes to economize on energy had other, perhaps even larger, implications. I believe the reevaluation of organizational processes and procedures stimulated by the oil shock also generated dramatic increases in efficiency beyond the original pure energy-saving projects. The original energy-motivated reexamination of corporate processes helped initiate a major reengineering of company practices and procedures that continues to accelerate throughout the world.

Since the oil price increases of the 1970s, we again have seen systematic overcapacity problems in many industries similar to those of the nineteenth century. While the reasons for this overcapacity nominally differ among industries, I doubt they are independent phenomena. We do not yet fully understand all the causes propelling the rise in excess capacity in the 1980s, yet I believe there were a few basic forces in operation.

Macro policies. Major deregulation of the American economy (including trucking, rail, airlines, telecommunications, banking, and financial services industries) under President Carter contributed to the requirements for exit in these industries (Vietor 1994), as did important changes in the U.S. tax laws that reduced tax advantages to real estate development, construction, and other activities. The end of the cold war has had obvious ramifications for the defense industry as well as less direct effects on the industry's suppliers. In addition, two generations of managerial focus on growth as a recipe for success caused many firms to overshoot their optimal capacity, setting the stage for cutbacks, especially in white collar corporate bureaucracies.

Specifically, in the decade from 1979 to 1989 the *Fortune* 100 firms lost 1.5 million employees, or 14% of their workforce (COMPUSTAT Financial Database).

Technology. Massive changes in technology are clearly part of the cause of the current industrial revolution and its associated excess capacity. Both within and across industries, technological developments have had far-reaching impact. Some examples are the widespread acceptance of radial tires (lasting three to five times longer than the older bias ply technology and providing better gas mileage), which caused excess capacity in the tire industry; the personal computer revolution, which forced contraction of the market for mainframes; the advent of aluminum and plastic alternatives, which reduced demand for steel and glass containers; and fiberoptic, satellite, digital (ISDN), and new compression technologies, which dramatically increased capacity in telecommunication. Wireless personal communications, such as cellular phones and their replacements, promise to further extend this dramatic change.

The changes in computer technology, including miniaturization, have not only revamped the computer industry but also redefined the capabilities of countless other industries. Some estimates indicate the price of computing capacity fell by a factor of 1,000 over the last decade.[13] This means that computer production lines now produce boxes with 1,000 times the capacity for a given price. Consequently, computers are commonplace—in cars, toasters, cameras, stereos, ovens, and so on. A change of similar magnitude in auto production technology would have reduced the price of a $20,000 auto in 1980 to under $20 today. Such increases in capacity and productivity in a basic technology have massive implications for the organization of work and society.

Organizational innovation. Overcapacity can be caused not only by changes in the physical technology, but also by changes in organizational practices and management technology. The vast improvements in telecommunications—including computer networks, electronic mail, teleconferencing, and facsimile transmission—are changing the manner in which people work and interact. It is far less valuable for people to be in the same geographical location to work together effectively, and this is encouraging smaller, more efficient, entrepreneurial organizing units that cooperate through technology.[14] This in turn leads to even more fundamental changes. Through competition "virtual organizations"—networked or transitory organizations where people come together temporarily to complete a task, then separate to pursue their individual specialties—are changing the structure of the traditionally large, bureaucratic organization and contributing to its shrinkage. Virtual organizations tap talented specialists, avoid many of the regulatory costs imposed on permanent structures, and bypass the inefficient work rules and high wages imposed by unions. In doing so, they increase efficiency and thereby further contribute to excess capacity.

In addition, Japanese management techniques such as total quality management, just-in-time production, and flexible manufacturing have significantly increased the efficiency of organizations where they have been successfully implemented throughout the world. Some experts argue that, properly implemented, these new management techniques can reduce defects and spoilage by an order of magnitude. These changes in managing and organizing principles have contributed significantly to the productivity of the world's capital stock and economized on the use of labor and raw materials, thus also contributing to the excess capacity problems.[15]

Globalization of trade. With the globalization of markets, excess capacity tends to occur worldwide. Japan, for example, is currently in the midst of substantial excess capacity caused, at least partially, by the breakdown in its own corporate control system;[16] it now faces the prospect of a massive restructuring of its economy (see Neff et al. 1993). Yet even if the requirement for exit were isolated in the United States, the interdependency of today's world economy would ensure that such overcapacity would have reverberating global implications. For example, the rise of efficient high quality producers of steel and autos in Japan and Korea has contributed to excess capacity in those industries worldwide. Between 1973 and 1990 total capacity in the U.S. steel industry fell by 38% from 156.7 million tons to 97 million tons, and total employment fell over 50% from 509,000 to 252,000.[17] From 1985 to 1989 multifactor productivity in the industry increased at an annual rate of 5.3% compared to 1.3% for the period 1958 to 1989 (Burnham 1993, table 1 and p. 15).

Revolution in political economy. The movement of formerly closed communist and socialist centrally planned economies to more market-oriented, open capitalist economies is likely to generate huge changes in the world economy over the next several decades. These changes promise to cause much conflict, pain, and suffering as world markets adjust, but also large profit opportunities.

More specifically, the rapid pace of the adoption of capitalism, the opening of closed economies, and the dismantlement of central control in communist and socialist states are occurring to various degrees in China, India, Indonesia, Pakistan, other Asian economies, and Africa.[18] This evolution will place a potential labor force of almost a billion people—whose current average income is less than $3 per day—on world markets.[19] Table 2.1 summarizes some of the population and labor force estimates relevant to this issue. The opening of Mexico and other Latin American countries and the transition of communist and socialist central and eastern European economies to open capitalist systems (at least some of which will make the transition in some form) could add almost 200 million laborers with average incomes of less than $14 per day to the world market.

For perspective, Table 2.1 shows that the average daily U.S. income per worker is slightly over $100, and the total labor force numbers about 125 million, and the European Economic Community (EEC) average wage is about $98 per day with a total labor force of about 180 million. The labor forces that have affected world trade extensively in the last several decades total only about 95 million (Hong Kong, Japan, Korea, Malaysia, Singapore, and Taiwan).[20]

While the changes associated with bringing a potential 1.2 billion low-cost laborers onto world markets will significantly increase average living standards throughout the world, they will also bring massive obsolescence of capital (manifested in the form of excess capacity) in Western economies as the adjustments sweep through the system. Western managers cannot count on the backward nature of these economies to limit competition from these new human resources. Experience in China and elsewhere indicates the problems associated with bringing relatively current technology on line with labor forces in these areas is possible with fewer difficulties than one might anticipate.[21]

The bottom line, of course, is that with even more excess capacity and the requirement for additional exit, the strains put on the internal control mechanisms of Western corporations are likely to worsen for decades to come.

In the 1980s managers and employees demanded protection from

Table 2.1 Labor force and manufacturing wage estimates of various countries and areas playing an actual or potential role in international trade in the past and in the future

Country/area	Total population[a] (millions)	Potential labor force[b] (millions)	Avg. daily earnings[c] (US $)
Major potential entrants from Asia			
China	1,232.08	579.23	$2.89
India	939.54	441.70	1.51
Indonesia	198.34	93.24	NA
Pakistan	134.15	63.07	2.38
Sri Lanka	18.31	8.61	2.59
Thailand	60.00	28.21	9.55
Vietnam	75.18	35.34	NA
Total (pop., labor force) or avg. (earnings)	2,657.60	1,249.40	$2.48[d]
Major potential entrants from Central and South America			
Argentina	35.22	16.56	$31.20
Brazil	157.87	74.22	NR
Chile	14.42	6.97	14.04
Colombia	35.63	16.75	4.64
Costa Rica	3.20	1.50	14.73
Mexico	96.58	45.40	10.57
Peru	23.95	11.26	10.33
Total/average	366.87	172.47	$13.31
Previous world market entrants from Asia			
Hong Kong	6.31	2.97	$ 38.38
Japan	125.76	59.12	128.35
Korea	45.54	21.41	NR
Malaysia	21.17	9.95	16.86
Singapore	3.61	1.70	78.32
Taiwan	NA	NA	NA
Total/average	202.39	95.15	$108.53
U.S. and EEC for comparison			
United States	265.45	124.79	$102.24
European Economic Community	384.76	180.88	98.21
Total/average	650.21	305.68	$ 99.86

NA = not available. NR = not reliable, due to extreme exchange rate fluctuations.

a. Population statistics from *Monthly Bulletin of Statistics* (United Nations, 1998), mid-year 1996 data.

b. Potential labor force estimated by applying the 47.01% labor force participation rate in the European Economic Community to the 1991 population estimates, using the most recent employment estimates from the *Yearbook of Labour Statistics* (United Nations, 1992) for each member country.

c. Unless otherwise noted, earnings come from the *Yearbook of Labour Statistics*, converted into 1996 dollars using 1996 year-average exchange rates from Oanda (www.oanda.com/converter/cc_table).

d. Average daily wage weighted according to projected labor force in each grouping.

the capital markets. Many are now demanding protection from international competition in the product markets (often under the guise of protecting jobs). The dispute over the North American Free Trade Agreement (NAFTA), which removed trade barriers between Canada, the United States, and Mexico, is but one general example of conflicts that are also occurring in the steel, automobile, computer chip, computer screen, and textile industries. In addition it would not be surprising to see a return to demands for protection from even domestic competition. This is currently under way in the deregulated airline industry, which is faced with significant excess capacity.

We should not underestimate the strains this continuing change will place on worldwide social and political systems. In both the First and Second Industrial Revolutions, the demands for protection from competition and for redistribution of income became intense. It is conceivable that Western nations could face the modern equivalent of the English Luddites who destroyed industrial machinery (primarily knitting frames) in the period 1811–1816, and were eventually subdued by the militia (Watson 1993). In the United States during the early 1890s, large groups of unemployed men (along with some vagrants and criminals), banding together under different leaders in the West, Midwest, and East, wandered cross-country in a march on Congress. These bands, known as "Coxey's industrial armies," formed to demand relief from "the evils of murderous competition; the supplanting of manual labor by machinery; the excessive Mongolian and pauper immigration; the curse of alien landlordism" (McMurray 1929, p. 128). Although the armies received widespread attention and enthusiasm at the onset, the groups were soon seen as implicit threats as they roamed from town to town, often stealing trains and provisions as they went. Of the 100,000 men anticipated by Coxey, only 1,000 actually arrived in Washington to protest on May 1, 1893. At the request of local authorities, the protestors disbanded and dispersed after submitting a petition to Congress (McMurray 1929, pp. 253–262).

We need look no further than central and eastern Europe or Asia to see the effects of policies that protect organizations from foreign and domestic competition. Hundreds of millions of people have been condemned to poverty as a result of governmental policies that protect firms from competition in the product markets (both domestic and foreign) and attempt to ensure prosperity and jobs by protecting organizations against decline and exit. Such policies are self-defeating, as employees of state-owned factories in these areas are now finding. Indeed, Porter (1990) finds that the most successful economies are those blessed with intense internal competition that forces efficiency through survival of the fittest.

The U.S. experience in the 1980s demonstrated that the capital markets can also play an important role—that capital market pressures, while not perfect, can significantly increase efficiency by bringing about earlier adjustments. Earlier adjustments avoid much of the waste generated when failure in the product markets forces exit.

2.4 The Difficulty of Exit

The Asymmetry between Growth and Decline

Exit problems appear to be particularly severe in companies that for long periods enjoyed rapid growth, commanding market positions, and high cash flow and profits. In these situations, the culture of the organization and the mindset of managers seem to make it extremely difficult for adjustment to take place until long after the problems have become severe, and in some cases even unsolvable. In a fundamental sense, there is an asymmetry between the growth stage and the contraction stage over the life of a firm. We have spent little time thinking about how to manage the contracting stage efficiently, or more importantly how to manage the growth stage to avoid sowing the seeds of decline.

In industry after industry with excess capacity, managers fail to recognize that they themselves must downsize; instead they leave the exit to others while they continue to invest. When all managers behave this way, exit is significantly delayed at substantial cost of real resources to society. The tire industry is an example. Widespread consumer acceptance of radial tires meant that worldwide tire capacity had to shrink by two-thirds (because radials last three to five times longer than bias ply tires). Nonetheless, the response by the managers of individual companies was often equivalent to: "This business is going through some rough times. We have to make major investments so that we will have a chair when the music stops." A. William Reynolds (1988), chairman and CEO of GenCorp (maker of General Tires), exemplified this reaction in his testimony before the Subcommittee on Oversight and Investigations (February 18, 1988), U.S. House Committee on Energy and Commerce:

The tire business was the largest piece of GenCorp, both in terms of annual revenues and its asset base. Yet General Tire was not GenCorp's strongest performer. Its relatively poor earnings performance was due in part to conditions affecting all of the tire industry . . . In 1985 worldwide tire manufacturing capacity substantially exceeded demand. At the same time, due to a series of technological improvements in the design of tires and the materials used to make them, the product life of tires had lengthened significantly. General Tire, and its competitors, faced an increasing imbalance between supply and demand. The economic pressure on our tire business was substantial. Because our unit volume was far below others in the industry, we had less competitive flexibility . . . We made several moves to improve our competitive position: We increased our investment in research and development. We increased our involvement in the high performance and light truck tire categories, two market segments which offered faster growth opportunities. We developed new tire products for those segments and invested heavily in an aggressive marketing program designed to enhance our presence in both markets. We made the difficult decision to reduce our overall manufacturing capacity by closing one of our older, less modern plants in Waco, TX . . . I believe that the General Tire example illustrates that we were taking a rational, long-term approach to improving GenCorp's overall performance and shareholder value . . . As a result of the takeover attempt, . . . [and] to meet the principal and interest payments on our vastly increased corporate debt, GenCorp had to quickly sell off valuable assets and abruptly lay-off approximately 550 important employees.

GenCorp sold its General Tire subsidiary to Continental AG of Hannover, Germany, for approximately $625 million. Despite Reynolds' good intentions and efforts, GenCorp's increased investment seems not to be a socially optimal response for managers in a declining industry with excess capacity.

Information problems. Information problems hinder exit because the high-cost capacity in the industry must be eliminated if resources are to be used efficiently. Firms often do not have good information on their own costs, much less the costs of their competitors; it is therefore sometimes unclear to managers that they are the high-cost firm that should exit the industry.[22] Even when managers do acknowledge the requirement for exit, it is often difficult for them to accept and initiate the shutdown decision. For the managers who must implement these decisions, shutting plants or liquidating the firm causes personal pain, creates uncertainty, and interrupts or sidetracks careers. Rather than confronting this pain, managers generally resist such actions as long as they have the cash flow to subsidize the losing operations. Indeed, firms with large positive cash flow will often invest in even more money-losing capacity—situations that illustrate vividly what I call the "agency costs of free cash flow" (Jensen 1986a).

Contracting problems. Explicit and implicit contracts in the organization can become major obstacles to efficient exit. Unionization, restrictive work rules, and lucrative employee compensation and benefits are other ways in which the agency costs of free cash flow can manifest themselves in a growing, cash-rich organization. Formerly dominant firms became unionized in their heyday (or effectively unionized when workers were implicitly promised jobs for life in organizations like IBM and Kodak) as managers spent some of the organization's free cash flow to buy labor peace. Faced with technical innovation and worldwide competition (often from new, more flexible, and nonunion organizations), these dominant firms cannot adjust fast enough to maintain their market dominance (see Burnham 1993; and DeAngelo 1991). Part of the problem is managerial and organizational defensiveness that inhibits learning and prevents managers from changing their model of the business (see Argyris 1990).

Implicit contracts with unions, other employees, suppliers, and communities add to formal union barriers to change by reinforcing organizational defensiveness and inhibiting change long beyond the optimal time—even beyond the survival point for the organization. In an environment like this a shock must occur to bring about effective change. We must ask why we cannot design systems that can adjust more continuously and therefore more efficiently.

The security of property rights and the enforceability of contracts are extremely important to the growth of real output, efficiency, and wealth. Much press coverage and official policy seems to be based on the notion that all implicit contracts should be unchangeable and rigidly enforced. Yet it is clear that, given the occurrence of unexpected events, not all contracts, whether explicit or implicit, can (or even should) be fulfilled. Implicit contracts, in addition to avoiding the costs incurred in the writing process, provide opportunity to revise the obligation if circumstances change; presumably, this is a major reason for their existence.

Indeed, the gradual abrogation of the legal notion of "at will" employment is coming closer to granting property rights in jobs to all employees.[23] While casual breach of implicit contracts will destroy trust in an organization and seriously reduce efficiency, all organizations must evolve a way to change contracts that are no longer optimal. For example, bankruptcy is essentially a state-supervised system for breaking (or more politely, rewriting) contracts that are mutually inconsistent and therefore unenforceable. All developed economies evolve such a system. Yet the problem is a very general one, given that the optimality of changing contracts must be one of the major reasons for leaving many of them implicit. Research into the optimal breach of contracts, and the bonding against opportunistic behavior that must accompany it, is an important topic that has received considerable attention in the law and economics literature (see Polinsky 1989) but is deserving of more attention by organization theorists.

2.5 The Role of the Market for Corporate Control

The Four Control Forces Operating on the Corporation

There are only four control forces operating on the corporation to resolve the problems caused by a divergence between managers' decisions and those that are optimal from society's standpoint. They are the

- capital markets,
- legal–political–regulatory system,
- product and factor markets, and
- internal control system headed by the board of directors.

As explained elsewhere (Chapter 3; Jensen 1989b, 1991; Roe 1990, 1991), the capital markets were relatively constrained by law and regulatory practice from about 1940 until their resurrection through hostile tender offers in the 1970s. Prior to the 1970s capital market discipline took place primarily through the proxy process. (Pound 1993 analyzes the history of the political model of corporate control.)

The legal–political–regulatory system is far too blunt an instrument to effectively handle the problems of wasteful managerial behavior. (The breakup and deregulation of AT&T, however, is one of the court system's outstanding successes. As described below, it helped create over $125 billion of increased value between AT&T and the Baby Bells.)

While the product and factor markets are slow to act as a control force, their discipline is inevitable—firms that do not supply the product that customers desire at a competitive price cannot survive. Unfortunately, when product and factor market disciplines take effect it can often be too late to save much of the enterprise. To avoid this waste of resources, it is important to learn how to make the other three organizational control forces more expedient and efficient.

Substantial data support the proposition that the internal control systems of publicly held corporations have generally failed to cause managers to maximize efficiency and value.[24] More persuasive than the formal statistical evidence is the fact that few firms ever restructure themselves or engage in a major strategic redirection without a crisis either in the capital markets, the legal–political–regulatory system, or the product and factor markets. But there are firms that have proved to be flexible in their responses to changing market conditions in an evolutionary way. For example, investment banking firms and consulting firms seem to be better at responding to changing market conditions.

Capital Markets and the Market for Corporate Control

The capital markets provide one mechanism for accomplishing change before losses in the product markets generate a crisis. While the corporate control activity of the 1980s has been widely criticized as counterproductive to American industry, few have recognized that many of these transactions were necessary to accomplish exit over the objections of current managers and other constituencies of the firm such as employees and communities. For example, the solution to excess capacity in the tire industry came about through the market for corporate control. Every major U.S. tire firm was either taken over or restructured in the 1980s.[25] In total, thirty-seven tire plants were shut down in the period 1977–1987 and total employment in the industry fell by over 40% (U.S. Bureau of the Census 1987, table 1a-1). The pattern in the U.S. tire industry is repeated elsewhere among the crown jewels of American business.

Capital market and corporate control transactions such as the repurchase of stock (or the purchase of another company) for cash or debt creates exit of resources in a very direct way. When Chevron acquired Gulf for $13.2 billion in cash and debt, the net assets devoted to the oil industry fell by $13.2 billion.[26] In the 1980s the oil industry had to shrink to accommodate the reduction in the quantity of oil demanded and the reduced rate of growth of demand. This meant paying out to shareholders its huge cash inflows, reducing exploration and development expenditures to bring reserves in line with reduced demands, and closing refining and distribution facilities. The leveraged acquisitions and equity repurchases helped accomplish this end for virtually all major U.S. oil firms (see Jensen 1986b, 1988).

Exit also resulted when Kohlberg, Kravis, and Roberts (KKR) acquired RJR-Nabisco for $25 billion in cash and debt in its 1986 LBO. Given the change in smoking habits in response to consumer awareness of health threats, the tobacco industry must shrink, and the payout of RJR's cash accomplished this to some extent. Furthermore, the LBO debt prohibits RJR from continuing to squander its cash flows on the wasteful projects it had undertaken prior to the buyout. Thus the buyout laid the groundwork for the efficient reduction of capacity by one of the major firms in the industry. Also, by eliminating some of the cash resources from the oil and tobacco industries, these capital market transactions promote an environment that reduces the rate of growth of human resources in the industries or even promotes outright reduction when that is the optimal policy.

The era of the control market came to an end, however, in late 1989 and 1990. Intense controversy and opposition from corporate managers, assisted by charges of fraud, the increase in default and bankruptcy rates, and insider trading prosecutions caused the shutdown of the control market through court decisions, state antitakeover amendments, and regulatory restrictions on the availability of financing (see Comment and Schwert 1995; Swartz 1992). In 1991 the total value of transactions fell to $96 billion from $340 billion in 1988.[27] Leveraged buyouts and management buyouts fell to slightly over $1 billion in 1991 from $80 billion in 1988.[28] The demise of the control market as an effective influence on American corporations has not ended the restructuring, but it has meant that organizations have typically postponed addressing the problems they face until forced to by financial difficulties generated by the product markets. Unfortunately the delay means that some of these organizations will not survive—or will survive as mere shadows of their former selves.

2.6   The Failure of Corporate Internal Control Systems

With the shutdown of the capital markets as an effective mechanism for motivating change, renewal, and exit, we are left to depend on the internal control system to act to preserve organizational assets, both human and nonhuman. Throughout corporate America, the problems that motivated much of the control activity of the 1980s are now reflected in lackluster performance, financial distress, and pressures for restructuring. Kodak, IBM, Xerox, ITT, and many others have faced or are now facing severe challenges in the product markets. We therefore must understand why these internal control systems have failed and learn how to make them work.

Organizations by nature abhor control systems, and ineffective governance is a major part of the problem with internal control mechanisms. They seldom respond in the absence of a crisis. General Motors (GM), one of the world's high-cost producers in a market with substantial excess capacity, avoided making major changes in its strategy for over a decade. Yet the board acted to remove the CEO, Robert Stempel, only in 1992, after the company had reported losses of $6.5 billion in 1990 and 1991 and (as we shall see in the next section) an opportunity loss of over $100 billion in its R&D and capital expenditure program from 1980 to 1990. Moreover, the changes to date are still too small to resolve the company's problems.

Unfortunately, GM is not an isolated example. IBM is another testimony to the failure of internal control systems: it failed to adjust to the substitution away from its mainframe business following the revolution in the workstation and personal computer market—ironically enough a revolution that it helped launch with the invention of the RISC technology in 1974 (Loomis 1993). Like GM, IBM was a high-cost producer in a market with substantial excess capacity. It too began to change its strategy significantly and removed its CEO only after reporting losses of $2.8 billion in 1991 and further losses in 1992 while losing almost 65% of its equity value.

Eastman Kodak, another major U.S. company formerly dominant in its market, also failed to adjust to competition and has performed poorly. Its $37 share price in 1992 was roughly unchanged from 1981. After several reorganizations, it only recently began to seriously change its incentives and strategy, and it appointed a chief financial officer well known for turning around troubled companies. (Unfortunately he resigned only several months later—after, according to press reports, running into resistance from the current management and board about the necessity for dramatic change.)

General Electric (GE) under Jack Welch, who has been CEO since 1981, is a counterexample to my proposition about the failure of corporate internal control systems. GE has accomplished a major strategic redirection, eliminating 104,000 of its 402,000-person workforce (through layoffs or sales of divisions) in the period 1980–1990 without the motivation of a threat from capital or product markets (GE annual reports). But there is little evidence to indicate this is due to anything more than the vision and persuasive powers of Jack Welch rather than the influence of GE's governance system.

General Dynamics (GD) provides another counterexample. The appointment of William Anders as CEO in September 1991 (coupled with large changes in its management compensation system that tied bonuses to increases in stock value) resulted in its rapid adjustment to excess capacity in the defense industry—again with no apparent threat from any outside force. GD generated $3.4 billion of increased value on a $1 billion company in just over two years (Murphy and Dial 1992, 1995). Sealed Air (Wruck 1994) is another particularly interesting example of a company that restructured itself without the threat of an immediate crisis. CEO Dermot Dumphy recognized the necessity for redirection, and after several attempts to rejuvenate the company to avoid future competitive problems in the product markets, created a crisis by voluntarily using the capital markets in a leveraged restructuring. Its value more than tripled over a three-year period. I hold these companies up as examples of successes of the internal control systems because each redirection was initiated without immediate crises in the product or factor markets, the capital markets, or in the legal–political–regulatory system. The problem is that they are far too rare.

Although the strategic redirection of General Mills provides another counterexample (Donaldson 1990), the fact that it took more than ten years to accomplish the change leaves serious questions about the social costs of continuing the waste caused by ineffective control. It appears that internal control systems have two faults: they react too late and they take too long to effect major change. Changes motivated by the capital market are generally accomplished quickly—within one and a half to three years. As yet no one has demonstrated the social benefit from relying on purely internally motivated change that offsets the costs of the decade-long delay exhibited by General Mills.

In summary, it appears that the infrequency with which large corporate organizations restructure or redirect themselves solely on the basis of the internal control mechanisms in the absence of crises in the product, factor, or capital markets or the regulatory sector is strong testimony to the inadequacy of these control mechanisms.

2.7 Direct Evidence of the Failure of Internal Control Systems

The Productivity of R&D and Capital Expenditures

The control market, corporate restructurings, and financial distress provide substantial evidence on the failings of corporate internal control systems. My purpose in this section is to provide another and more direct estimate of the effectiveness of internal control systems by measuring the productivity of corporate R&D and capital expenditures. The results reaffirm that many corporate control systems are not functioning well. While it is impossible to get an unambiguous measure of the productivity of R&D and capital expenditures, by using a period as long as a decade we can get some approximations. We cannot simply measure the performance of a corporation by the change in its market value over time (more precisely the returns to its shareholders) because this measure does not take account of the efficiency with which the management team manages internally generated cash flows. For example, consider a firm that provides dividends plus capital gains to its shareholders over a ten-year period that equal the cost of capital on the beginning of period share value. Suppose, however, that management spent $30 billion of internally generated cash flow on R&D and capital expenditures that generated no returns. In this case the firm's shareholders suffered an opportunity loss equal to the value that could have been created if the firm had paid the funds out to them and they had invested it in equivalently risky projects.

The opportunity cost of R&D and capital expenditures thus can be thought of as the returns that would have been earned by an investment in equivalent-risk assets over the same time period. We do not know exactly what that risk is, nor what the expected returns would be, but we can make a range of assumptions. A simple measure of performance would be the difference between the total value of the R&D plus capital and acquisition expenditures invested in a benchmark strategy and the total value the firm actually created with its investment strategy. The benchmark strategy can be thought of as the ending value of a comparable-risk bank account (with an expected return of 10%) into which the R&D and capital expenditures in excess of depreciation (hereinafter referred to as "net capital expenditures") had been deposited instead of invested in real projects. For simplicity I call this the "benchmark strategy." The technical details of the model are given in the Appendix to this chapter. The calculation of the performance measure takes account of all stock splits, stock dividends, equity issues and repurchases, dividends, debt issues and payments, and interest.

Three Measures of the Productivity of R&D and Net Capital Expenditures

Measure 1. Consider an alternative strategy that pays the same dividends and stock repurchases as the firm actually paid (and raises the same outside capital) and puts the R&D and capital and acquisition expenditures (in excess of depreciation) in marketable securities of the same risk as the R&D and capital expenditures, yielding expected returns equal to their cost of capital, i. Under the assumption that the zero investment and R&D strategy yields a terminal value of the firm equal to the ending debt plus the beginning value of equity (that is, investment equal to depreciation is sufficient to maintain the original equity value of the firm), Measure 1 is the difference between the actual ending total value of the firm and the value of the benchmark. The exact equations for this measure as well as for the next two measures of performance are given in the Appendix.

Unless capital and R&D expenditures are completely unproductive, this first crude measure of the productivity of R&D and capital expenditures will be biased downward. I define two additional measures that use different assumptions about the effect of the reduced R&D and capital expenditures on the ending value of the firm's equity and on the ability of the firm to make the intermediate cash dividend and stock repurchase payouts to shareholders. If R&D is required to maintain a competitive position in the industry, the ending value of the equity in the benchmark strategy is likely to be less than the initial value of equity even though nominal depreciation of the capital stock is being replaced. Moreover, with no R&D and maintenance only of the nominal value of the capital stock, the annual cash flows from operations are also likely to be lower than those actually realized (because organizational efficiency and product improvement will lag competitors, and new product introduction will be lower). I therefore use two more conservative measures that will yield higher estimates of the productivity of these expenditures.

Measure 2. The second measure assumes that replacement of depreciation and zero expenditures on R&D are sufficient to maintain the intermediate cash flows but, like a one-horse shay, the firm arrives at the end of the period still generating cash returns, but then collapses with no additional cash payments to equityholders, and equity value of zero as of the horizon date.

Measure 3. To allow for the effects of the reduced investment and R&D on intermediate cash flows, my third measure assumes that all intermediate cash flows are reduced in the benchmark investment strategy by the amount paid out to shareholders in the form of dividends and net share repurchases and that the original value of the equity is maintained. This measure is likely to yield an estimate of the productivity of R&D and capital expenditures that is biased upward.

The Data and Results

The analysis comprises 1,431 firms on COMPUSTAT for which data on R&D, capital expenditures, depreciation, dividends, and market value were available for the period December 31, 1979, through December 31, 1990. The estimates of the productivity of R&D are likely to be biased upward because the selection criteria uses only firms that managed to survive through the period and eliminates those that failed. I have calculated results for various rates of interest but report only those using a 10% rate of return. This rate is probably lower than the cost of capital for R&D expenditures at the beginning of the period when interest rates were in the high teens, and probably about right or on the high side at the end of the period when the cost of capital was probably on the order of 8–10%. A low approximation of the cost of capital appropriate to R&D and capital expenditures will bias the performance measures upward, so I am reasonably comfortable with these conservative assumptions.

Because they are interesting in their own right, Table 2.2 presents the data on annual R&D and capital expenditures of eight selected *Fortune 500* corporations and the total venture capital industry from January 1,

Table 2.2 Total R&D and capital expenditures for selected companies and the venture capital industry, 1980–1990 ($ billions)

Year	GM	IBM	Xerox	Kodak	Intel	GE	Venture capital industry	Merck	AT&T
Total R&D expenditures:									
1980	2.2	1.5	0.4	0.5	0.1	0.8	0.6	0.2	0.4
1981	2.2	1.6	0.5	0.6	0.1	0.8	1.2	0.3	0.5
1982	2.2	2.1	0.6	0.7	0.1	0.8	1.5	0.3	0.6
1983	2.6	2.5	0.6	0.7	0.1	0.9	2.6	0.4	0.9
1984	3.1	3.1	0.6	0.8	0.2	1.0	2.8	0.4	2.4
1985	3.6	3.5	0.6	1.0	0.2	1.1	2.7	0.4	2.2
1986	4.2	4.0	0.7	1.1	0.2	1.3	3.2	0.5	2.3
1987	4.4	4.0	0.7	1.0	0.3	1.2	4.0	0.6	2.5
1988	4.8	4.4	0.8	1.1	0.3	1.2	3.9	0.7	2.6
1989	5.2	5.2	0.8	1.3	0.4	1.3	3.4	0.8	2.7
1990	5.3	4.9	0.8	1.3	0.5	1.5	1.9	0.9	2.4
Total	39.8	36.8	7.1	10.2	2.5	11.8	27.8	5.3	19.4
Total capital expenditures:									
1980	7.8	6.6	1.3	0.9	0.2	1.9	NA	0.3	17.0
1981	9.7	6.8	1.4	1.2	0.2	2.0	NA	0.3	17.8
1982	6.2	6.7	1.2	1.5	0.1	1.6	NA	0.3	16.5
1983	4.0	4.9	1.1	0.9	0.1	1.7	NA	0.3	13.8
1984	6.0	5.5	1.3	1.0	0.4	2.5	NA	0.3	3.5
1985	9.2	6.4	1.0	1.5	0.2	2.0	NA	0.2	4.2
1986	11.7	4.6	1.0	1.4	0.2	2.0	NA	0.2	3.6
1987	7.1	4.3	0.3	1.7	0.3	1.8	NA	0.3	3.7
1988	5.5	5.4	0.5	1.9	0.5	1.9	NA	0.4	4.0
1989	7.4	6.4	0.4	2.1	0.4	2.2	NA	0.4	3.5
1990	7.4	6.5	0.4	2.0	0.7	2.1	NA	0.7	3.7
Total	82.0	64.2	10.2	16.1	3.2	21.9	NA	3.6	91.2

Net capital expenditures (capital expenditures − depreciation)

Year									
1980	3.6	3.8	0.5	0.5	0.1	1.2	NA	0.2	9.9
1981	5.3	3.5	0.6	0.7	0.1	1.1	NA	0.2	9.9
1982	1.7	3.1	0.4	0.9	0.1	0.6	NA	0.2	7.7
1983	−1.1	1.3	0.3	0.2	0.1	0.6	NA	0.1	3.9
1984	1.1	2.3	0.5	0.2	0.3	1.4	NA	0.1	0.7
1985	3.0	3.4	0.1	0.7	0.1	0.8	NA	0.1	0.9
1986	5.1	1.3	0.2	0.5	0.0	0.6	NA	0.0	−0.3
1987	0.9	0.8	−0.4	0.7	0.1	0.2	NA	0.1	−0.1
1988	0.0	1.5	−0.2	0.7	0.3	0.4	NA	0.2	0.3
1989	1.8	2.2	−0.2	0.8	0.2	0.7	NA	0.2	0.1
1990	1.6	2.3	−0.2	0.7	0.4	0.6	NA	0.4	0.2
Total	22.9	25.5	1.5	6.7	1.6	8.3	NA	1.8	33.4

Total value of R&D + net capital expenditures

	62.8	62.3	8.6	16.8	4.2	20.2	27.8	7.2	52.8

Ending equity value of the company, 12/90:

	20.8	64.6	3.2	13.5	7.7	50.1	>60	34.8	32.9

Source: Annual reports, COMPUSTAT, *Business Week R&D Scoreboard*, William Sahlman. *Venture Economics* for total disbursements by industry.
NA = not available.
Capital expenditures for the venture capital industry are included in the R&D expenditures, which are the total actual disbursements by the industry.

Table 2.3 Benefit-cost analysis of corporate R&D and investment programs: actual total value of company at 12/31/90 less total of the benchmark strategy ($r = 10\%$) (billions of dollars)

GM	IBM	Xerox	Kodak	Intel	GE	Venture capital industry	Merck	AT&T
Measure 1: Gain (loss) (assumes beginning value of equity is maintained)								
($109.1)	($72.8)	($20.5)	($26.8)	$0.2	$3.0	>$17	$19.4	($67.0)
Measure 2 (assumes ending equity value is zero)								
($94.4)	($35.2)	($15.3)	($19.0)	$1.6	$14.5	>$17	$24.8	($28.4)
Measure 3 (assumes ending equity value = beginning value and intermediate cash flows are smaller by the amount paid to equity under company's strategy)								
($91.4)	($25.3)	($16.6)	($13.0)	($1.4)	$24.2	>$17	$28.8	($44.7)

1980, through December 31, 1990. Table 2.3 contains calculations that provide some benchmarks for evaluating the productivity of these expenditures.

Total R&D expenditures over the eleven-year period range from $39.8 billion for GM to $2.5 billion for Intel. The individual R&D expenditures of GM and IBM were significantly greater than the $27.8 billion spent by the entire U.S. venture capital industry over the eleven-year period. Because venture capital data include both the R&D component and capital expenditures, we must add in corporate capital expenditures to get a proper comparison to the venture industry figures. Total capital expenditures range from $91.2 billion for AT&T and $82 billion for GM to $3.2 billion for Intel. Capital expenditures net of depreciation range from $33.4 billion for AT&T to $1.6 billion for Intel.

It is clear that GM's R&D and investment program produced massive losses. The company spent a total of $62.8 billion in excess of depreciation in the period and produced a firm with total ending value of equity (including the E and H shares) of $20.8 billion. Ironically, its expenditures were more than enough to pay for the entire equity value of Toyota and Honda, which in 1985 totaled $21.5 billion. If it had done this (and not changed the companies in any way), GM would have owned two of the world's low-cost, high-quality automobile producers.

As Table 2.3 shows, the difference between the value of GM's actual strategy and the value of the equivalent-risk bank account strategy amounts to $-94.4 billion by Measure 2 (which assumes the ending value of the company given no R&D or net capital expenditures is zero in the benchmark strategy), $-109.1 billion for Measure 1 (which assumes the original value of the equity is maintained), and $-91.4 billion by Measure 3 (which assumes cash flows fall by the amount of all intermediate cash outflows to shareholders and debtholders). I concentrate on Measure 2, which I believe is the best measure of the three. By this measure, IBM lost over $35 billion relative to the benchmark strategy (and this is prior to the $50 billion decline in its equity value in 1991 and 1992), while Xerox and Kodak were down $15.3 billion and $19 billion, respectively. GE and Merck were major success stories, with value creation in excess of the benchmark strategy of $14.5 billion and $24.8 billion, respectively. AT&T lost $28.4 billion over the benchmark strategy, after having gone through the court-ordered breakup and deregulation of the Bell system in 1984. The value gains of the seven Baby Bells totaled $125 billion by Measure 2 (not shown in the table), making the breakup and deregulation a nontrivial success given that prices to consumers have generally fallen in the interim.

The value created by the venture capital industry is difficult to estimate. We would like to have estimates of the 1990 total end-of-year value of all companies funded during the eleven-year period. This value is not available so I have relied on the $60 billion estimate of the total value of all initial public offerings (IPOs) during the period. This overcounts those firms that were funded prior to 1980 and counts as zero all those firms that had not yet come public as of 1990. Because of the pattern of increasing investment over the period from the mid-1970s, the overcounting problem is not likely to be as severe as the undercounting problem. Thus the value added by the industry over the bank account strategy is most probably greater than $17 billion as shown in Table 2.3. Since the venture capital industry is in Table 2.3 as another potential source of comparison, and since virtually its entire value creation is reflected in its ending equity value, I have recorded its value creation under each measure as the actual estimate of greater than $17 billion.

Because the extreme observations in the distribution are the most interesting, Table 2.4 gives the three performance measures for the thirty-five companies at the top of the list of 1,431 firms ranked in order on Measure 2 (Panel A), and for the thirty-five companies at the bottom of

Table 2.4 Difference between value of benchmark strategy for investing R&D and net capital expenditure and actual strategy under three assumptions regarding ending value of equity and intermediate cash flows for benchmark strategy (performance measures 1–3)

Rank	Company	Performance measure (millions)		
		1	2	3

Panel A: Performance measures for the 35 companies at the top of the ranked list of 1,431 companies in the period 1980–1990 on performance measure 2 ($r = 10\%$)

Rank	Company	1	2	3
1	Wal-Mart Stores	31,971	32,509	32,368
2	Bristol-Myers Squibb	24,823	27,247	30,287
3	Merck & Co.	19,360	24,802	28,671
4	Coca-Cola	20,515	24,778	30,430
5	British Gas PLC-ADR	11,623	21,894	11,623
6	BellSouth Corp.	11,623	21,793	19,572
7	Pacific Gas & Electric	17,615	21,481	17,615
8	British Telecom PLC-ADR	8,269	19,549	17,021
9	Southern Co.	15,618	18,265	15,618
10	Bell Atlantic Corp.	9,170	17,176	15,478
11	Southwestern Bell Corp.	9,174	16,216	14,534
12	Commonwealth Edison	13,297	16,130	13,297
13	Pacific Telesis Group	8,960	15,849	15,484
14	Ameritech Corp.	8,154	15,682	15,547
15	Scecorp	13,121	15,525	13,121
16	Squibb Corp.	13,741	15,463	15,855
17	Glaxo Holdings PLC-ADR	14,072	14,864	16,102
18	General Electric	3,009	14,543	24,029
19	Philip Morris Cos.	9,996	14,480	21,430
20	Warner Communications	11,537	12,530	10,660
21	Pepsico	10,229	12,492	14,025
22	Texas Utilities	9,994	12,092	9,994
23	American Electric Power	9,014	11,909	9,014
24	U.S. West	4,893	11,684	9,333
25	Abbott Laboratories	9,179	11,658	14,500
26	Smithkline Beecham PLC-ADS	4,560	11,356	7,292
27	Marion Merrell Dow	11,044	11,161	11,297
28	FPL Group	9,411	10,864	9,411
29	Duke Power	8,767	10,815	8,767
30	Procter & Gamble	4,365	10,712	11,647
31	Public Service Entrp.	8,765	10,679	8,765
32	Consolidated Edison of New York	7,966	10,196	7,966
33	Dominion Resources	8,540	10,193	8,540
34	Ito Yokado Co. LTD-ADR	9,346	10,109	9,084
35	Johnson & Johnson	5,226	10,077	12,244

Table 2.4 (continued)

Rank	Company	Performance measure (millions)		
		1	2	3

Panel B: Performance measures for the 35 companies ranked at the bottom of the ranked list of 1,431 companies in the period 1980–1990 on performance measure 2 (r = 10%)

Rank	Company	1	2	3
1,397	Imperial Chem. Inds. PLC-ADR	(12,446)	(7,778)	(8,582)
1,398	Digital Equipment	(10,076)	(7,812)	(12,104)
1,399	Lockheed Corp.	(8,515)	(8,059)	(8,749)
1,400	RCA Corp.	(9,764)	(8,096)	(9,015)
1,401	Unocal Corp.	(12,039)	(8,162)	(2,546)
1,402	Phillips Petroleum	(15,902)	(8,489)	(3,087)
1,403	Occidental Petroleum Corp.	(11,006)	(8,592)	(10,965)
1,404	McDonnell Douglas Corp.	(10,098)	(8,729)	(8,739)
1,405	Federated Dept. Stores	(10,155)	(8,851)	(7,833)
1,406	AMR Corp.—Del.	(9,352)	(8,954)	(10,363)
1,407	Mobil Corp.	(21,125)	(9,453)	(4,164)
1,408	Honda Motor Ltd.—AM Shares	(11,800)	(10,355)	(12,047)
1,409	Dome Petroleum Ltd.	(12,880)	(10,571)	(12,706)
1,410	Hewlett-Packard	(13,860)	(10,740)	(11,898)
1,411	Hitachi Ltd.-ADR	(13,403)	(10,952)	(13,019)
1,412	Canadian Pacific Ltd.-ORD	(14,110)	(11,650)	(13,979)
1,413	Tenneco	(16,344)	(11,900)	(10,440)
1,414	BCE	(15,725)	(12,690)	(14,722)
1,415	Exxon Corp.	(36,927)	(12,738)	(34,360)
1,416	Atlantic Richfield	(22,240)	(12,938)	(4,160)
1,417	Allied Signal	(14,655)	(13,041)	(10,037)
1,418	Sun Co.	(18,608)	(14,446)	(12,035)
1,419	United Technologies Corp.	(17,421)	(14,739)	(13,204)
1,420	Xerox Corp.	(20,488)	(15,261)	(16,649)
1,421	Unisys Corp.	(19,310)	(16,081)	(19,455)
1,422	Chrysler Corp.	(17,897)	(17,228)	(14,729)
1,423	Eastman Kodak	(26,808)	(19,041)	(13,013)
1,424	Chevron Corp.	(36,931)	(27,293)	(22,814)
1,425	American Telephone & Telegraph	(67,001)	(28,422)	(44,668)
1,426	Philips NV—NY Share	(32,577)	(30,712)	(31,936)
1,427	Du Pont (E. I.) de Nemours	(39,204)	(33,123)	(34,275)
1,428	IBM	(72,788)	(35,219)	(25,284)
1,429	British Petroleum PLC-ADR	(50,159)	(38,246)	(38,166)
1,430	Ford Motor Co.	(52,788)	(48,931)	(38,378)
1,431	General Motors	(109,134)	(94,382)	(91,391)

Table 2.5 Summary statistics on R&D, capital expenditures, and performance measures for 1,431 firms in the period 1980–1990 ($r = 10\%$) (millions of dollars)

Statistic	R&D expenditures	Net capital expenditures	Performance measure 1	Performance measure 2	Performance measure 3
Mean	$471	$668	($640)	$163	$94
Median	0	141	(93)	46	7
Minimum	0	(7,186)	(109,133)	(94,382)	(91,391)
Maximum	39,814	34,455	31,970	32,509	34,360
Standard deviation	2,161	2,469	5,963	5,069	5,132

the ranked list (Panel B). As the table shows, Wal-Mart created the most value in excess of the benchmark strategy, followed by Bristol-Myers, Merck, Coca-Cola, British Gas, BellSouth, Pacific Gas & Electric, British Telecom, Southern Co., and Bell Atlantic.[29] Panel B shows that GM ranked at the bottom of the performance list, preceded by Ford, British Petroleum, IBM, du Pont, Philips NV, AT&T, Chevron, and Kodak. Obviously many of the United States' largest and best-known companies appear on this list, along with Japan's Honda Motor company.

Table 2.5 provides summary statistics (including the minimum, mean, five fractiles of the distribution, maximum, and standard deviation) on R&D expenditures, net capital expenditures, and the three performance measures. The mean eleven-year R&D and net capital expenditures are $471 million and $668 million, respectively; the medians are $0 and $141 million. The average of Measure 2 over all 1,431 firms is $163 million with a t-value of 3.0, indicating that on average this sample of firms created value above that of the benchmark strategy. The average for Measures 1 and 3 are $640 million and $94 million, respectively. All productivity measures are biased upward because failed firms are omitted from the sample and because the decade of the eighties was a historical outlier in stock market performance. The median performance measures are $93 million, $46 million, and $7 million, respectively. The maximum performance measures range from $32 billion to $34.4 billion.

Although the average performance measures are positive, well-functioning internal control systems would substantially truncate the lower tail of the distribution. And given that the sample is subject to survivorship bias[30] and that the period was one in which stock prices performed historically above average, the results demonstrate major inefficiencies in the capital expenditure and R&D spending decisions of a substantial number of firms.[31] I believe we can improve these control systems substantially, but to do so we must attain a detailed understanding of how they work and the factors that lead to their success or failure.

2.8   Reviving Internal Corporate Control Systems

Remaking the Board as an Effective Control Mechanism

The problems with corporate internal control systems start with the board of directors. The board, at the apex of the internal control system, has the final responsibility for the functioning of the firm. Most importantly, it sets the rules of the game for the CEO. The job of the board is to hire, fire, and compensate the CEO and to provide high-level counsel. Few boards in the past decades have done this job well in the absence of external crises. This is particularly unfortunate given that the very purpose of the internal control mechanism is to provide an early warning system to put the organization back on track before difficulties reach a crisis stage. The reasons for the failure of the board are not completely understood, but we are making progress toward understanding these complex issues. The available evidence does suggest that CEOs are removed after poor performance,[32] although the effect, while statistically significant, seems too late and too small to meet the obligations of the board. I believe bad systems or rules, not bad people, underlie the general failings of boards of directors.

Some caution is advisable here because while resolving problems with boards can cure the difficulties associated with a nonfunctioning court of last resort, this alone cannot solve all the problems with defective internal control systems. I resist the temptation in an already lengthy chapter to launch into a discussion of other organizational and strategic issues that must be attacked. A well-functioning board, however, is capable of providing the organizational culture and supporting environment for a continuing attack on these issues.

Board culture. Board culture is an important component of board failure. The emphasis on politeness and courtesy at the expense of truth and frankness in boardrooms is both a symptom and cause of failure in the control system. CEOs have the same insecurities and defense mechanisms as other human beings; few will accept, much less seek, the monitoring and criticism of an active and attentive board. Magnet (1992, p. 86) gives an example of this environment. John Hanley, retired Monsanto CEO, accepted an invitation from a CEO

> to join his board—subject, Hanley wrote, to meeting with the company's general counsel and outside accountants as a kind of directorial due diligence. Says Hanley: "At the first board dinner the CEO got up and said, 'I think Jack was a little bit confused whether we wanted him to be a director or the chief executive officer.' I should have known right there that he wasn't going to pay a goddamn bit of attention to anything I said." So it turned out, and after a year Hanley quit the board in disgust.

The result is a continuing cycle of ineffectiveness: by rewarding consent and discouraging conflicts, CEOs have the power to control the board, which in turn ultimately reduces the CEO's and the company's performance. This downward spiral makes the resulting difficulties likely to be a crisis rather than a series of small problems met by a continuously self-correcting mechanism. The culture of boards will not change simply in response to calls for change from policy makers, the press, or the academic community. It only will follow, or be associated with, a general recognition that past practices have resulted in major failures and substantive changes in the rules and practices governing the system.

Information problems. Serious information problems limit the effectiveness of board members in the typical large corporation. For example, the CEO almost always determines the agenda and the information given to the board. This limitation on information severely hinders the ability of even highly talented board members to contribute effectively to the monitoring and evaluation of the CEO and the company's strategy.

Moreover, the board requires expertise to provide input into the financial aspects of planning—especially in forming the corporate objective and determining the factors that affect corporate value. Yet such financial expertise is generally lacking on today's boards. Consequently, boards (and management) often fail to understand why long-run market value maximization is generally the privately and socially optimal corporate objective, and they often fail to understand how to translate this objective into a feasible foundation for corporate strategy and operating policy.

Legal liability. The factors that motivate modern boards are generally inadequate. Boards are often motivated by substantial legal liabilities through class action suits initiated by shareholders, the plaintiffs' bar, and others—lawsuits that are often triggered by unexpected declines in stock price. These legal incentives are more often consistent with minimizing downside risk rather than maximizing value. Boards are also motivated by threats of adverse publicity from the media or from the political–regulatory authorities. Again, while these incentives often provide motivation for board members to cover their own interests, they do not necessarily provide proper incentives to take actions that create efficiency and value for the company.

Lack of management and board member equity holdings. Many problems arise from the fact that neither managers nor nonmanager board members typically own substantial fractions of their firm's equity. While the average CEO of the 1,000 largest firms (measured by market value of equity) held 2.7% of his or her firm's equity in 1991, the median holding is only 0.2%, and 75% of CEOs own less than 1.2% (Murphy 1992).[33] Encouraging outside board members to hold substantial equity interests would provide better incentives. Stewart (1990) outlines a useful approach using levered equity purchase plans or the sale of in-the-money options to executives to resolve this problem in large firms, where achieving significant ownership would require huge dollar outlays by managers or board members. By requiring significant outlays by managers for the purchase of these quasi-equity interests, Stewart's approach reduces the incentive problems created by the asymmetry of payoffs in the typical option plan.

Boards should have an implicit understanding or explicit requirement that new members must invest in the stock of the company. While the initial investment could vary, it should seldom be less than $100,000 from the new board member's personal funds; this investment would force new board members to recognize from the outset that their decisions affect their own wealth as well as that of remote shareholders. Over the long term the investment can be made much larger by options or other stock-based compensation. The recent trend to pay some board member fees in stock or options is a move in the right direction. Discouraging board members from selling this equity is important so that holdings will accumulate to a significant size over time.

Oversized boards. Keeping boards small can help improve their performance. When boards get beyond seven or eight people they are less likely to function effectively and are easier for the CEO to control.[34] Since the possibility for animosity and retribution from the CEO is too great, it is almost impossible for those who report directly to the CEO to participate openly and critically in effective evaluation and monitoring of the CEO. Therefore, the only inside board member should be the CEO. Insiders other than the CEO can be regularly invited to attend board meetings in an ex officio capacity. Indeed, board members should be given regular opportunities to meet with and observe executives below the CEO—both to expand their knowledge of the company and CEO succession candidates, and to increase other top-level executives' understanding of the thinking of the board and the board process.

Attempts to model the process after political democracy. Suggestions to model the board process after a democratic political model in which various constituencies are represented are likely to make the process even weaker. To see this we need look no further than the inefficiency of representative political democracies (whether at the local, state, or federal level), or at their management of such quasi-business organizations as the post office, schools, or power generation entities like the Tennessee Valley Authority (TVA). This does not mean, however, that the current corporate system is satisfactory as it stands; indeed, there is significant room for rethinking and revision.

For example, proxy regulations by the Securities and Exchange Commission (SEC) make the current process far less efficient than it otherwise could be. Specifically, it has been illegal for any shareholder to discuss company matters with more than ten other shareholders without prior filing with, and approval of, the SEC. The November 1992 relaxation of this restriction allows an investor to communicate with an unlimited number of other stockholders provided the investor owns less than 5% of the shares, has no special interest in the issue being discussed, and is not seeking proxy authority. These restrictions still have obvious shortcomings that limit effective institutional action by those shareholders most likely to pursue an issue.

As equity holdings become concentrated in institutional hands, it is easier to resolve some of the free-rider problems that limit the ability of thousands of individual shareholders to engage in effective collective action. In principle, such institutions can therefore begin to exercise corporate control rights more effectively. Legal and regulatory restrictions, however, have prevented financial institutions from playing a major corporate monitoring role. (Black 1990; Pound 1991; and Roe 1990, 1991 provide an excellent historical review of these restrictions.) If institutions are to aid in effective governance, therefore, we must continue to dismantle the rules and regulations that have prevented them and other large investors from accomplishing this coordination.

The CEO as chairman of the board. It is common in U.S. corporations for the CEO to also hold the position of chairman of the board. The function of the chairman is to run board meetings and oversee the process of hiring, firing, evaluating, and compensating the CEO. Clearly, the CEO cannot perform this function apart from his or her personal interest. Without the direction of an independent leader, it is much more difficult for the board to perform its critical function. Therefore, for the board to be effective, it is important to separate the CEO and chairman positions.[35] The independent chairman should, at a minimum, be given the rights to initiate board appointments, board committee assignments, and (jointly with the CEO) the setting of the board's agenda. All these recommendations, of course, will be made conditional on the ratification of the board.

An effective board will often manifest tension among its members as well as with the CEO. But I hasten to add that I am not advocating continuous war in the boardroom. In fact, in well-functioning organizations the board will generally be relatively inactive and will exhibit little conflict. It becomes important primarily when the rest of the internal control system is failing, and this should be a relatively rare event. The challenge is to create a system that will not lapse into complacency and inactivity during periods of prosperity and high-quality management, rendering it slow to respond to the challenge of correcting a failing management system. This is a difficult task because there are strong tendencies for boards to evolve a culture and social norms that reflect optimal behavior under prosperity, and these norms make it extremely difficult for the board to respond early to failure in its top management team.[36]

Resurrecting active investors. A major set of problems with internal control systems is associated with the curbing of what I call "active investors" (Chapter 3; Jensen 1989b). Active investors are individuals or institutions that simultaneously hold large debt and/or equity positions in a company and actively participate in its strategic direction. Active investors are important to a well-functioning governance system because they have the financial interest and independence to view firm management and policies in an unbiased way. They have the incentives to buck the system to correct problems early rather than late when the problems are obvious but difficult to correct. Financial institutions such as banks, pension funds, insurance companies, mutual funds, and money managers are natural active investors, but they have been shut out of boardrooms and firm strategy by the legal structure, by custom, and by their own practices.[37]

There is much we can do to dismantle the web of legal, tax, and regulatory apparatus that severely limits the scope of active investors in this country.[38] But even absent these regulatory changes, CEOs and boards can take actions to encourage investors to hold large positions in their debt and equity and to play an active role in the strategic direction of the firm and in monitoring the CEO.

Wise CEOs can recruit large block investors to serve on the board, even selling them new equity or debt to induce their commitment to the firm. Lazard Frères Corporate Partners Fund is an example of an institution set up specifically to perform this function, making new funds available to the firm and taking a board seat to advise and monitor management performance. Warren Buffett's activity through Berkshire Hathaway provides another example of a well-known active investor. He played an important role in helping Salomon Brothers through its recent legal and organizational difficulties following the government bond bidding scandal. Dobrzynski (1993) discusses many varieties of this phenomenon (which she calls "relationship investing") that are currently arising both in the United States and abroad.

Using LBOs and Venture Capital Firms as Models of Successful Organization, Governance, and Control

Organizational experimentation in the 1980s. Founded on the assumption that firm cash flows are independent of financial policy, the Modigliani-Miller (M&M) theorems on the independence of firm value, leverage, and payout policy have been extremely productive in helping the finance profession structure the logic of many valuation issues. The 1980s control activities, however, have demonstrated that the M&M theorems, while logically sound, are empirically incorrect. The evidence from LBOs, leveraged restructurings, takeovers, and venture capital firms has demonstrated dramatically that leverage, payout policy, and ownership structure (that is, who owns the firm's securities) do in fact affect organizational efficiency, cash flow, and, therefore, value.[39] Such organizational changes show these effects are especially important in low-growth or declining firms where the agency costs of free cash flow are large.[40]

Evidence from LBOs. LBOs provide a good source of estimates of value gain from changing leverage, payout policies, and the control and governance system because, to a first approximation, the company has the same managers and the same assets but a different financial policy and control system after the transaction.[41] Leverage increases from about 18% of value to 90%, large payouts to prior shareholders occur, equity becomes concentrated in the hands of managers (over 20% on average) and the board (about 60% on average), boards shrink to about seven or eight people, the sensitivity of managerial pay to performance rises, and the companies' equity usually becomes nonpublicly traded (although debt is often publicly traded).

The evidence of DeAngelo, DeAngelo, and Rice (1984a), Kaplan (1989b), Smith (1990), and others indicates that premiums to selling-firm shareholders are roughly 40–50% of the pre-buyout market value, cash flows increase by 96% from the year before the buyout to three years after the buyout, and value increases by 235% (96% market adjusted) from two months prior to the buyout offer to the time of going public, sale, or recapitalization about three years later on average.[42] Wruck and Palepu (1992) show that large value increases also occur in voluntary recapitalizations where the company stays public but buys back a significant fraction of its equity or pays out a significant dividend. Clinical studies of individual cases demonstrate that these changes in financial and governance policies generate value-creating changes in the behavior of managers and employees.[43]

A proven model of governance structure. LBO associations and venture capital funds provide a blueprint for managers and boards who wish to revamp their top-level control systems to make them more efficient. LBOs and venture capital funds are, of course, the preeminent examples of active investors in recent U.S. history, and they serve as excellent models that can be emulated in part or in total by virtually any corporation. The two have similar governance structures and have been successful in resolving the governance problems of both slow growth or declining firms (LBO associations) and high growth entrepreneurial firms (venture capital funds).[44]

Both LBO associations and venture capital funds, of which KKR and Kleiner Perkins are prominent examples, tend to be organized as limited partnerships. In effect, the institutions that contribute the funds to these organizations are delegating the task of being active investors to the general partners of the organizations. Both governance systems are characterized by

- limited partnership agreements at the top level that prohibit headquarters from cross-subsidizing one division with the cash from another,
- high equity ownership on the part of managers and board members,
- board members (mostly the LBO association partners or the venture capitalists) who in their funds directly represent a large fraction of the equity owners of each subsidiary company,
- small boards of directors (of the operating companies) typically consisting of no more than eight people,
- CEOs who are typically the only insider on the board, and
- CEOs who are seldom the chairman of the board.

LBO associations and venture funds also solve many of the information problems facing typical boards of directors. First, as a result of the due diligence process at the time the deal is done, both the managers and the LBO and venture partners have extensive and detailed knowledge of virtually all aspects of the business. In addition, these boards have frequent contact with management, often weekly or even daily during times of difficult challenges. This contact and information flow is facilitated by the fact that LBO associations and venture funds both have their own staff. They also often perform the corporate finance function for the operating companies, providing the major interface with the capital markets and investment banking communities.

Finally, the close relationship between the LBO partners or venture fund partners and the operating companies facilitates the infusion of expertise from the board during times of crisis. It is not unusual for a partner to join the management team, even as CEO, to help an organization through such emergencies. Very importantly, there are market forces that operate to limit the human tendency to micromanage and thereby overcentralize management in the headquarters staff. If headquarters develops a reputation for abusing the relationship with the CEO, the LBO or venture organization will find it more difficult to complete new deals (which frequently depend on the CEO's being willing to sell the company to the LBO fund or on the new entrepreneur's being willing to sell an equity interest in the new venture to the venture capital organization).

2.9   Implications for the Finance Profession

One implication of the foregoing discussion is that finance has failed to provide firms with an effective mechanism to achieve efficient corporate investment. While modern capital-budgeting procedures are implemented by virtually all large corporations, it appears that the net present value (or more generally, value-maximizing) rule imbedded in these procedures is far from universally followed by operating managers. In particular, the acceptance of negative-value projects tends to be common in organizations with substantial amounts of free cash flow (cash flow in excess of that required to fund all value-increasing investment projects) and in particular in firms and industries where downsizing and exit are required. The finance profession has concentrated on how capital investment decisions should be made, with little systematic study of how they actually *are* made in practice.[45] This narrowly normative view of investment decisions has led the profession to ignore what has become a major worldwide efficiency problem that will be with us for several decades to come.

Agency theory (the study of the inevitable conflicts of interest that occur when individuals engage in cooperative behavior) has fundamentally changed corporate finance and organization theory, but it has yet to affect substantially research on capital-budgeting procedures. No longer can we assume managers automatically act (in opposition to their own best interests) to maximize firm value.

Conflicts between managers and the firm's financial claimants were brought to center stage by the market for corporate control in the last two decades. This market brought widespread experimentation, teaching us not only about corporate finance but also about the effects of leverage, governance arrangements, and active investors on incentives and organizational efficiency. These events have taught us much about the interdependencies among the implicit and explicit contracts specifying the following three elements of organizations:

- Finance—I use this term narrowly here to refer to the definition and structure of financial claims on the firm's cash flows (e.g., equity, bond, preferred stock, and warrant claims).[46]
- Governance—the top-level control structure, consisting of the decision rights possessed by the board of directors and the CEO, the procedures for changing them, the size and membership of the board, and the compensation and equity holdings of managers and the board.[47]
- Organization—the nexus of contracts defining the internal "rules of the game" (the performance measurement and evaluation system, the reward and punishment system, and the system for allocating decision rights to agents in the organization) (Jensen 1983; Jensen and Meckling 1992).

The close interrelationships among these factors have dragged finance scholars into the analysis of governance and organization theory.[48] In addition, the perceived "excesses of the 1980s" have generated major reregulation of financial markets in the United States, affecting the control market, credit markets (especially the banking, thrift, and insurance industries), and market microstructure.[49] These changes have highlighted the importance of the political and regulatory environment to financial, organizational, and governance policies, and generated a new interest in what I call the "politics of finance."[50]

The dramatic growth of these new research areas has fragmented the finance profession, which can no longer be divided simply into the study of capital markets and corporate finance. Finance is now much less an exercise in valuing a given stream of cash flows (although this is still important) and much more the study of how to increase those cash flows—an effort that goes far beyond the capital asset-pricing model, Modigliani and Miller irrelevance propositions, and capital budgeting. This fragmentation is evidence of progress, not failure; but the inability to understand this maturation causes conflict in those quarters where research is judged and certified, including the academic journals and university departments. Specialists in different subfields have tended to react by labeling research in areas other than their own as "low-quality" and "illegitimate." Acknowledging this separation and nurturing communication among the subfields will help avoid this intellectual warfare with substantial benefit to the progress of the profession.

My review of macro and organizational trends in the previous pages has highlighted many areas for future research for finance scholars:

- The implications of the Third Industrial Revolution and how it will affect financial, product, and labor markets, as well as the level and distribution of worldwide income and wealth:
  - how industry-wide excess capacity arises, how markets and firms respond to such market pressures, and why exit is so difficult for organizations to deal with;
  - the implications of new technology for organizational downsizing;
  - the financial policies appropriate for the new virtual or network organizations that are arising.
- The weaknesses that cause internal corporate control systems to fail and how to correct them:
  - the reasons for the asymmetry between corporate growth and decline, and how to limit the organizational and strategic inefficiencies that seem to creep into highly successful rapidly growing organizations;
  - how capital budgeting decisions are actually made and how organizational practices can be implemented that will reduce the tendency to accept negative value projects;
  - the nature of implicit contracts, the optimal degree to which private contracts should be left open to abrogation or change, and how to bond or monitor to limit opportunistic behavior regarding those implicit contracts.
- How politics, the press, and public opinion affect the types of governance, financial, and organizational policies that firms adopt:
  - how capital market forces can be made a politically and economically efficient part of corporate control mechanisms;
  - how active investors can be resurrected and reconciled with a le-

gal structure that currently favors liquid and anonymous markets over the intimate illiquid market relations that seem to be required for efficient governance.

2.10   Conclusion

For those with a normative bent, making the internal control systems of corporations work is the major challenge facing economists and management scholars in the 1990s. For those who choose to take a purely positive approach, the major challenge is understanding how these systems work and how they interact with the other control forces (in particular the product and factor markets, legal, political, and regulatory systems, and the capital markets) impinging on the corporation. The reason we are interested in developing positive theories of the world is to make things work more efficiently. Without accurate positive theories of cause-and-effect relationships, normative propositions and decisions based on them will be wrong. Therefore, the two objectives are completely consistent.

Financial economists have a unique advantage in working on these control and organizational problems because we understand what determines value, and we know how to think about uncertainty and objective functions. To do this we have to understand even better than we do now the factors leading to organizational failures (and successes): we have to break open the black box called the "firm," and this means understanding how organizations and the people in them work. In short, we are facing the problem of developing a viable theory of organizations. To be successful we must continue to broaden our thinking to new topics and to learn and develop new analytical tools.

Appendix: Direct Estimates of the Productivity of R&D—the Model

Consider a firm in period t with cash flow from operations, C_t, available for:

R_t = R&D expenditures,
K_t = capital investment,
d_t = payments to shareholders in the form of dividends and net share repurchases,

b_t = interest and net debt payments,

a_t = acquisitions net of asset sales.

$d < 0, b < 0, a < 0$ mean respectively that new equity is raised in the form of capital contributions from equityholders, net bond issues exceed interest and debt repayments, and asset sales exceed acquisitions.

By definition $C_t = R_t + K_t + d_t + b_t + a_t$. The initial value of the firm equals the sum of the market values of equity and debt, $V_0 = S_0 + B_0$, and the final value at the end of period n is V_n. Assume for simplicity that taxes are zero and debt is riskless. If r is the riskless interest rate and r is the cost of equity capital, the total value, V_T, created by the firm's investment, R&D, and payout policy measured at the future horizon date n, is the final value of the firm plus the ending value of the dividend payments plus stock repurchases plus the ending value of the interest payments plus debt payments

$$V_T = V_n + \sum [d_t(1 + \rho)^{n-t} + b_t(1 + r)^{n-t}]$$

where the investor is assumed to reinvest all intermediate payouts from the firm at the cost of equity and debt, r and r respectively.

Consider an alternative strategy that pays the same dividends and stock repurchases d_t (and raises the same outside capital) and puts the R&D and capital and acquisition expenditures (in excess of depreciation) in marketable securities of the same risk as the R&D and capital expenditures, yielding expected returns equal to their cost of capital, i. Under the assumption that the zero investment and R&D strategy yields a terminal value, V_n, equal to the ending debt, B_n, plus the beginning value of equity, S_0 (that is, investment equal to depreciation is sufficient to maintain the original equity value of the firm), the value created by this strategy is

$$V'_n = S_0 + B_n + \sum(K_t + R_t + a_t)(1 + i)^{n-t}$$
$$+ \sum [d_t (1 + \rho)^{n-t} + b_t(1 + r)^{n-t}]$$

The difference between the terminal values of the two strategies is

$$V_T - V'_T = V_n - V'_n - \sum(K_t + R_t + a_t)(1 + i)^{n-t}$$
$$= S_n - S_0 - \sum(K_t + R_t + a_t)(1 + i)^{n-t} \qquad (1)$$

This is my first crude measure of the productivity of R&D and capital expenditures. Unless capital and R&D expenditures are completely unproductive, this measure will be biased downward. Therefore I define two more conservative measures that will yield higher estimates of the productivity of these expenditures. The second assumes that replacement of depreciation and zero expenditures on R&D are sufficient to maintain the intermediate cash flows but at the end of the period the firm has equity value of zero. This second measure is

$$V_T - V'_T = V_n - B_n - \sum(K_t + R_t + a_t)(1 + i)^{n-t} \qquad (2)$$

Alternatively, to allow for the effects of the reduced investment and R&D on intermediate cash flows, my third measure assumes that all intermediate cash flows are reduced in the benchmark investment strategy by the amount paid out to shareholders in the form of dividends and net share repurchases and that the original value of the equity is maintained. This measure is likely to yield an upward biased estimate of the productivity of R&D and capital expenditures. The measure is[51]

$$V_T - V'_T = V_n + \sum d_t(1 + \rho)^{n-t} - S_0$$
$$- B_n - \sum(K_t + R_t + a_t)(1 + i)^{n-t} \qquad (3)$$

3 | Active Investors, LBOs, and the Privatization of Bankruptcy

3.1 Introduction

The corporate sector of the U.S. economy has been experiencing major change, and the rate of change continues as we head into the last year of the 1980s. Over the past two decades the corporate control market has generated considerable controversy, first with the merger and acquisition movement of the 1960s, then with the hostile tender offers of the 1970s, and most recently with the leveraged buyouts (LBOs) and leveraged restructurings of the 1980s. The controversy has been renewed with the $25 billion LBO by Kohlberg, Kravis, and Roberts (KKR) of RJR-Nabisco, a transaction almost double the size of the largest previous acquisition to date, the $13.2 billion Chevron purchase of Gulf Oil in 1985.

These control transactions are the most visible aspect of a much larger phenomenon that is not yet well understood. Though controversy surrounds them, and despite the fact that they are not all productive, these transactions are the manifestation of powerful underlying economic forces that, on the whole, are productive for the economy. That understanding, however, is made difficult by the fact that change, as always, is threatening—and in this case the changes disturb many powerful interests.

One popular hypothesis offered for the current activity is that Wall Street is engineering transactions to buy and sell fine old firms out of pure greed. The notion is that these transactions reduce productivity but generate high fees for investment bankers and lawyers. The facts do not support this hypothesis even though mergers and acquisitions (M&A) professionals undoubtedly prefer more deals to less and thus

Originally published in *Journal of Applied Corporate Finance* 2, no. 1 (Spring 1989), pp. 35–44. Given as testimony before the House Ways and Means Committee, February 1, 1989.

sometimes encourage transactions (like diversification acquisitions) that are not productive.

There has been much study of corporate control activity, and although the results are not uniform, the evidence indicates control transactions generate value for shareholders. The evidence also suggests that this value comes from real increases in productivity rather than from simple wealth transfers to shareholders from other parties such as creditors, labor, government, customers, or suppliers.[1]

I have analyzed the causes and consequences of takeover activity in the United States elsewhere (Jensen 1986a, 1986b, 1988). My purpose here is to outline an explanation of the fundamental underlying cause of this activity that has to date received no attention. I propose to show how current corporate control activity is part of a larger development; to provide perspective on how LBOs, restructurings, and increased leverage in the corporate sector fit into the overall picture; and to discuss some reasons why high debt ratios and insolvency are less costly now than in the past. Because of its topical relevance, I pay particular attention to LBOs and their role in the restoration of competitiveness in the American corporation.

3.2   Active Investors and Their Importance

The role of institutional investors and financial institutions in the corporate sector has changed greatly over the last fifty years as institutions have been driven out of the role of active investors. By "active investor" I do not mean one who indulges in portfolio churning. I mean an investor who actually monitors management, sits on boards, is sometimes involved in dismissing management, is often intimately involved in the strategic direction of the company, and on occasion even manages. That description fits Carl Icahn, Irwin Jacobs, and KKR.

Before the mid-1930s, investment banks and commercial banks played a much more important role on boards of directors, monitoring and occasionally engineering changes in management. At the peak of their activities, J. P. Morgan and several of his partners served on the boards of directors and played a major role in the strategic direction of many firms.

Bankers' roles have changed over the past fifty years as a result of a number of factors. One important source of the change is a set of laws established in the 1930s that increased the costs of being actively involved in the strategic direction of a company while also holding large amounts of its debt and equity. For example, under the definitions of the 1934 Securities Exchange Act, an institution or individual is considered an "insider" if it owns more than 10% of a company, serves on its board of directors, or holds a position as officer. And the 16-b short swing profit rules in that act require an institution satisfying any insider conditions to pay the company 100% of the profits earned on investments held less than six months. Commercial bank equity holdings are significantly restricted and Glass Steagall restricts bank involvement in investment banking activities. The Chandler Act restricts the involvement by banks in the reorganization of companies in which they have substantial debt holdings. In addition, the 1940 Investment Company Act put restrictions on the maximum holdings of investment funds. These factors do much to explain why money managers do not serve on boards today and seldom think of getting involved in the strategy of their portfolio companies.

The restrictive laws of the 1930s were passed after an outpouring of populist attacks on the investment banking and financial community, exemplified by the Pecora hearings on the security markets in the 1930s and the earlier Pujo hearings in 1913. Current attacks on Wall Street are reminiscent of that era.

The result of these political and other forces over the past fifty years has been to leave managers increasingly unmonitored. In the United States at present, when the institutional holders of over 40% of corporate equity become dissatisfied with management, they have few options other than to sell their shares. Moreover, managers' complaints about the churning of financial institutions' portfolios ring hollow: one can guess they much prefer the churning system to one in which those institutions actually have direct power to correct a management problem. Few chief executive officers (CEOs) look kindly on the prospect of having institutions with substantial stock ownership sitting on their corporate board. That would bring about the monitoring of managerial activities by people who more closely bear the wealth consequences of managerial mistakes and who are not beholden to the CEO for their jobs. As financial institution monitors left the scene in the post-1940 period, managers commonly came to believe companies belonged to them and that stockholders were merely one of many stakeholders the firm had to serve.[2] This process took time, and the cultures of these organizations slowly changed as senior managers brought up in the old regime were replaced with younger managers.

The banning of financial institutions from fulfilling their critically important monitoring role has resulted in major inefficiencies. The increase in "agency costs" (loosely speaking, the efficiency loss resulting from the separation between ownership and control in widely held public corporations) appears to have peaked in the mid- to late 1960s when a substantial part of corporate America generated large cash flows but had few profitable investment projects. With this excess cash, these firms launched diversification programs that led to the assembly of conglomerates, a course since proven to be unproductive (Jensen 1986a, 1986b, 1988). While most attacks on takeovers have been directed at acquisitions by entrepreneurs such as Icahn and Goldsmith, it is the diversification acquisitions by the largest corporations (such as GE, GM, and the major oil companies) that have proven to be unproductive. The criticism leveled at takeovers seems misplaced given the evidence—especially given the lack of controversy surrounding the Philip Morris takeover of Kraft, which, if past evidence is any guide, will prove to be counterproductive.

The fact that takeover and restructuring premiums regularly average about 50% indicates managers have been able to destroy up to 30% of the value of the organizations they lead before facing serious threat of disturbance.[3] This destruction of value generates large profit opportunities, and the response to these incentives has been the creation of innovative financial institutions to recapture the lost value. Takeovers and LBOs are among the products of these institutions. My estimates indicate that over the years from 1975 to 1986, corporate control activities alone (i.e., mergers, tender offers, divestitures, spin-offs, buybacks, and LBOs) created more than $400 billion in value for investors.

Along with the takeover specialists came other new financial institutions such as the family funds (owned by the Bass Brothers, the Pritzkers, and the Bronfmans) as well as Warren Buffett's Berkshire Hathaway—institutions that discovered ways to bear the cost associated with insider status. Coniston Partners is another version of this new organizational response to the monitoring problem, and so is the Lazard Frères Corporate Partners Fund. These new institutions have discovered ways different from those of J. P. Morgan to resolve the monitoring problem. They purchase entire companies and play an active role in them; in fact, they often *are* the board of directors.

The modern trend toward merchant banking in which Wall Street firms take equity positions in their own deals is another manifestation of this phenomenon. KKR is much more than an expediter of LBO transactions. It plays an important role in management after the transaction. In general, LBO specialists control the boards of directors in the companies they help take private. They choose the managers of the firm and influence corporate strategy in important ways. Buyout specialists are very different from the usual outside or public directors who supposedly represent shareholders. Buyout specialists own, or represent in their buyout funds, an average of 60% of the firm's equity and therefore have great incentive to take the job seriously, in contrast to public directors with little or no equity interest (see Kaplan 1990).

The development of new financial institutions as a response to problems caused by the lack of effective monitoring of corporate managers continues to grow. Such innovation is likely to continue unless handicapped by new legislation, tax penalties, or unfavorable public opinion. The attack on Wall Street and investment bankers that has been progressing in recent years may be the modern equivalent to the populist attacks in the decades prior to 1940 that led to the crippling of American corporations in the 1960s and 1970s.

3.3   The LBO Association: A New Organizational Form

It is instructive to think about LBO associations such as KKR and Forstmann-Little as new organizational forms—in effect a new model of general management. These organizations are similar in many respects to diversified conglomerates or to Japanese groups of firms known as "keiretsu." It is noteworthy that the corporate sectors in Japan and Germany are significantly different from the American corporate model of diffuse ownership monitored by public directors. In both these economies, banks and associations of firms are more important than in the United States. Indeed, one way to see the current conflict between the Business Roundtable and Wall Street is that Wall Street is now a direct competitor to the corporate headquarters office of the typical conglomerate.

LBO associations such as KKR are one alternative to conglomerate organizations and, judging from their past performance, they apparently generate large increases in efficiency. Figure 3.1 illustrates the similarities and differences between these organizational forms. LBO associations, shown in the lower part of the figure, are run by partnerships instead of the headquarters office, as in the typical large, multi-business diversified corporation. These partnerships perform the monitoring and peak coordination function with a staff numbering in the tens of people, and replace the typical corporate headquarters staff of thousands. The leaders of these partnerships have large equity ownership in the outcomes and direct fiduciary relationships as general partners to the limited partner investors in their buyout funds.

The LBO partnerships play a role that is similar in many ways to that of the main banks in the Japanese groups of companies. The banks (and LBO partnerships) hold substantial amounts of equity and debt in their client firms and are deeply involved in the monitoring and strategic direction of these firms. Moreover, the business unit heads in the typical LBO association, unlike those in Westinghouse or GE, also have substantial equity ownership that gives them a pay-to-performance sensitivity that, on average, is twenty times higher than that of the average corporate CEO. In a sample of LBOs examined by Steven Kaplan (1990), the average CEO receives $64 per $1,000 change in shareholder wealth from his 6.4% equity interest alone. The typical corporate CEO, by contrast, is paid in a way that is insensitive to performance. In a study I conducted with Kevin Murphy, we found that the average CEO in the Forbes 1,000 firms receives total pay (including salary, bonus, deferred compensation, stock options, and equity) that changes about $3.25 per $1,000 change in stockholder value (Jensen and Murphy 1990b).

The proper comparison, however, of the pay-performance sensitivity of the compensation package of the conglomerate CEO is not with the CEOs of the LBOs but rather with the managing partner or partners of the partnership headquarters (e.g., the KKRs of this world). Little is publicly known about the compensation plans of these partnerships, but the pay-for-performance sensitivity (including ownership interests, of course) appears to be very large, even compared to that of the managers of the LBOs. The effective ownership interest in the gains realized by the buyout pool generally runs about 20% or more for the general partners as a group. LBO business unit heads also have far less bureaucracy to deal with and far more decision rights in the running of their businesses. In effect, the LBO association substitutes incentives provided by compensation and ownership plans for the direct monitoring

TYPICAL DIVERSIFIED FIRM

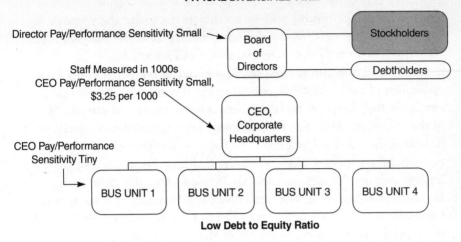

TYPICAL LBO ASSOCIATION
(KKR, Forstmann-Little)

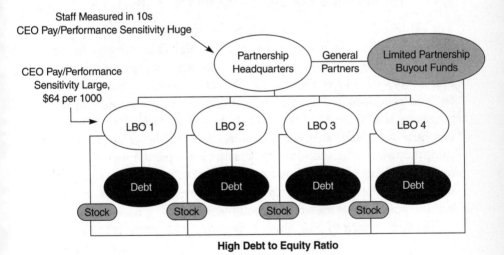

Figure 3.1 Correspondence between the typical diversified firm and the typical LBO association, which are competing organizational forms. The LBO association is headed by a small partnership organization that substitutes compensation incentives (mostly through equity ownership) and top-level oversight by a board with large equity ownership for the bureaucratic monitoring of the typical large corporate headquarters. For simplicity the board of directors of each LBO firm has been omitted. The LBO partnership headquarters generally hold 60% of the stock in their own name or that of the limited partnership fund and control each of these boards.

and often centralized decision making in the typical corporate bureaucracy. The compensation and ownership plans make the rewards to managers highly sensitive to the performance of their business unit, something that rarely occurs in major corporations.[4]

In addition, the contractual relation between the partnership headquarters and the suppliers of capital to the buyout funds is very different from that between the corporate headquarters and stockholders in the diversified firm. The buyout funds are organized as limited partnerships, in which the managers of the partnership headquarters are the general partners. Unlike the diversified firm, the contract with the limited partners denies partnership headquarters the right to transfer cash or other resources from one LBO business unit to another. Generally all cash payouts from each LBO business unit must be paid out directly to the limited partners of the buyout funds. This reduces the waste of free cash flow that is so prevalent in most diversified corporations.[5]

3.4 The Empirical Evidence on the Source of LBO Gains

The evidence on LBOs and management buyouts is growing rapidly. In general, this evidence shows that abnormal gains to stockholders are significantly positive and in the same range as gains from takeovers. Stock prices rise about 14–25% on the announcement of the offer, and the estimated average total premium to public shareholders ranges from 40 to 56%.[6] The recent study by Kaplan (1990) shows that for those buyouts that eventually come back public or are otherwise sold, the total value (adjusted for market movements) increases 96% from two months before a buyout to the final sale about five years after the buyout. Pre-buyout shareholders earn premiums of about 38%, and the post-buyout investors earn about 42%.[7]

This 42% return to post-buyout investors, it is important to note, is measured on the *total purchase price* of the pre-buyout equity and not the equity of the post-buyout firm. The median net-of-market return on the post-buyout equity alone is about 785%, but these returns are distorted by the fact that the equity is highly leveraged. In effect, the equity returns are almost a pure risk premium and therefore independent of the amount invested. Calculating the returns on the entire capital base used to purchase the pre-buyout equity, or the fraction of the total wealth gains that goes to the pre-buyout shareholders, gives a better picture of the distribution of the total wealth created in the buyout. Average total buyout fees amount to 5.5% of equity two months prior to the buyout proposal.

Some assert that post-buyout shareholders, especially managers, earn "too much" in these transactions and that managers are exploiting shareholders by using their inside information about the firm to buy it at below-market prices. Kaplan, however, finds evidence that managers holding substantial amounts of equity who are not part of the post-buyout management team are systematically selling their shares into the buyout. This is irrational behavior if the buyout is significantly underpriced in light of inside information and if such nonparticipating insiders have the same inside information as the continuing management team. Moreover, shareholders have many legal forums to press their claims because virtually all announcements of buyouts are followed by suits from the plaintiffs' bar. In addition, buyout firms systematically underperform the post-buyout projections they make in the proxy materials provided to selling shareholders (Kaplan 1990).

If, however, the buyout gains are due to the major changes in ownership and debt that occur at the buyout and the real changes in operations they engender, there may be no alternative but to allow managers to acquire substantial equity interests. These equity interests give them the incentive to make such highly leveraged companies successful and compensate them for the risks they take with their careers. One of the major risks, as Ross Johnson of RJR-Nabisco found out, is that a substantial fraction of proposed buyouts fail, and competing bids are an important reason for this failure.

Managers are subject to severe conflicts of interest in buyout transactions because they cannot simultaneously act as both buyer and agent for the seller. The system seems to work well, however, to protect shareholder interests. Directors are liable if they behave inappropriately and sacrifice shareholder interests in favor of managers, and shareholders receive protection from the fact that a bid significantly below the real value of the company (risk adjusted, of course) is likely to be met by competing outside bids. This is exactly what happened in the RJR case, where the initial management bid of $75 per share was topped by two outside bidders for an eventual stated price of $109 per share, an increase of $7.7 billion. In this case the system worked well to ensure that shareholder interests were served.

There are several credible studies that have examined the operating characteristics of large samples of post-buyout LBOs and have found real increases in productivity. The Kaplan (1990) study finds average increases in operating earnings of 42% from the year prior to the buyout to the third year after the buyout, and increases of 25% when adjusted for industry and business cycle trends. He finds 96% increases in cash flow in the same period (80% after adjustment for industry and business cycle trends).

A study by Abbie Smith (1990) also finds significant increases in operating earnings and net cash flows. In addition, she documents improvements in profit margins, sales per employee, working capital, inventories, and receivables, and finds no evidence of delays in payments to suppliers. She finds no changes in maintenance, repairs, and advertising as a fraction of sales, and no evidence that these items are being cut in ways that harm the long-run health of the enterprise (Smith 1990).

Corporate debt rises significantly, from about 20% of assets to almost 90%, after a buyout.[8] Some argue that a major part of the shareholder benefit is simply wealth transfers from bondholders who suffer when their bonds are left outstanding in the new company with its massive total debt. While it is undoubtedly true that some bondholders have lost in these transactions, there is no evidence that bondholders lose on average. Convertible bond- and preferred stockholders generally gain a statistically significant amount in such transactions, while straight bondholders show no significant gains or losses (Marais, Schipper, and Smith 1989). This result is somewhat surprising because the old bonds, in the majority of cases, experience significant downgradings by rating agencies.

The bondholder loss issue has been prominent in the press as Metropolitan Life has filed suit against RJR-Nabisco for restitution of the losses it experienced on its RJR-Nabisco bondholdings. The press, however, has greatly exaggerated the amount of the wealth loss to the RJR bondholders. The original announcement of the Johnson/Shearson Lehman offer occurred on October 20, 1988. From September 29 to November 29, the bondholders of RJR-Nabisco suffered losses of slightly under $300 million.[9] This loss is trivial relative to the $12.1 billion gain to RJR shareholders (calculated at the stated price of $109 per share).

In any event the expropriation of wealth from bondholders is not a continuing problem because the technology is available to protect bondholders from losses in the event of substantial restructuring and increases in debt. Poison puts or other covenant provisions that require repurchase of the bonds on such events can be used to eliminate such restructuring risk. One view of the RJR situation is that the Met and other purchasers of the bonds gambled that no restructuring would occur in order to reap the premium they would have given up if the protection had been included in the bonds they bought in 1988. Having gambled and lost, they are now asking for compensation.

The effects of LBOs on labor have not been thoroughly studied to date, but evidence in the Kaplan (1990) study indicates that median employment increases by 4.9% after a buyout, although, adjusted for industry conditions, it falls by 6.2%.[10] Thus employment does not systematically fall after a buyout. No data have been found that allow inference on whether wages are cut after a buyout.

There is also concern about the effect of LBOs on research and development (R&D) expenditures. This concern seems unwarranted because the low-growth, old-line firms that make good candidates for highly leveraged LBOs do not typically invest in R&D. Kaplan (1990) and Smith (1990), for example, each found only seven firms in their respective samples of seventy-six and fifty-eight firms that engaged in enough R&D to report in their financial statements.

Another area of controversy is the amount of value transferred from the U.S. Treasury in the form of tax subsidies to buyout transactions. The argument is that the massive increases in tax-deductible interest payments virtually eliminate tax obligations for buyout firms. In the year following the buyout, Kaplan (1990) finds that 50% of the firms pay no taxes. Because of operating improvements and the retirement of some debt, however, average tax payments are essentially back to the pre-buyout level by the third year after the buyout. Moreover, these subsidy arguments ignore five sources of added tax revenues:

1. the large increases in tax payments generated by the buyout in the form of capital gains tax payments by pre-buyout shareholders who are forced to realize all the gains in their holdings;
2. the capital gains taxes paid on the sale of assets by LBO firms;
3. the tax payments on the large increases in operating earnings caused by the buyout;
4. the tax payments by the buyout firm creditors who receive the interest payments; and
5. the increased taxes generated by the more efficient use of the firm's capital.

Direct estimates of the total effect on Treasury tax revenues taking account of all such gains and losses indicate the present value of revenues actually *increases* by about $110 million under the 1986 tax rules on the average buyout with a price of $500 million. Converted to an equivalent annual increase of $11 million in perpetuity, these revenues represent an annual increase of approximately 61% over the average $18 million tax payment by buyout firms in the year prior to the buyout. On a current account basis—that is, considering only the tax effects in the year after the buyout—the Treasury gains $41 million over the average pre-buyout tax payments.[11] Conservative estimates indicate that, at worst, the Treasury is unlikely to be a net loser from these transactions. If the value increases are the result of real productivity changes, rather than merely transfers of wealth from other parties, then it is not surprising that the Treasury is a winner. In the controversial RJR-Nabisco case, the $12 billion plus gains are likely to generate net incremental tax revenues to the Treasury totaling $3.8 billion in present value terms, and about $3.3 billion solely in the year following the buyout. Before the buyout, RJR-Nabisco was paying about $370 million in federal taxes.

3.5   High Leverage and the Privatization of Bankruptcy

One important and interesting characteristic of the LBO organization is its intensive use of debt. The debt-to-value ratio in the business units of these organizations averages close to 90% on a book value basis (Kaplan 1990). LBOs, however, are not the only organizations that are making use of high debt ratios. Public corporations are also following suit as witnessed by recapitalizations, highly leveraged mergers, and stock repurchases.

There has been much concern in the press and in public policy circles about the dangers of high debt ratios in these new organizations. What is not generally recognized, however, is that high debt has benefits as a monitoring and incentive device, especially in slow-growing or shrinking firms. Even less well known is that the costs for a firm in insolvency—the situation in which a firm cannot meet its contractual obligations to make payments—are likely to be much smaller in the new world of high leverage ratios than they have been historically. The reason is illustrated in Figure 3.2 (p. 76).

In a world of 20% debt-to-value ratios (with value based on the going concern value of a healthy company), the liquidation or salvage value is much closer to the face value of the debt than in the same company with an 85% debt-to-value ratio.[12] Figure 3.2 shows a $100 million company under these two leverage ratios and assumes that the salvage or liquidation value of the assets is 10% of the going concern value, or $10 million. Thus, if the company experiences such a decline in value during bad times that it cannot meet its payments on $20 million of debt, it is also likely that its value is below its liquidation value.

An identical company with an 85% debt ratio, however, is nowhere near liquidation when it experiences times sufficiently difficult to cause it to be unable to meet the payments on its $85 million of debt. That situation could occur when the company still has total value in excess of $80 million. In this case there is $70 million in value that can be preserved by resolving the insolvency problem in a fashion that minimizes the value lost through the bankruptcy process. In the former case, when the firm is worth less than $20 million, there may be so little value left that the economically sensible action is liquidation, with all its attendant conflicts and dislocation.

The incentives to preserve value in the new leverage model imply that a very different set of institutional arrangements and practices will arise to substitute for the usual bankruptcy process. In effect, bankruptcy will be taken out of the courts and "privatized." This institutional innovation will take place to recognize the large economic value that can be preserved by resolving the conflicts of interest among claimants to the firm.

When the going concern value of the firm is vastly greater than the liquidation value, it is likely to be more costly to trigger the cumbersome court-supervised bankruptcy process that diverts management time and attention away from managing the enterprise to focus on the abrogation of contracts that the bankruptcy process is designed to accomplish.

These large potential losses provide incentives for the parties to accomplish reorganization of the claims more efficiently outside the courtroom. This fact is reflected in the strip financing practices commonly observed in LBOs whereby claimants hold approximately proportional strips of all securities and thereby reduce the conflicts of interest among classes of claimants (Jensen 1988). Incentives to manage the insolvency process better are also reflected in the extremely low fre-

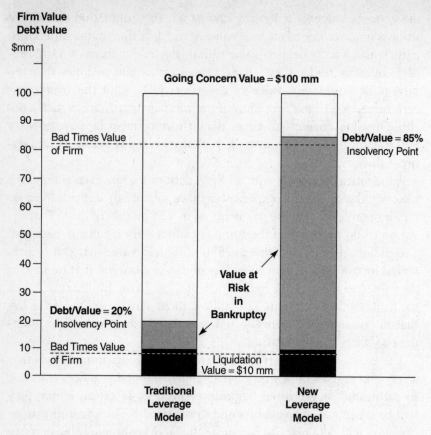

Figure 3.2 Relation between the insolvency point and liquidation value when the debt-value ratio is low versus high. The darkly shaded area represents the liquidation value for a given firm with assumed healthy-going-concern value of $100 million. Traditionally leveraged, the firm would have about a 20% debt-value ratio, while it would have about 85% debt in the new leverage model characterizing LBO and restructuring transactions. The lightly shaded areas represent the value at risk in bankruptcy. The much larger value at risk in the new leverage model if the firm should go into bankruptcy provides larger incentives to reorganize outside the courts.

quency with which these new organizations actually enter bankruptcy. The recent Revco case is both the largest such bankruptcy of an LBO and one of only a handful that have occurred.

LBOs frequently get into trouble, but they seldom enter formal bankruptcy. Instead, they are reorganized in a short period of time (several months is common), often under new management, and at apparently lower cost than would occur in the courts. In addition Kaplan's (1989a, 1992) detailed analysis of Campeau shows that an LBO can get into trouble, go bankrupt, and yet still create value for society because the value gains swamp the costs of bankruptcy.

Some assert that the success of LBOs has been ensured by the greatest bull market in history. The story is not that simple, however, because during the last eight years, major sectors of the economy have experienced bad times, and buyouts have occurred in many of these sectors. So, although they have not been tested by a general recession, they have survived well the trials of subsectors of the economy in the recent past (textiles and apparel are examples).

In addition, there are indications that organizations such as Drexel Burnham Lambert (which has been most active in facilitating the intensive use of debt) have anticipated these problems. They seem sensitive to the potential gains from innovation in the work-out and reorganization process. Such innovation is to be expected when there are large efficiency gains to be realized from new reorganization and recontracting procedures to deal with insolvency.

There is reason to believe, however, that actions by regulatory authorities will generate serious bankruptcy problems among Drexel's clients if its ability to handle the reorganization and work-out process is hampered. Drexel's position in the high-yield bond market gives it a unique ability to perform this function and no substitute is likely to emerge soon.

There has been much concern about the ability of LBO firms to withstand sharp increases in interest rates, given that the bank debt, which frequently amounts to 50% of the total debt, is primarily at floating rates. This problem is mitigated by the fact that most LBOs now protect themselves against sharp increases in interest rates by purchasing caps that limit any increase or by using swaps that convert the floating-rate debt to fixed rates. Indeed, it has become common for banks to require such protection for the buyout firm as a condition for lending. These new financial techniques are another means whereby some of the risks can be hedged away in the market, and therefore the total risks to the buyout firm are less than they would have been in past years at equivalent debt levels.

It will undoubtedly take time for the institutional innovation in reorganization practices to mature and for participants in the process to understand that insolvency will be a more frequent and less costly event than it has been historically. It is also reasonable to predict that this will be an area of intense future academic study.

3.6   Conclusion

LBOs are an interesting example of control transfers that highlight the effect of changes in organizational form and incentives on productivity. There appears to be no explanation for most of the gains other than real increases in operating efficiencies. That in itself is interesting because these are generally situations in which the same managers with the same assets are able, when provided with better incentives, to almost double the productivity and value of the enterprise. It is also surprising that it is so difficult to find losers in these transactions. Some middle and upper managers lose their jobs as the inefficient and bloated corporate staffs are replaced by LBO partnership headquarters units. Such LBO associations rely on incentives (created by equity ownership, performance-sensitive compensation, and high debt obligations) and decentralized decision making as substitutes for direct involvement by corporate headquarters in decision making.

As major innovations in corporate organization continue, mistakes will be made. This is natural and not counterproductive. How can we learn without pushing new policies to the margin? The surprising thing to me is that there have been so few major mistakes or problems in a revolution in business practice as large as that occurring over the last decade. Many of the proposed changes in public policy toward these transactions threaten to stifle this re-creation of the competitiveness of the American corporation. Perhaps the most dangerous of these policy proposals are those that, like that by the American Law Institute (ALI), would limit the formation of debt and the distribution of resources from corporations by imposing various tax penalties.[13] Removal of biases towards higher debt in the tax system would be desirable, but not if the proposed solutions create large inefficiencies as the ALI's now threaten to do.

The best and simplest way to remove any tax-induced bias toward debt is to eliminate the double taxation of dividends by making them tax deductible at the corporate level. This change would generate large additional efficiency gains in the economy because it would reduce the incentives for corporations to retain substantial amounts of funds even when they have no profitable projects in which to invest. This change would eliminate some of the most inefficient acquisitions that take place. These acquisitions are frequently engineered by managers flooded with free cash flow they are unable to invest in the businesses they understand but are reluctant to pay out to shareholders for reinvestment elsewhere in the economy. Some of the best examples of this have occurred in the oil, tire, and tobacco industries—all industries that have been forced to shrink their operations in the last decade. As in the past, elimination of double taxation of dividends is likely to be opposed by corporate managers who wish to avoid pressure for increased payouts to shareholders. Reforming the bankruptcy process to limit the courts' abrogation of contractual priority of claims voluntarily agreed to by security holders is also an important function that policy makers should address.

PART II   Agency Costs, Residual Claims, and Incentives

4

Theory of the Firm: Managerial Behavior, Agency Costs, and Ownership Structure

> The directors of such [joint-stock] companies, however, being the managers rather of other people's money than of their own, it cannot well be expected, that they should watch over it with the same anxious vigilance with which the partners in a private copartnery frequently watch over their own. Like the stewards of a rich man, they are apt to consider attention to small matters as not for their master's honour, and very easily give themselves a dispensation from having it. Negligence and profusion, therefore, must always prevail, more or less, in the management of the affairs of such a company.
>
> —Adam Smith, *The Wealth of Nations*

4.1 Introduction

In this chapter we draw on progress in the theory of (1) property rights, (2) agency, and (3) finance to develop a theory of ownership structure[1] for the firm. In addition to tying together elements of the theory of each of these three areas, our analysis casts new light on and has implications for a variety of issues in the professional and popular literature, including the definition of the firm, the "separation of ownership and control," the "social responsibility" of business, the definition of a "corporate objective function," the determination of an optimal capital structure, the specification of the content of credit agreements, the theory of organizations, and the supply side of the completeness of markets problems.

Our theory helps explain

1. why an entrepreneur or manager in a firm that has a mixed financial structure (containing both debt and outside equity claims) will choose a set of activities for the firm such that the total value of the firm is *less* than it would be if he were the sole

By Michael C. Jensen and William H. Meckling; originally published in *Journal of Financial Economics* 3, no. 4 (October 1976), pp. 305–360, with permission from Elsevier Science.

owner and why this result is independent of whether the firm operates in monopolistic or competitive product or factor markets;

2. why his failure to maximize the value of the firm is perfectly consistent with efficiency;

3. why the sale of common stock is a viable source of capital even though managers do not literally maximize the value of the firm;

4. why debt was relied upon as a source of capital before debt financing offered any tax advantage relative to equity;

5. why preferred stock would be issued;

6. why accounting reports would be provided voluntarily to creditors and stockholders, and why independent auditors would be engaged by management to testify to the accuracy and correctness of such reports;

7. why lenders often place restrictions on the activities of firms to whom they lend, and why firms would themselves be led to suggest the imposition of such restrictions;

8. why some industries are characterized by owner-operated firms whose sole outside source of capital is borrowing;

9. why highly regulated industries such as public utilities or banks will have higher debt-equity ratios for equivalent levels of risk than the average nonregulated firm; and

10. why security analysis can be socially productive even if it does not increase portfolio returns to investors.

Theory of the Firm: An Empty Box?

While the literature of economics is replete with references to the "theory of the firm," the material generally subsumed under that heading is not actually a theory of the firm but rather a theory of markets in which firms are important actors. The firm is a "black box" operated so as to meet the relevant marginal conditions with respect to inputs and outputs, thereby maximizing profits, or more accurately, present value. Except for a few recent and tentative steps, however, we have no theory that explains how the conflicting objectives of the individual participants are brought into equilibrium so as to yield this result. The limitations of this black box view of the firm have been cited by Adam Smith and Alfred Marshall, among others. More recently, popular and professional debates over the "social responsibility" of corporations, the separation of ownership and control, and the rash of reviews of the literature on the "theory of the firm" have evidenced continuing concern with these issues.[2]

A number of major attempts have been made during recent years to construct a theory of the firm by substituting other models for profit or value maximization, with each attempt motivated by a conviction that the latter is inadequate to explain managerial behavior in large corporations.[3] Some of these reformulation attempts have rejected the fundamental principle of maximizing behavior as well as the more specific profit-maximizing model. We retain the notion of maximizing behavior on the part of all individuals in the analysis that follows.[4]

Property Rights

An independent stream of research with important implications for the theory of the firm has been stimulated by the pioneering work of Coase, and extended by Alchian, Demsetz, and others.[5] A comprehensive survey of this literature is given by Furubotn and Pejovich (1972). While the focus of this research has been "property rights,"[6] the subject matter encompassed is far broader than that term suggests. What is important for the problems addressed here is that specification of individual rights determines how costs and rewards will be allocated among the participants in any organization. Since the specification of rights is generally effected through contracting (implicit as well as explicit), individual behavior in organizations, including the behavior of managers, will depend upon the nature of these contracts. We focus in this chapter on the behavioral implications of the property rights specified in the contracts between the owners and managers of the firm.

Agency Costs

Many problems associated with the inadequacy of the current theory of the firm can also be viewed as special cases of the theory of agency relationships, in which there is a growing literature.[7] This literature has developed independently of the property rights literature even though the problems with which it is concerned are similar; the approaches are in fact highly complementary to each other.

We define an agency relationship as a contract under which one or

more persons—the principal(s)—engage another person—the agent—
to perform some service on their behalf that involves delegating some
decision-making authority to the agent. If both parties to the relationship are utility maximizers, there is good reason to believe that the
agent will not always act in the best interests of the principal. The *principal* can limit divergences from her interest by establishing appropriate
incentives for the agent in the contracts they create and by incurring
monitoring costs designed to limit the aberrant activities of the agent.
In addition, in some situations it will pay the *agent* to expend resources
(bonding costs) to guarantee that he will not take certain actions that
would harm the principal or to ensure that the principal will be compensated if he does take such actions. However, it is generally impossible for the principal or the agent at zero cost to ensure that the agent
will make optimal decisions from the principal's viewpoint. In most
agency relationships, the principal and the agent will incur positive
monitoring and bonding costs (non-pecuniary as well as pecuniary),
and in addition there will be some divergence between the agent's
decisions[8] and those decisions that would maximize the welfare of the
principal. The dollar equivalent of the reduction in welfare experienced
by the principal as a result of this divergence is also a cost of the agency
relationship, and we refer to this latter cost as the "residual loss." We
define *agency costs* as the sum of

1. the costs of creating and structuring contracts between the
   principal and the agent,[9]
2. the monitoring expenditures by the principal,[10]
3. the bonding expenditures by the agent, and
4. the residual loss.

Note also that agency costs arise in any situation involving cooperative
effort (such as the coauthoring of this chapter) by two or more people
even though there is no clear-cut principal-agent relationship. Viewed
in this light, it is clear that our definition of agency costs and their importance to the theory of the firm bears a close relationship to the problem of shirking and monitoring of team production which Alchian and
Demsetz (1972) raise in their paper on the theory of the firm.

Since the relationship between the stockholders and the managers of
a corporation fits the definition of a pure agency relationship, it should
come as no surprise to discover that the issues associated with the "separation of ownership and control" in the modern diffuse ownership

corporation are intimately associated with the general problem of agency. We show below that an explanation of why and how the agency costs generated by the corporate form are borne leads to a theory of the ownership (or capital) structure of the firm.

Before moving on, however, it is worthwhile to point out the generality of the agency problem. The problem of inducing an "agent" to behave as if he were maximizing the "principal's" welfare is quite general. It exists in all organizations and in all cooperative efforts—at every level of management in firms,[11] in universities, in mutual companies, in cooperatives, in governmental authorities and bureaus, in unions, and in relationships actually called "agency relationships," such as those common in the performing arts and the market for real estate. The development of theories to explain the form agency costs take in each of these situations (where the contractual relations differ significantly), and how and why they are borne will lead to a rich theory of organizations presently lacking in economics and the social sciences generally. We confine our attention in this chapter to only a small part of this general problem—the analysis of agency costs generated by the contractual arrangements between the owners and top managers of the corporation.

Our approach to the agency problem here differs fundamentally from most of the existing literature. That literature focuses almost exclusively on the normative aspects of the agency relationship; that is, how to structure the contractual relation (including compensation incentives) between the principal and agent to provide appropriate incentives for the agent to make choices that will maximize the principal's welfare, given that uncertainty and imperfect monitoring exist. We focus almost entirely on the positive aspects of the theory. That is, we assume individuals solve these normative problems, and given that only stocks and bonds can be issued as claims, we investigate the incentives faced by each of the parties and the elements entering into the determination of the equilibrium contractual form characterizing the relationship between the manager (i.e., agent) of the firm and the outside equity- and debtholders (i.e., principals).

General Comments on the Definition of the Firm

Ronald Coase (1937) in his seminal paper entitled "The Nature of the Firm" pointed out that economics had no positive theory to determine the bounds of the firm. He characterized the bounds of the firm as that range of exchanges over which the market system was suppressed and where resource allocation was accomplished instead by authority and direction. He focused on the cost of using markets to effect contracts and exchanges and argued that activities would be included within the firm whenever the costs of using markets were greater than the costs of using direct authority. Alchian and Demsetz (1972) object to the notion that activities within the firm are governed by authority, and correctly emphasize the role of contracts as a vehicle for voluntary exchange. They emphasize the role of monitoring in situations in which there is joint input or team production.[12] We are sympathetic to the importance they attach to monitoring, but we believe the emphasis that Alchian and Demsetz place on joint input production is too narrow and therefore misleading. Contractual relations are the essence of the firm, not only with employees but with suppliers, customers, creditors, and so on. The problem of agency costs and monitoring exists for all of these contracts, independent of whether there is joint production in their sense; that is, joint production can explain only a small fraction of the behavior of individuals associated with a firm.

It is important to recognize that most organizations are simply legal fictions[13] that serve as a nexus for a set of contracting relationships among individuals. This includes firms, nonprofit institutions such as universities, hospitals, and foundations, mutual organizations such as mutual savings banks and insurance companies and cooperatives, some private clubs, and even governmental bodies such as cities, states, and the federal government, government enterprises such as the Tennessee Valley Authority (TVA), the post office, transit systems, and so forth.

The private corporation is simply one form of legal fiction that serves as a nexus for contracting relationships and is also characterized by the existence of divisible residual claims on the assets and cash flows of the organization which can generally be sold without permission of the other contracting individuals. This definition of the firm is important because it emphasizes the essential contractual nature of firms and other organizations and focuses attention on a crucial set of questions—why particular sets of contractual relations arise for various types of organizations, what the consequences of these contractual relations are, and how they are affected by changes exogenous to the organization. Viewed this way, it makes little or no sense to try to distinguish those things that are "inside" the firm (or any other organization) from those things that are "outside" of it. What there really is instead is a multitude of complex relationships (i.e., contracts) between the legal fiction (the firm) and the owners of labor, material, and capital inputs and the consumers of output.[14]

Viewing the firm as the nexus of a set of contracting relationships among individuals also serves to make it clear that the personalization of the firm implied by asking questions such as "What should be the objective function of the firm?" or "Does the firm have a social responsibility?" is seriously misleading. The firm is not an individual. It is a legal fiction that serves as a focus for a complex process in which the conflicting objectives of individuals (some of whom may "represent" other organizations) are brought into equilibrium within a framework of contractual relations. In this sense the "behavior" of the firm is like the behavior of a market: the outcome of a complex equilibrium process. We seldom fall into the trap of characterizing the wheat or stock market as an individual, but we often make this error by thinking about organizations as if they were persons with motivations and intentions.[15]

Overview of the Chapter

We develop our theory in stages. Sections 4.2 and 4.4 provide analyses of the agency costs of equity and debt, respectively. These form the major foundation of the theory. In Section 4.3, we pose some questions regarding the existence of the corporate form of organization and examine the role of limited liability. Section 4.5 provides a synthesis of the basic concepts derived earlier into a theory of the corporate ownership structure that takes account of the trade-offs available to the entrepreneur-manager between inside and outside equity and debt. Some qualifications and extensions of the analysis are discussed in Section 4.6, and Section 4.7 contains a brief summary and conclusions.

4.2 The Agency Costs of Outside Equity

Overview

In this section we analyze the effect of outside equity on agency costs by comparing the behavior of a manager who owns 100% of the residual claims on a firm with the behavior of a manager who sells off a portion of those claims to outsiders. If a wholly owned firm is managed by the owner, he will make operating decisions that maximize his utility. These decisions will involve not only the benefits derived from pecuniary returns but also the utility generated by various non-pecuniary aspects of his entrepreneurial activities, such as the physical appointments of the office, the attractiveness of the office staff, the level of employee discipline, the kind and amount of charitable contributions, personal relations ("friendship," "respect," and so on) with employees, a larger than optimal computer to play with, or purchase of production inputs from friends. The optimum mix (in the absence of taxes) of the various pecuniary and non-pecuniary benefits is achieved when the marginal utility derived from an additional dollar of expenditure (measured net of any productive effects) is equal for each non-pecuniary item and equal to the marginal utility derived from an additional dollar of after-tax purchasing power (wealth).

In the case of the owner-manager who sells equity claims on the corporation that are identical to his own (i.e., that share proportionately in the profits of the firm and have limited liability), agency costs will be generated by the divergence between his interest and those of the outside shareholders, since he will then bear only a fraction of the costs of any non-pecuniary benefits he takes out in maximizing his own utility. If the manager owns only 95% of the stock, he will expend resources to the point where the marginal utility derived from a dollar's expenditure of the firm's resources on such items equals the marginal utility of an additional 95 cents in general purchasing power (i.e., *his* share of the wealth reduction) and not one dollar. Such activities, on his part, can be limited (but probably not eliminated) by the expenditure of resources on monitoring activities by the outside stockholders. But as we show below, the owner will bear the entire wealth effects of these expected costs so long as the equity market anticipates these effects. Prospective minority shareholders will realize that the owner-manager's interests will diverge somewhat from theirs; hence the price that they will pay for shares will reflect the monitoring costs and the effect of the divergence between the manager's interest and theirs. Nevertheless, ignoring for the moment the possibility of borrowing against his wealth, the owner will find it desirable to bear these costs as long as the welfare increment he experiences from converting his claims on the firm into general purchasing power[16] is large enough to offset them.

As the owner-manager's fraction of the equity falls, his fractional claim on the outcomes falls and this will tend to encourage him to ap-

propriate larger amounts of the corporate resources in the form of perquisites. This also makes it desirable for the minority shareholders to
expend more resources in monitoring his behavior. Thus, the wealth
costs to the owner of obtaining additional cash in the equity markets
rise as his fractional ownership falls.

We will continue to characterize the agency conflict between the
owner-manager and outside shareholders as deriving from the manager's tendency to appropriate perquisites out of the firm's resources for
personal consumption. We do not mean to leave the impression, however, that this is the only or even the most important source of conflict.
Indeed, it is likely that the most important conflict arises from the fact
that as the manager's ownership claim falls, his incentive to devote significant effort to creative activities such as searching out new profitable
ventures falls. He may in fact avoid such ventures simply because it requires too much trouble or effort on his part to manage or to learn
about new technologies. Avoidance of these personal costs and the anx-
ieties that go with them also represents a source of on-the-job utility to
him, and it can result in the value of the firm being substantially lower
than it otherwise could be.

A Simple Formal Analysis of the Sources of Agency Costs of Equity and Who Bears Them

In order to develop some structure for the analysis to follow, we make
two sets of assumptions. The first set (permanent assumptions) carry
through almost all of the analysis in Sections 4.2–4.5. The effects of re-
laxing some of these are discussed in Section 4.6. The second set (temporary assumptions) are made only for expositional purposes and are
relaxed as soon as the basic points have been clarified.

Permanent assumptions
(P.1) All taxes are zero.
(P.2) No trade credit is available.
(P.3) All outside equity shares are nonvoting.
(P.4) No complex financial claims such as convertible bonds or
    preferred stock or warrants can be issued.
(P.5) Outside owners do not gain utility from ownership in a firm in
    any way other than through its effect on their wealth or cash
    flows.

(P.6) All dynamic aspects of the multiperiod nature of the problem are ignored by assuming there is only one production-financing decision to be made by the entrepreneur.

(P.7) The entrepreneur-manager's money wages are held constant throughout the analysis.

(P.8) There exists a single manager (the peak coordinator) with ownership interest in the firm.

Temporary assumptions

(T.1) The size of the firm is fixed.

(T.2) No monitoring or bonding activities are possible.

(T.3) No debt financing through bonds, preferred stock, or personal borrowing (secured or unsecured) is possible.

(T.4) All elements of the owner-manager's decision problem involving portfolio considerations induced by the presence of uncertainty and the existence of diversifiable risk are ignored.

Define:

X = $\{x_1, x_2, \ldots, x_n\}$ = vector of quantities of all factors and activities within the firm from which the manager derives non-pecuniary benefits;[17] the x_i are defined such that his marginal utility is positive for each of them;

$C(X)$ = total dollar cost of providing any given amount of these items;

$P(X)$ = total dollar value to the firm of the productive benefits of X;

$B(X)$ = $P(X) - C(X)$ = net dollar benefit to the firm of X ignoring any effects of X on the equilibrium wage of the manager.

Ignoring the effects of X on the manager's utility and therefore on his equilibrium wage rate, the optimum levels of the factors and activities X are defined by X^* such that

$$\frac{\partial B(X^*)}{\partial X^*} = \frac{\partial P(X^*)}{\partial X^*} - \frac{\partial C(X^*)}{\partial X^*} = 0.$$

Thus for any vector $X \geq X^*$ (i.e., where at least one element of X is greater than its corresponding element of X^*), $F \equiv B(X^*) - B(X) > 0$ measures the dollar cost to the firm (net of any productive effects) of providing the increment $X - X^*$ of the factors and activities that generate utility to the manager. We assume henceforth that for any given level of cost to the firm, F, the vector of factors and activities on which F

is spent are those, $\hat{X}$, that yield the manager maximum utility. Thus $F \equiv B(X^*) - B(\hat{X})$.

We have thus far ignored in our discussion the fact that these expenditures on X occur through time and therefore there are trade-offs to be made across time as well as between alternative elements of X. Furthermore, we have ignored the fact that the future expenditures are likely to involve uncertainty (i.e., they are subject to probability distributions) and therefore some allowance must be made for their riskiness. We resolve both of these issues by defining C, P, B, and F to be the *current market values* of the sequence of probability distributions on the period-by-period cash flows involved.[18]

Given the definition of F as the current market value of the stream of manager's expenditures on non-pecuniary benefits, we represent the constraint a single owner-manager faces in deciding how much non-pecuniary income to extract from the firm by the line $\overline{V}F$ in Figure 4.1. This is analogous to a budget constraint. The market value of the firm is measured along the vertical axis and the market value of the manager's stream of expenditures on non-pecuniary benefits, F, is measured along the horizontal axis. $O\overline{V}$ is the value of the firm when the amount of non-pecuniary income consumed is zero. By definition $\overline{V}$ is the maximum market value of the cash flows generated by the firm for a given money wage for the manager when his consumption of non-pecuniary benefits is zero. At this point all the factors and activities within the firm that generate utility for the manager are at the level X^* defined above. There is a different budget constraint $\overline{V}F$ for each possible scale of the firm (i.e., level of investment, I) and for alternative levels of money wage, W, for the manager. For the moment we pick an arbitrary level of investment (which we assume has already been made) and hold the scale of the firm constant at this level. We also assume that the manager's money wage is fixed at the level W^*, which represents the current market value of his wage contract[19] in the optimal compensation package consisting of both wages, W^*, and non-pecuniary benefits, F^*. Since one dollar of current value of non-pecuniary benefits withdrawn from the firm by the manager reduces the market value of the firm by $1, by definition, the slope of $\overline{V}F$ is -1.

The owner-manager's taste for wealth and non-pecuniary benefits is represented in Figure 4.1 by a system of indifference curves, U_1, U_2, and so on.[20] The indifference curves will be convex as drawn as long as the owner-manager's marginal rate of substitution between non-pecuniary

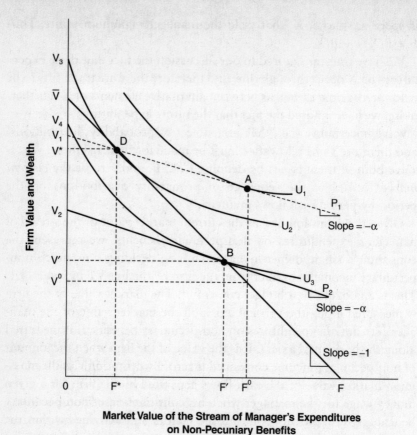

Figure 4.1   The value of the firm *(V)* and the level of non-pecuniary benefits consumed *(F)* when the fraction of outside equity is $(1-\alpha)$, and $U_j(j = 1,2,3)$ represents the owner's indifference curves between wealth and non-pecuniary benefits.

benefits and wealth diminishes with increasing levels of the benefits. For the 100% owner-manager, this presumes that there are not perfect substitutes for these benefits available on the outside, that is, to some extent they are job-specific. For the fractional owner-manager this presumes that the benefits cannot be turned into general purchasing power at a constant price.[21]

When the owner has 100% of the equity, the value of the firm will be V^* where indifference curve U_2 is tangent to $\overline{V}F$, and the level of non-pecuniary benefits consumed is F^*. If the owner sells the entire equity but remains as manager, and if the equity buyer could, at zero cost, force the old owner (as manager) to take the same level of non-pecuniary benefits as he did as owner, then V^* is the price the new owner would be willing to pay for the entire equity.[22]

In general, however, we cannot expect the new owner to be able to enforce identical behavior on the old owner at zero costs. If the old owner sells a fraction of the firm to an outsider, he, as manager, will no longer bear the full cost of any non-pecuniary benefits he consumes. Suppose the owner sells a share of the firm, $1 - \alpha$ $(0 < \alpha < 1)$, and retains for himself a share, α. If the prospective buyer believes that the owner-manager will consume the same level of non-pecuniary benefits as he did as full owner, the buyer will be willing to pay $(1 - \alpha)V^*$ for a fraction $(1 - \alpha)$ of the equity. Given that an outsider now holds a claim to $(1 - \alpha)$ of the equity, however, the *cost* to the owner-manager of consuming $1 of non-pecuniary benefits in the firm will no longer be $1. Instead, it will be $\alpha \times \$1$. If the prospective buyer actually paid $(1 - \alpha)V^*$ for his share of the equity, and if thereafter the manager could choose whatever level of non-pecuniary benefits he liked, his budget constraint would be V_1P_1 in Figure 4.1 and has a slope equal to $-\alpha$. Including the payment the owner receives from the buyer as part of the owner's post-sale wealth, his budget constraint, V_1P_1, must pass through D, since he can if he wishes have the same wealth and level of non-pecuniary consumption he enjoyed as full owner.

But if the owner-manager is free to choose the level of perquisites, F, subject only to the loss in wealth he incurs as a part owner, his welfare will be maximized by increasing his consumption of non-pecuniary benefits. He will move to point A where V_1P_1 is tangent to U_1, representing a higher level of utility. The value of the firm falls from V^* to V^0, that is, by the amount of the cost to the firm of the increased non-pecuniary expenditures, and the owner-manager's consumption of non-pecuniary benefits rises from F^* to F^0.

If the equity market is characterized by rational expectations, the buyers will be aware that the owner will increase his non-pecuniary consumption when his ownership share is reduced. If the owner's response function is known or if the equity market makes unbiased estimates of the owner's response to the changed incentives, the buyer will not pay $(1 - \alpha)V^*$ for $(1 - \alpha)$ of the equity.

Theorem. For a claim on the firm of $(1 - \alpha)$ the outsider will pay only $(1 - \alpha)$ times the value he expects the firm to have given the induced change in the behavior of the owner-manager.

Proof. For simplicity we ignore any element of uncertainty introduced by the lack of perfect knowledge of the owner-manager's response function. Such uncertainty will not affect the final solution if the equity market is large as long as the estimates are rational (i.e., unbiased) and the errors are independent across firms. The latter condition ensures that this risk is diversifiable and therefore that equilibrium prices will equal the expected values.

Let W represent the owner's total wealth after he has sold a claim equal to $1 - \alpha$ of the equity to an outsider. W has two components. One is the payment, S_o, made by the outsider for $1 - \alpha$ of the equity; the rest, S_i, is the value of the owner's (i.e., insider's) share of the firm, so that W, the owner's wealth, is given by

$$W = S_o + S_i = S_o + \alpha V(F, \alpha),$$

where $V(F, \alpha)$ represents the value of the firm given that the manager's fractional ownership share is α and that he consumes perquisites with current market value of F. Let $V_2 P_2$, with a slope of $-\alpha$ represent the trade-off the owner-manager faces between non-pecuniary benefits and his wealth after the sale. Given that the owner has decided to sell a claim $1 - \alpha$ of the firm, his welfare will be maximized when $V_2 P_2$ is tangent to some indifference curve such as U_3 in Figure 4.1. A price for a claim of $(1 - \alpha)$ on the firm that is satisfactory to both the buyer and the seller will require that this tangency occur along $\overline{V}F$, that is, that the value of the firm must be V'. To show this, assume that such is not the case—that the tangency occurs to the left of the point B on the line $\overline{V}F$. Then, since the slope of $V_2 P_2$ is negative, the value of the firm will be larger than V'. The owner-manager's choice of this lower level of consumption of non-pecuniary benefits will imply a higher value both to the firm as a whole and to the fraction of the firm $(1 - \alpha)$ the outsider has acquired; that is, $(1 - \alpha)V' > S_o$. From the owner's viewpoint, he has sold $1 - \alpha$ of the firm for less than he could have, given the (assumed) lower level of non-pecuniary benefits he enjoys. On the other hand, if the tangency point B is to the right of the line $\overline{V}F$, the owner-manager's higher consumption of non-pecuniary benefits means the value of the firm is less than V', and hence $(1 - \alpha)V(F, \alpha) < S_o = (1 - \alpha)V'$. The outside owner then has paid more for his share of the equity than it is worth. S_o will be a mutually satisfactory price if and only if

$(1 - \alpha)V' = S_o$. But this means that the owner's post-sale wealth is equal to the (reduced) value of the firm V', since

$$W = S_o + \alpha V' = (1 - \alpha)V' + \alpha V' = V'.$$

Q.E.D.

The requirement that V' and F' fall on $\overline{VF}$ is thus equivalent to requiring that the value of the claim acquired by the outside buyer be equal to the amount he pays for it, and conversely for the owner. This means that the decline in the total value of the firm $(V^* - V')$ is entirely imposed on the owner-manager. His total wealth after the sale of $(1 - \alpha)$ of the equity is V' and the decline in his wealth is $V^* - V'$.

The distance $V^* - V'$ is the reduction in the market value of the firm engendered by the agency relationship and is a measure of the "residual loss" defined earlier. In this simple example the residual loss represents the total agency costs engendered by the sale of outside equity because monitoring and bonding activities have not been allowed. The welfare loss the owner incurs is less than the residual loss by the value to him of the increase in non-pecuniary benefits $(F' - F^*)$. In Figure 4.1 the difference between the intercepts on the Y axis of the two indifference curves U_2 and U_3 is a measure of the owner-manager's welfare loss due to the incurrence of agency costs,[23] and he would sell such a claim only if the increment in welfare he achieved by using the cash amounting to $(1 - \alpha)V'$ for other things was worth more to him than this amount of wealth.

Determination of the Optimal Scale of the Firm:
The Case of All-Equity Financing

Consider the problem faced by an entrepreneur with initial pecuniary wealth, W, and monopoly access to a project requiring investment outlay, I, subject to diminishing returns to scale in I. Figure 4.2 portrays the solution to the optimal scale of the firm taking into account the agency costs associated with the existence of outside equity. The axes are as defined in Figure 4.1 except we now plot on the vertical axis the total wealth of the owner, that is, his initial wealth, W, plus $V(I) - I$, the net increment in wealth he obtains from exploitation of the investment opportunities. The market value of the firm, $V = V(I,F)$, is now a

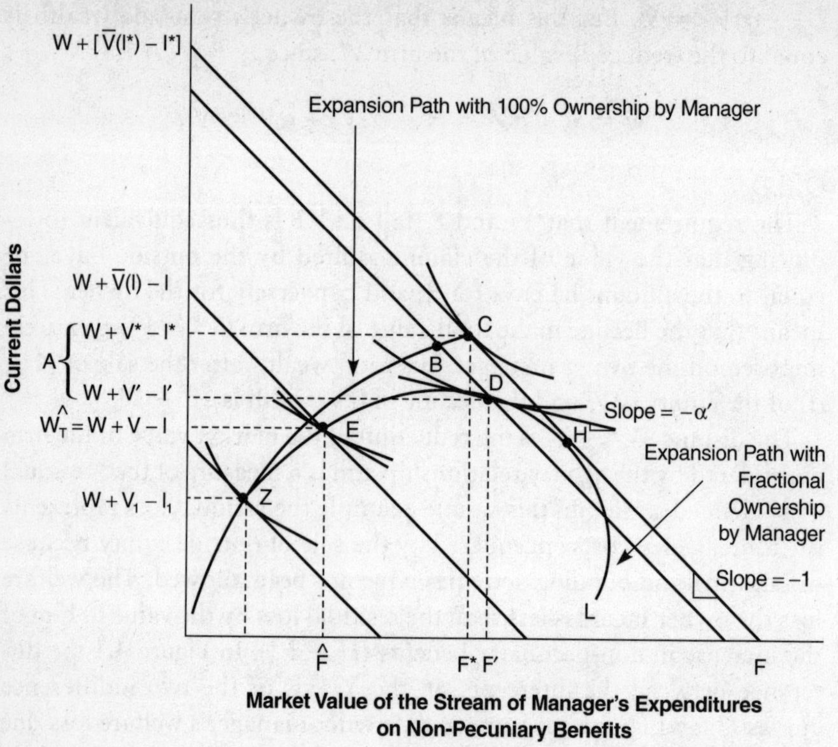

W + [V̄(I*) – I*]
Expansion Path with 100% Ownership by Manager
Current Dollars
W + V̄(I) – I
W + V* – I*
A
W + V′ – I′
Ŵ_T = W + V – I
W + V_1 – I_1
C
B
D
E
Z
H
L
Slope = –α′
Expansion Path with Fractional Ownership by Manager
Slope = –1
F̂
F* F′
F
Market Value of the Stream of Manager's Expenditures on Non-Pecuniary Benefits

Figure 4.2 Determination of the optimal scale of the firm in the case where no monitoring takes place. Point *C* denotes optimum investment, I^*, and non-pecuniary benefits, F^*, when investment is 100% financed by the entrepreneur. Point *D* denotes optimum investment, I', and non-pecuniary benefits, F', when outside equity financing is used to help finance the investment and the entrepreneur owns a fraction α' of the firm. The distance *A* measures the gross agency costs.

function of the level of investment, *I*, and the current market value of the manager's expenditures of the firm's resources on non-pecuniary benefits, *F*. Let $\overline{V}(I)$ represent the value of the firm as a function of the level of investment when the manager's expenditures on non-pecuniary benefits, *F*, are zero. The schedule with intercept labeled $W + [\overline{V}(I^*) - I^*]$ and slope equal to -1 in Figure 4.2 represents the locus of combinations of post-investment wealth and dollar cost to the firm of non-pecuniary benefits that are available to the manager when investment is carried to the value-maximizing point, I^*. At this point $\Delta\overline{V}(I) - \Delta I = 0$. If the manager's wealth were large enough to cover the investment required to reach this scale of operation, I^*, he would consume F^* in non-pecuniary benefits and have pecuniary wealth with value $W + V^*$ $- I^*$. If, however, outside financing is required to cover the investment, he will not reach this point if monitoring costs are non-zero.[24]

The expansion path $OZBC$ represents the equilibrium combinations of wealth and non-pecuniary benefits, F, which the manager could obtain if he had enough personal wealth to finance all levels of investment up to I^*. It is the locus of points such as Z and C that present the equilibrium position for the 100% owner-manager at each possible level of investment, I. As I increases we move up the expansion path to the point C where $V(I) - I$ is at a maximum. Additional investment beyond this point reduces the net value of the firm, and as it does the equilibrium path of the manager's wealth and non-pecuniary benefits retraces (in the reverse direction) the curve $OZBC$. We draw the path as a smooth concave function only as a matter of convenience.

If the manager obtained outside financing and if there were zero costs to the agency relationship (perhaps because monitoring costs were zero), the expansion path would also be represented by $OZBC$. Therefore, this path represents what we might call the "idealized" solutions, that is, those that would occur in the absence of agency costs.

Assume the manager has sufficient personal wealth to completely finance the firm only up to investment level I_1, which puts him at point Z. At this point $W = I_1$. To increase the size of the firm beyond this point he must obtain outside financing to cover the additional investment required, and this means reducing his fractional ownership. But doing this incurs agency costs, and the lower his ownership fraction, the larger are the agency costs he incurs. If the investments requiring outside financing are sufficiently profitable, however, his welfare will continue to increase.

The expansion path $ZEDHL$ in Figure 4.2 portrays one possible path of the equilibrium levels of the owner's non-pecuniary benefits and wealth at each possible level of investment higher than I_1. This path is the locus of points such as E or D where (1) the manager's indifference curve is tangent to a line with slope equal to $-\alpha$ (his fractional claim on the firm at that level of investment), and (2) the tangency occurs on the "budget constraint" with slope $= -1$ for the firm value and non-pecuniary benefit trade-off at the same level of investment.[25] As we move along $ZEDHL$ his fractional claim on the firm continues to fall as he raises larger amounts of outside capital. This expansion path represents his complete opportunity set for combinations of wealth and non-pecuniary benefits, given the existence of the costs of the agency relationship with the outside equity holders. Point D, where this opportunity set is tangent to an indifference curve, represents the solution that maximizes his welfare. At this point, the level of investments is I', his fractional ownership share in the firm is α', his wealth is $W + V' - I'$, and he consumes a stream of non-pecuniary benefits with current market value of F'. The gross agency costs (denoted by A) are equal to $(V^* - I^*) - (V' - I')$. Given that no monitoring is possible, I' is the socially optimal level of investment as well as the privately optimal level.

We can characterize the optimal level of investment as that point, I', that satisfies the following condition for small changes:

$$\Delta V - \Delta I + \alpha' \Delta F = 0. \tag{1}$$

$\Delta V - \Delta I$ is the change in the net market value of the firm, and $\alpha' \Delta F$ is the dollar value to the manager of the incremental fringe benefits he consumes (which cost the firm ΔF dollars); see note 26 for the proof and eq. (2).[26] Furthermore, recognizing that $V = \overline{V} - F$, where $\overline{V}$ is the value of the firm at any level of investment when $F = 0$, we can substitute into the optimum condition to get

$$(\Delta \overline{V} - \Delta 1) - (1 - \alpha') \Delta F = 0 \tag{3}$$

as an alternative expression for determining the optimum level of investment.

The idealized or zero agency cost solution, I^*, is given by the condition $(\Delta \overline{V} - \Delta I) = 0$, and since ΔF is positive the actual welfare maximizing level of investment I' will be less than I^*, because $(\Delta \overline{V} - \Delta I)$ must be positive at I' if (3) is to be satisfied. Since $-\alpha'$ is the slope of the indifference curve at the optimum and therefore represents the manager's demand price for incremental non-pecuniary benefits, ΔF, we know that $\alpha' \Delta F$ is the dollar value to him of an increment of fringe benefits costing the firm ΔF dollars. The term $(1 - \alpha') \Delta F$ thus measures the dollar "loss" to the firm (and himself) of an additional ΔF dollars spent on non-pecuniary benefits. The term $\Delta \overline{V} - \Delta I$ is the gross increment in the value of the firm ignoring any changes in the consumption of non-pecuniary benefits. Thus, the manager stops increasing the size of the firm when the gross increment in value is just offset by the incremental "loss" involved in the consumption of additional fringe benefits due to his declining fractional interest in the firm.[27]

The Role of Monitoring and Bonding Activities in Reducing Agency Costs

In the above analysis we have ignored the potential for controlling the behavior of the owner-manager through monitoring and other control activities. In practice, it is usually possible by expending resources to alter the opportunity the owner-manager has for capturing non-pecuniary benefits. These methods include auditing, formal control systems, budget restrictions, incentive compensation systems that serve to identify the manager's interests more closely with those of the outside equity holders, and so forth. Figure 4.3 portrays the effects of monitoring and other control activities in the simple situation portrayed in Figure 4.1. Figures 4.1 and 4.3 are identical except for the curve BCE in Figure 4.3, which depicts a "budget constraint" derived when monitoring possibilities are taken into account. Without monitoring, and with outside equity of $(1 - \alpha)$, the value of the firm will be V' and non-pecuniary expenditures F'. By incurring monitoring costs, M, the equity holders can restrict the manager's consumption of perquisites to amounts less than F'. Let $F(M, \alpha)$ denote the maximum perquisites the manager can consume for alternative levels of monitoring expenditures, M, given his ownership share α. We assume that increases in monitoring reduce F, and reduce it at a decreasing rate, that is, $\partial F/\partial M < 0$ and $\partial^2 F/\partial M^2 > 0$.

Since the current value of expected future monitoring expenditures by the outside equity holders reduces the value of any given claim on the firm to them dollar for dollar, the outside equity holders will take this into account in determining the maximum price they will pay for any given fraction of the firm's equity. Therefore, given positive monitoring activity the value of the firm is given by $V = \overline{V} - F(M,\alpha) - M$ *and the locus of these points for various levels of M* and for a given level of α lie on the line BCE in Figure 4.3. The vertical difference between the $\overline{V}F$ and BCE curves is M, the current market value of the future monitoring expenditures.

If it is possible for the outside equity holders to make these monitoring expenditures and thereby to impose the reductions in the owner-manager's consumption of F, he will voluntarily enter into a contract with the outside equity holders giving them the right to restrict his consumption of non-pecuniary items to F''. He finds this desirable because it will cause the value of the firm to rise to V''. Given the contract, the optimal monitoring expenditure on the part of the outsiders, M, is the

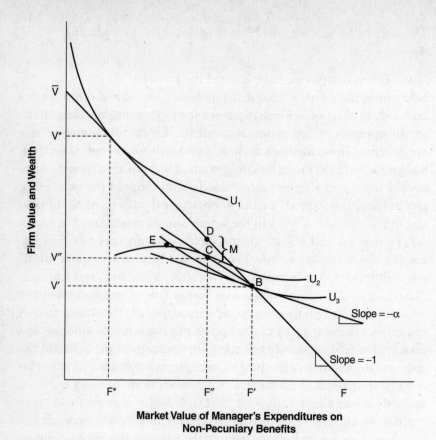

Figure 4.3 The value of the firm *(V)* and level of non-pecuniary benefits *(F)* when outside equity is $(1-\alpha)$, U_1, U_2, U_3 represent owner's indifference curves between wealth and non-pecuniary benefits, and monitoring (or bonding) activities impose opportunity set *BCE* as the trade-off constraint facing the owner.

amount $D - C$. The entire increase in the value of the firm that accrues will be reflected in the owner's wealth, but his welfare will be increased by less than this because he forgoes some non-pecuniary benefits he previously enjoyed.

If the equity market is competitive and makes unbiased estimates of the effects of monitoring expenditures on *F* and *V*, potential buyers will be indifferent between the following two contracts:

1. Purchase of a share $(1-\alpha)$ of the firm at a total price of $(1-\alpha)V'$ and no rights to monitor or control the manager's consumption of perquisites.

2. Purchase of a share $(1-\alpha)$ of the firm at a total price of $(1-\alpha)V''$ and the right to expend resources up to an amount equal to $D - C$ which will limit the owner-manager's consumption of perquisites to F''.

Given the contract (2) the outside shareholders would find it desirable to monitor to the full rights of their contract because it will pay them to do so. If the equity market is competitive, however, the total benefits (net of the monitoring costs) will be capitalized into the price of the claims. Thus, not surprisingly, the owner-manager reaps all the benefits of the opportunity to write and sell the monitoring contract.[28]

An analysis of bonding expenditures. We can also see from the analysis of Figure 4.3 that it makes no difference who actually makes the monitoring expenditures—the owner bears the full amount of these costs as a wealth reduction in all cases. Suppose that the owner-manager could expend resources to guarantee to the outside equity holders that he would limit his activities that cost the firm F. We call these expenditures "bonding costs," and they would take such forms as contractual guarantees to have the financial accounts audited by a public account, explicit bonding against malfeasance on the part of the manager, and contractual limitations on the manager's decision-making power (which impose costs on the firm because they limit his ability to take full advantage of some profitable opportunities as well as limiting his ability to harm the stockholders while making himself better off).

If incurring bonding costs were entirely under the control of the manager and if they yielded the same opportunity set BCE for him in Figure 4.3, he would incur them in amount $D - C$. This would limit his consumption of perquisites to F'' from F', and the solution is exactly the same as if the outside equity holders had performed the monitoring. The manager finds it in his interest to incur these costs as long as the net increments in his wealth they generate (by reducing the agency costs and therefore increasing the value of the firm) are more valuable than the perquisites given up. This optimum occurs at point C in both cases under our assumption that the bonding expenditures yield the same opportunity set as the monitoring expenditures. In general, of course, it will pay the owner-manager to engage in bonding activities and to write contracts that allow monitoring as long as the marginal benefits of each are greater than their marginal cost.

Optimal scale of the firm in the presence of monitoring and bonding activities. If we allow the outside owners to engage in (costly) monitoring activities to limit the manager's expenditures on non-pecuniary benefits and allow the manager to engage in bonding activities to guarantee to the outside owners that he will limit his consumption of F, we get an expansion path such as that illustrated in Figure 4.4 on which Z and G lie. We have assumed in drawing Figure 4.4 that the cost functions involved in monitoring and bonding are such that some positive levels of the activities are desirable, that is, yield benefits greater than their cost. If this is not true, the expansion path generated by the expenditure of resources on these activities would lie below ZD and no such activity would take place at any level of investment. Points Z, C, and D and the two expansion paths they lie on are identical to those portrayed in Figure 4.2. Points Z and C lie on the 100% ownership expansion path, and points Z and D lie on the fractional ownership, zero monitoring and bonding activity expansion path.

The path on which points Z and G lie is the one given by the locus of equilibrium points for alternative levels of investment characterized by the point labeled C in Figure 4.3, which denotes the optimal level of monitoring and bonding activity and the resulting values of the firm and non-pecuniary benefits to the manager given a fixed level of investment. If any monitoring or bonding is cost effective, the expansion path on which Z and G lie must be above the nonmonitoring expansion path over some range. Furthermore, if it lies anywhere to the right of the indifference curve passing through point D (the zero monitoring-bonding solution), the final solution to the problem will involve positive amounts of monitoring and bonding activities. On the basis of the discussion above, we know that as long as the contracts between the manager and outsiders are unambiguous regarding the rights of the respective parties, the final solution will be at that point where the new expansion path is just tangent to the highest indifference curve. At this point the optimal level of monitoring and bonding expenditures is M'' and b''; the manager's post-investment-financing wealth is given by $W + V'' - I'' - M'' - b''$ and his non-pecuniary benefits are F''. The total gross agency costs, A, are given by $A(M'', b'', \alpha'', I'') = (V^* - I^*) - (V'' - I'' - M'' - b'')$.

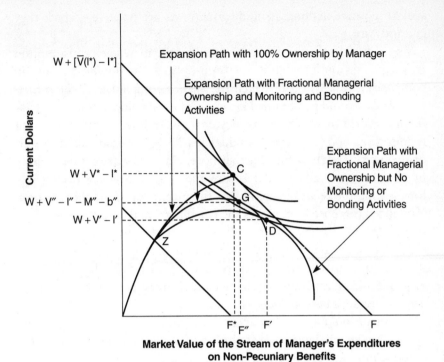

Expansion Path with 100% Ownership by Manager

Expansion Path with Fractional Managerial Ownership and Monitoring and Bonding Activities

Expansion Path with Fractional Managerial Ownership but No Monitoring or Bonding Activities

$W + [\overline{V}(I^*) - I^*]$

$W + V^* - I^*$

$W + V'' - I'' - M'' - b''$

$W + V' - I'$

Current Dollars

F^* F'' F' F

Market Value of the Stream of Manager's Expenditures on Non-Pecuniary Benefits

Figure 4.4 Determination of optimal scale of the firm allowing for monitoring and bonding activities. Optimal monitoring costs are M'' and bonding costs are b'', and the equilibrium scale of firm, manager's wealth, and consumption of non-pecuniary benefits is at point G.

Pareto Optimality and Agency Costs in Manager-Operated Firms

In general we expect to observe both bonding and external monitoring activities, and the incentives are such that the levels of these activities will satisfy the conditions of efficiency. They will not, however, result in the firms being run in a manner so as to maximize its value. The difference between V^*, the efficient solution under zero monitoring and bonding costs (and therefore zero agency costs), and V'', the value of the firm given positive monitoring costs, is the total gross agency costs defined earlier in the introduction. These are the costs of the separation of ownership and control Adam Smith focused on in the passage quoted at the beginning of this chapter and that Berle and Means (1932) were to popularize 157 years later. The solutions outlined above to our highly simplified problem imply that agency costs will be positive as long as monitoring costs are positive—which they certainly are.

The reduced value of the firm caused by the manager's consumption of perquisites outlined above is "non-optimal" or inefficient only in comparison to a world in which the agent's compliance to the principal's wishes could be obtained at zero cost or in comparison to a *hypothetical* world in which the agency costs were lower. But the costs of monitoring, bonding, and "residual loss" are an unavoidable result of the agency relationship. Furthermore, since they are borne entirely by the decision maker (in this case the original owner) responsible for creating the relationship, he has the incentives to see that they are minimized (because he captures the benefits from their reduction). Furthermore, these agency costs will be incurred only if the benefits to the owner-manager from their creation are great enough to outweigh them. In our current example these benefits arise from the availability of profitable investments requiring capital investment in excess of the original owner's personal wealth.

In conclusion, finding that agency costs are non-zero (i.e., that there are costs associated with the separation of ownership and control in the corporation) and concluding therefrom that the agency relationship is non-optimal, wasteful, or inefficient is equivalent in every sense to comparing a world in which iron ore is a scarce commodity (and therefore costly) to a world in which it is freely available at zero resource costs, and concluding that the first world is "non-optimal"—a perfect example of the fallacy criticized by Coase (1964) and what Demsetz (1969) characterizes as the "Nirvana" form of analysis.[29]

Factors Affecting the Size of the Divergence from Ideal Maximization

The magnitude of the agency costs discussed above will vary from firm to firm. It will depend on the tastes of managers, the costs of monitoring and bonding activities, and the ease with which managers can use their decision-making responsibilities to exercise their own preferences as opposed to the owners' preferences.[30] The agency costs will also depend upon the cost of measuring the manager's (agent's) performance and evaluating it, the cost of devising and applying an index for compensating the manager that correlates with the owner's (principal's) welfare, and the cost of devising and enforcing specific behavioral rules or policies. Where the manager has less than a controlling interest in the firm, it will also depend upon the labor market for managers. Competition from other potential managers limits the costs of obtaining managerial services (including the extent to which a given manager can diverge from the idealized solution that would obtain if all monitoring and bonding costs were zero). The size of the divergence (the agency costs) will be directly related to the cost of replacing the manager. If his responsibilities require very little knowledge specialized to the firm, if it is easy to evaluate his performance, and if replacement search costs are modest, the divergence from the ideal will be relatively small and vice versa.

The divergence will also be constrained by the market for the firm itself, that is, by capital markets. Owners always have the option of selling their firm, either as a unit or in pieces. Owners of manager-operated firms can and do sample the capital market from time to time. If they discover that the value of the future earnings stream to others is higher than the value of the firm to them given that it is to be manager-operated, they can exercise their right to sell. It is conceivable that other owners could be more efficient at monitoring or even that a single individual with appropriate managerial talents and with sufficiently large personal wealth would elect to buy the firm. In this latter case the purchase by such a single individual would completely eliminate the agency costs. If there were a number of such potential owner-manager purchasers (all with talents and tastes identical to the current manager), the owners would receive in the sale price of the firm the full value of the residual claimant rights including the capital value of the eliminated agency costs plus the value of the managerial rights.

Monopoly, competition, and managerial behavior. It is frequently argued that the existence of competition in product (and factor) markets will constrain the behavior of managers to idealized value maximization—that is, that monopoly in product (or monopsony in factor) markets will permit larger divergences from value maximization.[31] Our analysis does not support this hypothesis. The owners of a firm with monopoly power have the same incentives to limit divergences of the manager from value maximization (i.e., the ability to increase their wealth) as do the owners of competitive firms. Furthermore, competition in the market for managers will generally make it unnecessary for the owners to share rents with the manager. The owners of a monopoly firm need only pay the supply price for a manager.

Since the owner of a monopoly has the same wealth incentives to minimize managerial costs as would the owner of a competitive firm, both will undertake that level of monitoring that equates the marginal cost of monitoring to the marginal wealth increment from reduced consumption of perquisites by the manager. Thus the existence of monopoly will not increase agency costs.

Furthermore the existence of competition in product and factor markets will not eliminate the agency costs due to managerial control problems, as has often been asserted (see Friedman 1970). All firms will incur agency costs; competitive pressure will be felt only by firms with higher agency costs than their competitors.

The existence and size of the agency costs depends on the nature of the monitoring costs, the tastes of managers for non-pecuniary benefits, and the supply of potential managers who are capable of financing the entire venture out of their personal wealth. If monitoring costs are zero, agency costs will be zero, or if there are enough 100% owner-managers available to own and run all the firms in an industry (competitive or not) then agency costs in that industry will also be zero.[32]

4.3 Some Unanswered Questions Regarding the Existence of the Corporate Form

The analysis to this point has left us with a basic puzzle: Why, given the existence of positive costs of the agency relationship, do we find the usual corporate form of organization with widely diffuse ownership so widely prevalent? If one takes seriously much of the literature regarding the "discretionary" power held by managers of large corporations, it is difficult to understand the historical fact of enormous growth in equity in such organizations, not only in the United States but throughout the world. Paraphrasing Alchian (1968): How does it happen that millions of individuals are willing to turn over a significant fraction of their wealth to organizations run by managers who have so little interest in their welfare? What is even more remarkable, why are they willing to make these commitments purely as residual claimants, that is, on the anticipation that managers will operate the firm so that there will be earnings that accrue to the stockholders?

There is certainly no lack of alternative ways that individuals might invest, including entirely different forms of organizations. Even if consideration is limited to corporate organizations, there are clearly alternative ways capital might be raised: through fixed claims of various sorts, bonds, notes, mortgages, and so forth. Moreover, the corporate income tax seems to favor the use of fixed claims since interest is treated as a tax-deductible expense. Those who assert that managers do not behave in the interest of stockholders have generally not addressed a very important question: Why, if non-manager-owned shares have such a serious deficiency, have they not long since been driven out by fixed claims?[33]

Some Alternative Explanations of the Ownership Structure of the Firm

The role of limited liability. Manne (1967) and Alchian and Demsetz (1972) argue that one of the attractive features of the corporate form vis-à-vis individual proprietorships or partnerships is the limited liability feature of equity claims in corporations. Without this provision each and every investor purchasing one or more shares of a corporation would be potentially liable to the full extent of his personal wealth for the debts of the corporation. Few individuals would find this a desirable risk to accept and the major benefits to be obtained from risk reduction through diversification would be to a large extent unobtainable. This argument, however, is incomplete since limited liability does not eliminate the basic risk, it merely shifts it. The argument must rest ultimately on transaction costs. If all stockholders of GM were liable for GM's debts, the maximum liability for an individual shareholder would be greater than it would be if his shares had limited liability. However, given that many other stockholders also exist and that each would be liable for the unpaid claims in proportion to his ownership, it is highly unlikely that the maximum payment each would have to make would be large in the event of GM's bankruptcy since the total wealth of those stockholders would also be large. The existence of unlimited liability, however, would impose incentives for each shareholder to keep track of both the liabilities of GM and the wealth of the other GM owners. It is easily conceivable that the costs of so doing would, in the aggregate, be much higher than simply paying a premium in the form of higher interest rates to the creditors of GM in return for their acceptance of a contract that grants limited liability to the shareholders. The creditors would then bear the risk of any nonpayment of debts in the event of GM's bankruptcy.

It is also not generally recognized that limited liability is merely a necessary condition for explaining the magnitude of the reliance on equities, not a sufficient condition. Ordinary debt also carries limited liability.[34] If limited liability is all that is required, why do we not observe large corporations, individually owned, with a tiny fraction of the capital supplied by the entrepreneur, and the rest simply borrowed?[35] At first this question seems silly to many people (as does the question regarding why firms would ever issue debt or preferred stock under conditions where there are no tax benefits obtained from the treatment of interest or preferred dividend payments).[36] We have found that this question is often misinterpreted to ask why firms obtain capital. The issue is not why they obtain capital, but why they obtain it through the particular forms we have observed for such long periods of time. The fact is that no well-articulated answer to this question currently exists in the literature of either finance or economics.

The "irrelevance" of capital structure. In their pathbreaking article on the cost of capital, Modigliani and Miller (1958) demonstrated that in the absence of bankruptcy costs and tax subsidies on the payment of interest, the value of the firm is independent of the financial structure. They later (Modigliani and Miller 1963) demonstrated that the existence of tax subsidies on interest payments would cause the value of the firm to rise with the amount of debt financing by the amount of the capitalized value of the tax subsidy. But this line of argument implies that the firm should be financed almost entirely with debt. Realizing the inconsistency with observed behavior, Modigliani and Miller comment (1963, p. 442):

> It may be useful to remind readers once again that the existence of a tax advantage for debt financing . . . does not necessarily mean that corporations should at all times seek to use the maximum amount of debt in their capital structures . . . [T]here are as we pointed out, limitations imposed by lenders . . . as well as many other dimensions (and kinds of costs) in real-world problems of financial strategy which are not fully comprehended within the framework of static equilibrium models, either our own or those of the traditional variety. These additional considerations, which are typically grouped under the rubric of "the need for

preserving flexibility," will normally imply the maintenance by the corporation of a substantial reserve of untapped borrowing power.

Modigliani and Miller are essentially left without a theory of the determination of the optimal capital structure, and Fama and Miller (1972, p. 173), commenting on the same issue, reiterate this conclusion: "And we must admit that at this point there is little in the way of convincing research, either theoretical or empirical, that explains the amounts of debt that firms do decide to have in their capital structure."

The Modigliani-Miller theorem is based on the assumption that the probability distribution of the cash flows to the firm is independent of the capital structure. It is now recognized that the existence of positive costs associated with bankruptcy and the presence of tax subsidies on corporate interest payments will invalidate this irrelevance theorem precisely because the probability distribution of future cash flows changes as the probability of the incurrence of the bankruptcy costs changes, that is, as the ratio of debt to equity rises. We believe the existence of agency costs provides stronger reasons for arguing that the probability distribution of future cash flows is *not* independent of the capital or ownership structure.

While the introduction of bankruptcy costs in the presence of tax subsidies leads to a theory that defines an optimal capital structure,[37] we argue that this theory is seriously incomplete since it implies that no debt should ever be used in the absence of tax subsidies if bankruptcy costs are positive. Since we know debt was commonly used prior to the existence of the current tax subsidies on interest payments, this theory does not capture what must be some important determinants of the corporate capital structure.

In addition, neither bankruptcy costs nor the existence of tax subsidies can explain the use of preferred stock or warrants that have no tax advantages, and there is no theory that tells us anything about what determines the fraction of equity claims held by insiders as opposed to outsiders, which our analysis in Section 4.2 indicates is so important. We return to these issues later after analyzing in detail the factors affecting the agency costs associated with debt.

4.4   The Agency Costs of Debt

In general, if the agency costs engendered by the existence of outside owners are positive it will pay the absentee owner (i.e., shareholders) to sell out to an owner-manager who can avoid these costs.[38] This could be accomplished in principle by having the manager become the sole equity holder by repurchasing all of the outside equity claims with funds obtained through the issuance of limited liability debt claims and the use of his own personal wealth. This single-owner corporation would not suffer the agency costs associated with outside equity. There must therefore be some compelling reasons why we find the diffuse-owner corporate firm financed by equity claims so prevalent as an organizational form.

An ingenious entrepreneur eager to expand has open to him the opportunity to design a whole hierarchy of fixed claims on assets and earnings, with premiums paid for different levels of risk.[39] Why do we not observe large corporations individually owned with a tiny fraction of the capital supplied by the entrepreneur in return for 100% of the equity and the rest simply borrowed? We believe there are a number of reasons: (1) the incentive effects associated with highly leveraged firms; (2) the monitoring costs these incentive effects engender; and (3) bankruptcy costs. Furthermore, all of these costs are simply particular aspects of the agency costs associated with the existence of debt claims on the firm.

Incentive Effects and Agency Costs of Debt

We do not find many large firms financed almost entirely with debt-type claims (i.e., non-residual claims) because of the effect such a financial structure would have on the owner-manager's behavior. Potential creditors will not loan $100,000,000 to a firm in which the entrepreneur has an investment of $10,000. With that financial structure the owner-manager will have a strong incentive to engage in activities (investments) that promise very high payoffs if successful even if they have a very low probability of success. If they turn out well, he captures most of the gains; if they turn out badly, the creditors bear most of the costs.[40]

To illustrate the incentive effects associated with the existence of debt and to provide a framework within which we can discuss the effects of monitoring and bonding costs, wealth transfers, and the incidence of agency costs, we again consider a simple situation. Assume we have a manager-owned firm with no debt outstanding in a world in which there are no taxes. The firm has the opportunity to take one of two mutually exclusive equal cost investment opportunities, each of which yields a random payoff, $\overline{X}_j, T$ periods in the future ($j = 1,2$). Production and monitoring activities take place continuously between time 0 and time T, and markets in which the claims on the firm can be traded are open continuously over this period. After time T the firm has no productive activities, so the payoff $\overline{X}_j$ includes the distribution of all remaining assets. For simplicity, we assume that the two distributions are log-normally distributed and have the same expected total payoff, $E(\overline{X})$, where $\overline{X}$ is defined as the logarithm of the final payoff. The distributions differ only by their variances with $\sigma_1^2 \sigma_2^2$. The systematic or covariance risk of each of the distributions, β_j, in the Sharpe (1964)–Lintner (1965a) capital asset pricing model, is assumed to be identical. Assuming asset prices are determined according to the capital asset ... the preceding assumptions imply that the total market ... these distributions is identical, and we represent this

... ager has the right to decide which investment pro-
... after he decides this he has the opportunity to sell
... ns on the outcomes in the form of either debt or
... different between the two investments.[41]
... the owner has the opportunity *first* to issue debt, then to
which of the investments to take, and then to sell all or part of
his remaining equity claim on the market, he will not be indifferent between the two investments. The reason is that by promising to take the low variance project, selling bonds, and then taking the high variance project, he can transfer wealth from the (naive) bondholders to himself as equity holder.

Let X^* be the amount of the "fixed" claim in the form of a non-coupon bearing bond sold to the bondholders such that the total payoff to them R_j($j = 1,2$ denotes the distribution the manager chooses) is

$$R_j = X^*, \text{ if } \overline{X}_j \geq X^*,$$
$$= X_j, \text{ if } \overline{X}_j \leq X^*.$$

Let B_1 be the current market value of bondholder claims if investment 1 is taken, and let B_2 be the current market value of bondholder claims if investment 2 is taken. Since in this example the total value of the firm, V, is independent of the investment choice and also of the financing decision, we can use the Black-Scholes (1973) option pricing model to determine the values of the debt, B_j, and equity, S_j, under each of the choices.[42]

Black and Scholes derive the solution for the value of a European call option (one that can be exercised only at the maturity date) and argue that the resulting option pricing equation can be used to determine the value of the equity claim on a leveraged firm. That is, the stockholders in such a firm can be viewed as holding a European call option on the total value of the firm with exercise price equal to X^* (the face value of the debt), exercisable at the maturity date of the debt issue. More simply, the stockholders have the right to buy the firm back from the bondholders for a price of X^* at time T. Merton (1973, 1974) shows that as the variance of the outcome distribution rises, the value of the stock (i.e., call option) rises; and since our two distributions differ only in their variances, $\sigma_2^2 > \sigma_1^2$, the equity value S_1 is less than S_2. This implies $B_1 > B_2$, since $B_1 = V - S_1$, and $B_2 = V - S_2$.

Now if the owner-manager could sell bonds with face value X^* under the conditions that the potential bondholders believed this to be a claim on distribution 1, he would receive a price of B_1. After selling the bonds, his equity interest in distribution 1 would have value S_1. But we know S_2 is greater than S_1, and thus the manager can make himself better off by changing the investment to take the higher variance distribution 2, thereby redistributing wealth from the bondholders to himself. All this assumes of course that the bondholders could not prevent him from changing the investment program. If the bondholders cannot do so, and if they perceive that the manager has the opportunity to take distribution 2, they will pay the manager only B_2 for the claim X^*, realizing that his maximizing behavior will lead him to choose distribution 2. In this event there is no redistribution of wealth between bondholders and stockholders (and in general with rational expectations there never will be) and no welfare loss. It is easy to construct a case, however, in which these incentive effects do generate real costs.

Let cash flow distribution 2 in the previous example have an expected value, $E(X_2)$, which is lower than that of distribution 1. Then we know that $V_1 > V_2$, and if ΔV, which is given by

$$\Delta V = V_1 - V_2 = (S_1 - S_2) + (B_1 - B_2),$$

is sufficiently small relative to the reduction in the value of the bonds, the value of the stock will increase.[43] Rearranging the expression for which helps to explain why debt does not completely dominate capital structures—the existence of bankruptcy and reorganization costs.

It is important to emphasize that bankruptcy and liquidation are very different events. The legal definition of bankruptcy is difficult to specify precisely. In general, it occurs when the firm cannot meet a current payment on a debt obligation,[50] or when one or more of the other indenture provisions providing for bankruptcy is violated by the firm. In this event the stockholders have lost all claims on the firm,[51] and the remaining loss, the difference between the face value of the fixed claims and the market value of the firm, is borne by the debtholders. Liquidation of the firm's assets will occur only if the market value of the future cash flows generated by the firm is less than the opportunity cost of the assets, that is, the sum of the values that could be realized if the assets were sold piecemeal.

If there were no costs associated with the event called "bankruptcy," the total market value of the firm would not be affected by increasing the probability of its incurrence. However, it is costly, if not impossible, to write contracts representing claims on a firm that clearly delineate the rights of holders for all possible contingencies. Thus even if there were no adverse incentive effects in expanding fixed claims relative to equity in a firm, the use of such fixed claims would be constrained by the costs inherent in defining and enforcing those claims. Firms incur obligations daily to suppliers, to employees, to different classes of investors, and so forth. So long as the firm is prospering, the adjudication of claims is seldom a problem. When the firm has difficulty meeting some of its obligations, however, the issue of the priority of those claims can pose serious problems. This is most obvious in the extreme case where the firm is forced into bankruptcy. If bankruptcy were costless, the reorganization would be accompanied by an adjustment of the claims of various parties and the business could, if that proved to be in the interest of the claimants, simply go on (although perhaps under new management).[52]

In practice, bankruptcy is not costless but generally involves an adjudication process that itself consumes a fraction of the remaining value of the assets of the firm. Thus the costs of bankruptcy will be of concern to potential buyers of fixed claims in the firm because their existence will reduce the payoffs to them in the event of bankruptcy. These are examples of the agency costs of cooperative efforts among individuals (although in this case perhaps "non-cooperative" would be a better term). The price buyers will be willing to pay for fixed claims will thus be inversely related to the probability of the incurrence of these costs, that is, to the probability of bankruptcy. Using a variant of the argument employed above for monitoring costs, it can be shown that the total value of the firm will fall, and the owner-manager equity holder will bear the entire wealth effect of the bankruptcy costs as long as potential bondholders make unbiased estimates of their magnitude at the time they initially purchase bonds.[53]

Empirical studies of the magnitude of bankruptcy costs are almost nonexistent. Warner (1977), in a study of eleven railroad bankruptcies between 1930 and 1955, estimates the average costs of bankruptcy[54] as a fraction of the value of the firm three years prior to bankruptcy to be 2.5% (with a range of 0.4–5.9%). The average dollar costs were $1.88 million. Both of these measures seem remarkably small and are consistent with our belief that bankruptcy costs themselves are unlikely to be the major determinant of corporate capital structures. It is also interesting to note that the annual amount of defaulted funds has fallen significantly since 1940. (See Atkinson 1967.) One possible explanation for this phenomenon is that firms are using mergers to avoid the costs of bankruptcy. This hypothesis seems even more reasonable if, as is frequently the case, reorganization costs represent only a fraction of the costs associated with bankruptcy.

In general the revenues or the operating costs of the firm are not independent of the probability of bankruptcy and thus the capital structure of the firm. As the probability of bankruptcy increases, both the operating costs and the revenues of the firm are adversely affected, and some of these costs can be avoided by merger. For example, a firm with a high probability of bankruptcy will also find that it must pay higher salaries to induce executives to accept the higher risk of unemployment. Furthermore, in certain kinds of durable-goods industries the demand function for the firm's product will not be independent of the probability of bankruptcy. The computer industry is a good example. There, the buyer's welfare is dependent to a significant extent on the ability to maintain the equipment and on continuous hardware and software development. Furthermore, the owner of a large computer often receives benefits from the software developments of other users. Thus if the manufacturer leaves the business or loses its software support and development experts because of financial difficulties, the value of the equipment to its users will decline. The buyers of such services have a continuing interest in the manufacturer's viability not unlike that of a bondholder, except that their benefits come in the form of continuing services at lower cost rather than principal and interest payments. Service facilities and spare parts for automobiles and machinery are other examples.

In summary, then, the agency costs associated with debt[55] consist of:

- the costs of creating and structuring the debt contract;
- the opportunity wealth loss caused by the impact of debt on the investment decisions of the firm;
- the monitoring and bonding expenditures by the bondholders and the owner-manager (i.e., the firm); and
- the bankruptcy and reorganization costs.

Why Are the Agency Costs of Debt Incurred?

We have argued that the owner-manager bears the entire wealth effects of the agency costs of debt and that he captures the gains from reducing them. Thus the agency costs associated with debt discussed above will tend, in the absence of other mitigating factors, to discourage the use of corporate debt. What are the factors that encourage its use?

One factor is the tax subsidy on interest payments. (This will not explain preferred stock where dividends are not tax deductible.)[56] Modigliani and Miller (1963) originally demonstrated that the use of riskless perpetual debt will increase the total value of the firm (ignoring the agency costs) by an amount equal to τB, where τ is the marginal and average corporate tax rate and B is the market value of the debt. Fama and Miller (1972, chap. 4) demonstrate that for the case of risky debt the value of the firm will increase by the market value of the (uncertain) tax subsidy on the interest payments. Again, these gains will accrue entirely to the equity and will provide an incentive to utilize debt to the point where the marginal wealth benefits of the tax subsidy are just equal to the marginal wealth effects of the agency costs discussed above.

Even in the absence of these tax benefits, however, debt would be utilized if the ability to exploit potentially profitable investment opportunities is limited by the resources of the owner. If the owner of a project cannot raise capital, he will suffer an opportunity loss represented by the increment in value offered to him by the additional investment opportunities. Thus even though he will bear the agency costs from selling debt, he will find it desirable to incur them to obtain additional capital as long as the marginal wealth increments from the new investment projects are greater than the marginal agency costs of debt, and these agency costs are in turn less than those caused by the sale of additional equity discussed in Section 4.2. Furthermore, this solution is optimal from the social viewpoint. However, in the absence of tax subsidies on debt these projects must be unique to this firm[57] or they would be taken by other competitive entrepreneurs (perhaps new ones) who possess the requisite personal wealth to fully finance the projects[58] and therefore are able to avoid the existence of debt or outside equity.

4.5   A Theory of the Corporate Ownership Structure

In the previous sections we discussed the nature of agency costs associated with outside claims on the firm—both debt and equity. Our purpose here is to integrate these concepts into the beginnings of a theory of the corporate ownership structure. We use the term "ownership structure" rather than "capital structure" to highlight the fact that the crucial variables to be determined are not just the relative amounts of debt and equity but also the fraction of the equity held by the manager. Thus, for a given size firm we want a theory to determine three variables:[59]

S_i: inside equity (held by the manager);
S_o: outside equity (held by anyone outside of the firm); and
B: debt (held by anyone outside of the firm).

The total market value of the equity is $S = S_i + S_o$, and the total market value of the firm is $V = S + B$. In addition, we also wish to have a theory that determines the optimal size of the firm, that is, its level of investment.

Determination of the Optimal Ratio of Outside Equity to Debt

Consider first the determination of the optimal ratio of outside equity to debt, S_o/B. To do this let us hold the size of the firm constant. V, the actual value of the firm for a given size, will depend on the agency costs incurred, hence we use as our index of size V^*, the value of the firm at a given scale when agency costs are zero. For the moment we also hold

the amount of outside financing $(B + S_o)$ constant. Given that a specified amount of financing $(B + S_o)$ is to be obtained externally, our
problem is to determine the optimal fraction $E^* \equiv S^*_o/(B + S_o)$ to be
financed with equity.

We argued above that (1) as long as capital markets are efficient (i.e.,
characterized by rational expectations) the prices of assets such as debt
and outside equity will reflect unbiased estimates of the monitoring
costs and redistributions that the agency relationship will engender,
and (2) the selling owner-manager will bear these agency costs. Thus
from the owner-manager's standpoint the optimal proportion of outside funds to be obtained from equity (versus debt) *for a given level of
internal equity* is that E which results in minimum total agency costs.

Figure 4.5 presents a breakdown of the agency costs into two separate components: Define $A_{S_o}(E)$ as the total agency costs (a function of
E) associated with the "exploitation" of the outside equity holders by
the owner-manager, and $A_B(E)$ as the total agency costs associated with
the presence of debt in the ownership structure. $A_T(E) = A_{S_o}(E) +
A_B(E)$ is the total agency cost.

Consider the function $A_{S_o}(E)$. When $E \equiv S_o/(B + S_o)$ is zero (i.e.,
when there is no outside equity), the manager's incentive to exploit the
outside equity is at a minimum (zero) since the changes in the value of
the *total* equity are equal to the changes in *his* equity.[60] As E increases
to 100% his incentives to exploit the outside equity holders increase
and hence the agency costs $A_{S_o}(E)$ increase.

The agency costs associated with the existence of debt, $A_B(E)$ are
composed mainly of the value reductions in the firm and monitoring
costs caused by the manager's incentive to reallocate wealth from the
bondholders to himself by increasing the value of his equity claim.
They are at a maximum where all outside funds are obtained from
debt, that is, where $S_o = E = 0$. As the amount of debt declines to zero,
these costs also go to zero because, as E goes to 1, his incentive to reallocate wealth from the bondholders to himself falls. These incentives
fall for two reasons: (1) the total amount of debt falls, and therefore
it is more difficult to reallocate any given amount away from the debtholders; and (2) his share of any reallocation that is accomplished is
falling since S_o is rising and therefore $S_i/(S_o + S_i)$, his share of the total
equity, is falling.

The curve $A_T(E)$ represents the sum of the agency costs from various combinations of outside equity and debt financing, and as long as

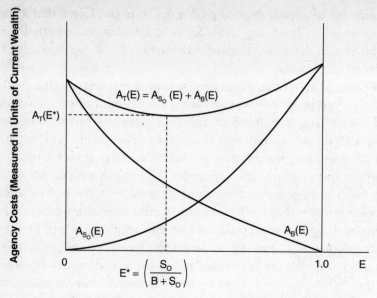

Figure 4.5 Total agency costs, $A_T(E)$, as a function of the ratio of outside equity to total outside financing, $E \equiv S_o/(B+S_o)$, for a given firm size V^* and given total amounts of outside financing $(B+S_o)$. $A_{s_o}(E) \equiv$ agency costs associated with outside equity. $A_B(E) \equiv$ agency costs associated with debt, B. $A_T(E^*) =$ minimum total agency costs at optimal fraction of outside financing E^*.

$A_{s_o}(E)$ and $A_B(E)$ are as we have drawn them, the minimum total agency cost for a given size firm and outside financing will occur at some point such as $A_T(E^*)$ with a mixture of both debt and equity.[61]

A caveat. Before proceeding further we point out that the issue regarding the exact shapes of the functions drawn in Figure 4.5 and several others discussed below is essentially an open question at this time. In the end, the shape of these functions is a question of fact and can only be settled by empirical evidence. We outline some a priori arguments that we believe lead to some plausible hypotheses about the behavior of the system, but confess that we are far from understanding the many conceptual subtleties of the problem. We are fairly confident of our arguments regarding the signs of the first derivatives of the functions, but the second derivatives are also important to the final solution and much more work (both theoretical and empirical) is required before we can have much confidence regarding these parameters. We anticipate the work of others as well as our own to cast more light on these issues. Moreover, we suspect the results of such efforts will generate revisions to the details of what follows. We believe it is worthwhile to delineate the overall framework in order to demonstrate, if only in a simplified fashion, how the major pieces of the puzzle fit together into a cohesive structure.

Effects of the Scale of Outside Financing

In order to investigate the effects of increasing the amount of outside financing, $B + S_o$, and therefore reducing the amount of equity held by the manager, S_i, we continue to hold the scale of the firm, V^*, constant. Figure 4.6 presents a plot of the agency cost functions $A_{S_o}(E)$, $A_B(E)$, and $A_T(E) = A_{S_o}(E) + A_B(E)$, for two different levels of outside financing. Define an index of the amount of outside financing to be

$$K = (B + S_o)/V^*,$$

and consider two different possible levels of outside financing K_o and K_1 for a given scale of the firm such that $K_o < K_1$.

As the amount of outside equity increases, the owner's fractional claim on the firm, α, falls. He will be induced thereby to take additional non-pecuniary benefits out of the firm because his share of the cost falls. This also increases the marginal benefits from monitoring activities and therefore will tend to increase the optimal level of monitoring. Both of these factors will cause the locus of agency costs $A_{S_o}(E;K)$ to shift upward as the fraction of outside financing, K, increases. This is depicted in Figure 4.6 by the two curves representing the agency costs of equity, one for the low level of outside financing, $A_{S_o}(E;K_o)$, the other for the high level of outside financing, $A_{S_o}(E;K_1)$. The locus of the latter lies above the former everywhere except at the origin, where both are zero.

The agency cost of debt will similarly rise as the amount of outside financing increases. This means that the locus of $A_B(E;K_1)$ for high outside financing, K_1, will lie above the locus of $A_B(E;K_o)$ for low outside financing, K_o because the total amount of resources that can be reallocated from bondholders increases as the total amount of debt increases. However, since these costs are zero when the debt is zero for both K_o and K_1, the intercepts of the $A_B(E;K)$ curves coincide at the right axis.

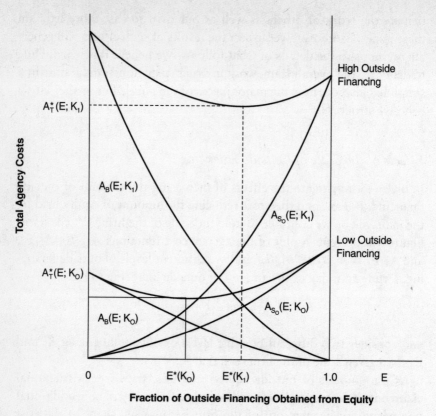

Figure 4.6 Agency cost functions and optimal outside equity as a fraction of total outside financing, $E^*(K)$, for two different levels of outside financing, K, for a given size firm, $V^* : K_1 > K_0$.

The net effect of the increased use of outside financing given the cost functions assumed in Figure 4.6 is (1) to increase the total agency costs from $A_T(E^*;K_0)$ to $A_T(E^*;K_1)$, and (2) to increase the optimal fraction of outside funds obtained from the sale of outside equity. We draw these functions for illustration only and are unwilling to speculate at this time on the exact form of $E^*(K)$ that gives the general effects of increasing outside financing on the relative quantities of debt and equity.

The locus of points $A_T(E^*;K)$ where agency costs are minimized (not drawn in Figure 4.6) determines $E^*(K)$, the optimal proportions of equity and debt to be used in obtaining outside funds as the fraction of outside funds, K, ranges from 0 to 100%. The solid line in Figure 4.7 is a plot of the minimum total agency costs as a function of the amount

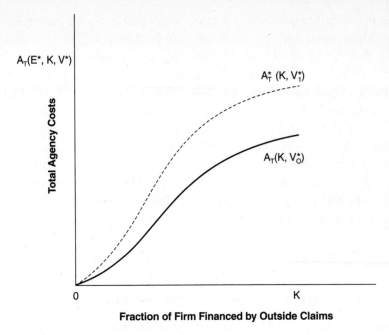

Figure 4.7 Total agency costs as a function of the fraction of the firm financed by outside claims for two firm sizes, $V_1^* > V_0^*$.

of outside financing for a firm with scale V_0^*. The dotted line shows the total agency costs for a larger firm with scale $V_1^* > V_0^*$. That is, we hypothesize that the larger the firm becomes, the larger are the total agency costs because it is likely that the monitoring function is inherently more difficult and expensive in a larger organization.

Risk and the Demand for Outside Financing

The model we have used to explain the existence of minority shareholders and debt in the capital structure of corporations implies that the owner-manager, if he resorts to any outside funding, will have his entire wealth invested in the firm. The reason is that he can thereby avoid the agency costs that additional outside funding imposes. This suggests he would not resort to outside funding until 100% of his personal wealth was invested in the firm—an implication that is not consistent with what we generally observe. Most owner-managers hold personal wealth in a variety of forms, and some have only a relatively small fraction of their wealth invested in the corporation they manage.[62] Diversification on the part of owner-managers can be explained by risk aversion and optimal portfolio selection.

If the returns from assets are not perfectly correlated, an individual can reduce the riskiness of the returns on his portfolio by dividing his wealth among many different assets, that is, by diversifying.[63] Thus a manager who invests all of his wealth in a single firm (his own) will generally bear a welfare loss (if he is risk averse) because he is bearing more risk than necessary. He will, of course, be willing to pay something to avoid this risk, and the costs of accomplishing this diversification will be the agency costs outlined above. He will suffer a wealth loss as he reduces his fractional ownership because prospective shareholders and bondholders will take into account the agency costs. Nevertheless, the manager's desire to avoid risk will contribute to his becoming a minority stockholder.

Determination of the Optimal Amount of Outside Financing, K*

Assume for the moment that the owner of a project (i.e., the owner of a prospective firm) has enough wealth to finance the entire project himself. The optimal scale of the corporation is then determined by the condition that $\Delta V - \Delta I = 0$. In general if the returns to the firm are uncertain, the owner-manager can increase his welfare by selling off part of the firm either as debt or equity and reinvesting the proceeds in other assets. If he does this with the optimal combination of debt and equity (as in Figure 4.6), the total wealth reduction he will incur is given by the agency cost function, $A_T(E^*,K;V^*)$ in Figure 4.7. The functions $A_T(E^*,K;V^*)$ will be S-shaped (as drawn) if total agency costs for a given scale of firm increase at an increasing rate at low levels of outside financing, and at a decreasing rate for high levels of outside financing as monitoring imposes more and more constraints on the manager's actions.

Figure 4.8 shows marginal agency costs as a function of K, the fraction of the firm financed with outside funds assuming the total agency cost function is as plotted in Figure 4.7, and assuming the scale of the firm is fixed. The demand by the owner-manager for outside financing is shown by the remaining curve in Figure 4.8. This curve represents the marginal value of the increased diversification the manager can obtain by reducing his ownership claims and optimally constructing a diversified portfolio. It is measured by the amount he would pay to be allowed to reduce his ownership claims by a dollar in order to increase

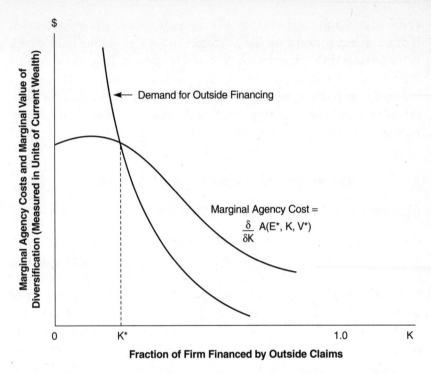

Figure 4.8 Determination of the optimal amount of outside financing, K^*, for a given scale of firm.

his diversification. If the liquidation of some of his holdings also influences the owner-manager's consumption set, the demand function plotted in Figure 4.8 also incorporates the marginal value of these effects. The intersection of these two schedules determines the optimal fraction of the firm to be held by outsiders, and this in turn determines the total agency costs borne by the owner. This solution is Pareto-optimal; there is no way to reduce the agency costs without making someone worse off.

Determination of the Optimal Scale of the Firm

While the details of the solution of the optimal scale of the firm are complicated when we allow for the issuance of debt, equity, and monitoring and bonding, the general structure of the solution is analogous to the case where monitoring and bonding are allowed for the outside equity example (see Figure 4.4).

If it is optimal to issue any debt, the expansion path taking full account of such opportunities must lie above the curve ZG in Figure 4.4. If this new expansion path lies anywhere to the right of the indifference curve passing through point G, debt will be used in the optimal financing package. Furthermore, the optimal scale of the firm will be determined by the point at which this new expansion path touches the highest indifference curve. In this situation the resulting level of the owner-manager's welfare must therefore be higher.

4.6   Qualifications and Extensions of the Analysis

Multiperiod Aspects of the Agency Problem

We have assumed throughout our analysis that we are dealing only with a single investment-financing decision by the entrepreneur and have ignored the issues associated with the incentives affecting future financing-investment decisions that might arise after the initial set of contracts are consummated between the entrepreneur-manager, outside stockholders, and bondholders. These are important issues which are left for future analysis.[64] Their solution will undoubtedly introduce some changes in the conclusions of the single decision analysis. It seems clear, for instance, that the expectation of future sales of outside equity and debt will change the costs and benefits facing the manager in making decisions that benefit him at the (short-run) expense of the current bondholders and stockholders. If he develops a reputation for such dealings, he can expect this to unfavorably influence the terms at which he can obtain future capital from outside sources. This will tend to increase the benefits associated with "sainthood" and will tend to reduce the size of the agency costs. Given the finite life of any individual, however, such an effect cannot reduce these costs to zero, because at some point these future costs will begin to weigh more heavily on his successors and therefore the relative benefits to him of acting in his own best interests will rise.[65] Furthermore, it will generally be impossible for him to fully guarantee to the outside interests that his successor will continue to follow his policies.

The Control Problem and the Outside Owner's Agency Costs

The careful reader will notice that nowhere in the analysis thus far have we taken into account many of the details of the relationship between the part owner-manager and the outside stockholders and bondhold-ers. In particular, we have assumed that all outside equity is nonvoting. If such equity does have voting rights, then the manager will be con-cerned about the effects on his long-run welfare of reducing his frac-tional ownership below the point where he loses effective control of the corporation—that is, below the point where it becomes possible for the outside equity holders to fire him. A complete analysis of this is-sue will require a careful specification of the contractual rights involved on both sides, the role of the board of directors, and the coordina-tion (agency) costs borne by the stockholders in implementing policy changes. This latter point involves consideration of the distribution of the outside ownership claims. Simply put, forces exist to determine an equilibrium distribution of outside ownership. If the costs of reducing the dispersion of ownership are lower than the benefits to be obtained from reducing the agency costs, it will pay some individual or group of individuals to buy shares in the market to reduce the dispersion of ownership. We occasionally witness these conflicts for control that in-volve outright market purchases, tender offers, and proxy fights. Fur-ther analysis of these issues is left to the future.

A Note on the Existence of Inside Debt and Some Conjectures on the Use of Convertible Financial Instruments

We have been asked[66] why debt held by the manager (i.e., "inside debt") plays no role in our analysis. We have as yet been unable to in-corporate this dimension formally into our analysis in a satisfactory way. The question is a good one and suggests some potentially impor-tant extensions of the analysis. For instance, it suggests an inexpensive way for the owner-manager with both equity and debt outstanding to eliminate a large part (perhaps all) of the agency costs of debt. If he binds himself contractually to hold a fraction of the total debt equal to his fractional ownership of the total equity, he would have no incentive whatsoever to reallocate wealth from the debtholders to the stockhold-ers. Consider the case where

$$B_i/S_i = B_o/S_o, \tag{4}$$

where S_i and S_o are as defined earlier, B_i is the dollar value of the inside debt held by the owner-manager, and B_o is the debt held by outsiders. In this case, if the manager changes the investment policy of the firm to re-allocate wealth between the debt- and equity holders, the net effect on the total value of his holdings in the firm will be zero. Therefore, his incentives to perform such reallocations are zero.[67]

Why then do we not observe practices or formal contracts that accomplish this elimination or reduction of the agency costs of debt? Maybe we do for smaller privately held firms (we have not attempted to obtain this data), but for large, diffuse-owner corporations the practice does not seem to be common. One reason for this, we believe, is that in some respects the claim that the manager holds on the firm in the form of his wage contract has some of the characteristics of debt.[68] If true, this implies that even with zero holdings of formal debt claims he still has positive holdings of a quasi-debt claim and this may accomplish the satisfaction of condition (4). The problem here is that any formal analysis of this issue requires a much deeper understanding of the relationship between formal debt holdings and the wage contract; that is, how much debt is it equivalent to?

This line of thought also suggests some other interesting issues. Suppose the implicit debt characteristics of the manager's wage contract result in a situation equivalent to

$$B_i/S_i > B_o/S_o.$$

Then he would have incentives to change the operating characteristics of the firm (i.e., reduce the variance of the outcome distribution) to transfer wealth from the stockholders to the debtholders, which is the reverse of the situation we examined in Section 4.4. Furthermore, this seems to capture some of the concern often expressed regarding the fact that managers of large publicly held corporations seem to behave in a risk-averse way to the detriment of the equity holders. One solution to this would be to establish incentive compensation systems for management or to grant stock options that in effect give managers a claim on the upper tail of the outcome distribution. This also seems to be a commonly observed phenomenon.

This analysis also suggests some additional issues we have yet to formally analyze regarding the costs and benefits associated with the use of more complicated financial claims such as warrants, convertible bonds, and convertible preferred stock. Warrants, convertible bonds, and convertible preferred stock have some of the characteristics of nonvoting shares, although they can be converted into voting shares under some terms. Alchian and Demsetz (1972) provide an interesting analysis regarding the use of nonvoting shares. They argue that some shareholders with strong beliefs in the talents and judgments of the manager will want to be protected against the possibility that some other shareholders will take over and limit the actions of the manager (or fire him). Given that the securities exchanges prohibit the use of nonvoting shares by listed firms, the use of the option-type securities might be a substitute for these claims.

In addition, warrants represent a claim on the upper tail of the distribution of outcomes, and convertible securities can be thought of as securities with nondetachable warrants. It seems that the incentive effect of warrants would tend to offset to some extent the incentive effects of the existence of risky debt because the owner-manager would be sharing part of the proceeds associated with a shift in the distribution of returns with the warrant holders. Thus, we conjecture that potential bondholders will find it attractive to have warrants attached to the risky debt of firms in which it is relatively easy to shift the distribution of outcomes to expand the upper tail of the distribution to transfer wealth from bondholders. It would also then be attractive to the owner-manager because of the reduction in the agency costs he would bear. This argument also implies that it would make little difference if the warrants were detachable (and therefore saleable separately from the bonds) since their mere existence would reduce the incentives of the manager (or stockholders) to increase the riskiness of the firm (and therefore increase the probability of bankruptcy). Furthermore, the addition of a conversion privilege to fixed claims such as debt or preferred stock would also tend to reduce the incentive effects of the existence of such fixed claims and therefore lower the agency costs associated with them. The theory predicts that these phenomena should be more frequently observed in cases where the incentive effects of such fixed claims are high than when they are low.

Monitoring and the Social Product of Security Analysts

One of the areas in which further analysis is likely to lead to high payoffs is that of monitoring. We currently have little work that could be glorified by the title of "A Theory of Monitoring," and yet this is a crucial building block of the analysis. We would expect monitoring activities to become specialized to those institutions and individuals who possess comparative advantages in these activities. One of the groups that seem to play a large role in these activities is composed of the security analysts employed by institutional investors, brokers, and investment advisory services as well as the analysis performed by individual investors in the normal course of investment decision making.

There is a large body of evidence that security prices incorporate in an unbiased manner all publicly available information and much of what might be called "private information."[69] There is also a large body of evidence that the security analysis activities of mutual funds and other institutional investors are not reflected in portfolio returns, that is, they do not increase risk-adjusted portfolio returns over a naive random selection buy-and-hold strategy.[70] Therefore, some have been tempted to conclude that the resources expended on such research activities to find undervalued or overvalued securities is a social loss. Jensen (1979) argues that this conclusion cannot be unambiguously drawn because there is a large consumption element in the demand for these services.

Furthermore, the analysis of this chapter would seem to indicate that to the extent that security analysis activities reduce the agency costs associated with the separation of ownership and control, they are indeed socially productive. Moreover, if this is true, we expect the major benefits of the security analysis activity to be reflected in the higher capitalized value of the ownership claims to corporations and *not* in the period-to-period portfolio returns of the analyst. Equilibrium in the security analysis industry requires that the private returns to analysis (i.e., portfolio returns) must be just equal to the private costs of such activity,[71] and this will not reflect the social product of this activity that will consist of larger output and higher *levels* of the capital value of ownership claims. Therefore, the argument implies that if there is a nonoptimal amount of security analysis being performed, it is too much,[72] not too little (since shareholders would be willing to pay directly to have the "optimal" monitoring performed), and we do not seem to observe such payments.

Specialization in the Use of Debt and Equity

Our previous analysis of agency costs suggests at least one other testable hypothesis: namely, that in those industries where the incentive effects of outside equity or debt are widely different, we would expect to see specialization in the use of the low agency cost financing arrangement. In industries where it is relatively easy for managers to lower the mean value of the outcomes of the enterprise by outright theft, special treatment of favored customers, ease of consumption of leisure on the job, and so forth (e.g., the bar and restaurant industry), we would expect to see the ownership structure of firms characterized by relatively little outside equity (i.e., 100% ownership of the equity by the manager) with almost all outside capital obtained through the use of debt.

The theory predicts the opposite would be true where the incentive effects of debt are large relative to the incentive effects of equity. Firms like conglomerates, in which it would be easy to shift outcome distributions adversely for bondholders (by changing the acquisition or divestiture policy), should be characterized by relatively lower utilization of debt. Conversely, in industries where the freedom of management to take riskier projects is severely constrained (e.g., regulated industries such as public utilities), we should find more intensive use of debt financing.

The analysis suggests that in addition to the fairly well-understood role of uncertainty in the determination of the quality of collateral, there is at least one other element of great importance—the ability of the owner of the collateral to change the distribution of outcomes by shifting either the mean outcome or the variance of the outcomes. A study of bank lending policies should reveal these to be important aspects of the contractual practices observed there.

Application of the Analysis to the Large Diffuse-Ownership Corporation

While we believe the structure outlined in the preceding pages is applicable to a wide range of corporations, it is still in an incomplete state. One of the most serious limitations of the analysis is that, as it stands, we have not worked out its application to the very large modern corporation whose managers own little or no equity. We believe our approach can be applied to this case, but the details must await future work.

The Supply Side of the Incomplete Markets Question

The analysis of this chapter is also relevant to the incomplete markets issue considered by Arrow (1964a), Diamond (1967), Hakansson (1974,

1976, 1978), Rubenstein (1974), Ross (1974b), and others. The problems addressed in this literature derive from the fact that whenever the available set of financial claims on outcomes in a market fails to span the underlying state space (see Arrow 1964a; Debreu 1959), the resulting allocation is Pareto-inefficient. A disturbing element in this literature surrounds the fact that the inefficiency conclusion is generally drawn without explicit attention in the analysis to the costs of creating new claims or of maintaining the expanded set of markets called for to bring about the welfare improvement.

The demonstration of a possible welfare improvement from the expansion of the set of claims by the introduction of new basic contingent claims or options can be thought of as an analysis of the demand conditions for new markets. Viewed from this perspective, what is missing in the literature on this problem is the formulation of a positive analysis of the supply of markets (or the supply of contingent claims). That is, what is it in the maximizing behavior of individuals in the economy that causes them to create and sell contingent claims of various sorts?

The analysis in this chapter can be viewed as a small first step in the direction of formulating an analysis of the supply of markets issue, which is founded in the self-interested maximizing behavior of individuals. We have shown why it is in the interest of a wealth-maximizing entrepreneur to create and sell claims such as debt and equity. Furthermore, as we have indicated, it appears that extensions of these arguments will lead to a theory of the supply of warrants, convertible bonds, and convertible preferred stock. We are not suggesting that the specific analysis offered in this chapter is likely to be sufficient to lead to a theory of the supply of the wide range of contracts (both existing and merely potential) in the world at large. We do believe, however, that framing the question of the completeness of markets in terms of the joining of both the demand and supply conditions will be very fruitful instead of implicitly assuming that new claims spring forth from some (costless) wellhead of creativity unaided or unsupported by human effort.

4.7   Conclusions

The publicly held business corporation is an awesome social invention. Millions of individuals voluntarily entrust billions of dollars, francs, pesos, and so on of personal wealth to the care of managers on the basis of a complex set of contracting relationships that delineate the rights of the parties involved. The growth in the use of the corporate form as well as the growth in market value of established corporations suggests that, at least up to the present, creditors and investors have by and large not been disappointed with the results, despite the agency costs inherent in the corporate form.

Agency costs are as real as any other costs. The level of agency costs depends, among other things, on statutory and common law and human ingenuity in devising contracts. Both the law and the sophistication of contracts relevant to the modern corporation are the products of a historical process in which there were strong incentives for individuals to minimize agency costs. Moreover, there were alternative organizational forms available, and opportunities to invent new ones. Whatever its shortcomings, the corporation has thus far survived the market test against potential alternatives.

5

Stockholder, Manager, and Creditor Interests: Applications of Agency Theory

5.1   Introduction

The modern corporate form of organization is a highly productive social invention. It accounts for a large fraction of nonagricultural output and employment in the West. Despite its importance, scholars had not until the 1980s developed a knowledge of the factors that make it so productive. Our purpose here is to review some of the work in agency theory that has implications for the structure of the corporation: in particular the resolution of conflicts of interest among stockholders, managers, and creditors.

We view the corporation as a legal entity that serves as a nexus for a complex set of explicit and implicit contracts among disparate individuals (Jensen and Meckling 1976, pp. 310–11, and Chapter 4 of this volume). The nexus-of-contracts view provides useful insights. For example, it helps to dispel the tendency to treat organizations as if they were persons; organizations do not have preferences and they do not choose in the conscious and rational sense that we attribute to people. Instead, the behavior of an organization is the equilibrium behavior of a complex contractual system made up of maximizing agents with diverse and conflicting objectives. In this sense, the behavior of the organization is like the equilibrium behavior of a market.

Construction of a theory of organizations involves describing the equilibrium behavior of these complex contractual systems where the individual agent is the elementary unit of analysis. In such a theory the exogenous variables are individuals' preferences and opportunity

By Michael C. Jensen and Clifford W. Smith, Jr.; originally published in *Recent Advances in Corporate Finance,* ed. E. I. Altman and M. G. Subrahmanyam (Homewood, Ill.: Irwin, 1985), pp. 93–131.

sets, including the impact of the contracting technology on opportunity sets. The structure of contracts, the forms of institutions, and the firm's investment, financing, dividend, insurance, accounting, production, and marketing policies are all endogenous, that is, determined within the system.

Agency Theory

Narrowly defined, an agency relationship is a contract in which one or more persons—the principal(s)—engage another person—the agent—to take actions on behalf of the principal(s) that involve the delegation of some decision-making authority to the agent. Spence and Zeckhauser (1971) and Ross (1973) provide early formal analyses of the problems associated with structuring the agent's compensation to align the agent's incentives with the interest of the principal. In Chapter 4, Jensen and Meckling argue that agency problems emanating from conflicts of interest are general to virtually all cooperative activity among individuals, whether or not they occur in the hierarchical fashion suggested by the principal-agent analogy.

The substantial attention devoted to developing a theory of agency has resulted in two approaches, which we refer to as the "positive theory of agency" and the "principal-agent" literatures. Although they differ in many respects, both literatures address the contracting problem among self-interested individuals and assume that in any contracting relationship total agency costs are minimized. The principal-agent literature is generally mathematical and nonempirically oriented, whereas the positive-agency literature is generally nonmathematical and empirically oriented. The principal-agent literature has concentrated more on analysis of the effects of preferences and asymmetric information and less on the effects of the technology of contracting and control. We focus here on the positive-agency literature. Jensen (1983) provides additional comparison of the two approaches.

In Chapter 4, Jensen and Meckling define agency costs as the sum of the out-of-pocket costs of structuring, administering, and enforcing contracts (both formal and informal) plus the residual loss. Enforcement costs include both monitoring and bonding costs, that is, the resources expended by the principal and agent, respectively, to ensure contract enforcement. It pays to expend resources on enforcement only to the point where the reduction in the loss from noncompliance equals the increase in enforcement costs. The residual loss represents the opportunity loss remaining when contracts are optimally but imperfectly enforced. Thus agency costs include all costs frequently referred to as contracting costs, transaction costs, moral-hazard costs, and information costs.

The key to understanding the agency problem is recognizing that the parties to a contract bear the agency costs of the relationship. Therefore, for any given scale of activity, self-interested maximizing agents will minimize the agency costs in any contracting relationship. It pays to write contracts that provide monitoring and bonding activities, but only to the point where their marginal cost equals the marginal gains from reducing the residual loss. Specifically, parties to a contract can make themselves better off by forecasting the activities to be accomplished and structuring contracts to facilitate the anticipated activities. This means that, in the absence of externalities, incentives to utilize resources efficiently are inherent in the contracting process. By "externalities" we mean situations in which the actions of one party have a physical effect on others and the acting party does not have to pay for costs imposed on others or cannot charge for benefits granted to others. Air and water pollution are examples.

Competition, Contracts, Survival, and Efficiency

Competition is as pervasive among social and economic agents as among species in nature. Long ago, Alchian (1950, p. 218) argued that success is associated with relative superiority and that "whenever successful enterprises are observed, the elements common to those observed successes will be associated with success and copied by others in their pursuit of profits or success." Since most goods and services can be produced by any form of organization, different organizational forms compete for survival in any activity just as different species compete for survival in nature. Competition among organizational forms occurs in numerous dimensions, not only in their pricing and other marketing policies but also, for example, in their investment, financing, compensation, dividend, leasing, insurance, and accounting policies. Fama and Jensen (1983a, 1983b) define the survival criterion by which the economic environment chooses among organizational forms as follows: absent fiat, the form of organization that survives in an activity is the form that delivers the product demanded by consumers at the lowest price while covering costs. Under general conditions, competition and survivorship produce an efficient utilization of resources.

Overview

In the next section we examine the conflicts between residual claimants and managers. This leads to examination of the theory of the determination of organizational forms. We analyze the nature of residual claims and the separation of management and risk bearing in the corporation. This analysis provides a theory based on trade-offs of the risk sharing and other advantages of the corporate form with its agency costs to explain the survival of the corporate form in large-scale, complex, nonfinancial activities. In such activities, the corporation tends to dominate other organizational forms such as nonprofits, proprietorships, partnerships, and mutuals. Since the primary distinction among organizational forms is the nature of their residual or equity claims, analysis of the survival of alternative organizational forms addresses the question: What type of equity claim should an organization issue? Although this question has not been widely examined in the literature, determination of the nature of the equity claim is a natural predecessor to the determination of the optimal quantity of debt relative to equity—the capital structure issue—that has long been discussed in finance. We also examine how managerial compensation contracts, labor markets, and the market for corporate control help to control the conflicts of interest between managers and stockholders in corporations.

In the following section, the conflicts of interest between creditors and stockholders are examined. We discuss the structure of corporate bond, lease, and insurance contracts, and show how agency theory can be used to analyze contractual provisions for monitoring and bonding to help control the conflicts of interest between these fixed claim holders and stockholders.

Other factors are important to a complete understanding of organizational structure and practices. We focus on the positive-agency literature to the exclusion of both tax and signaling issues. Hamanda and Scholes (1985) review a major part of the literature on the effect of taxes on the structure of corporate contracts. The signaling literature focuses on the implications of asymmetric costs of information. Important work in this area is by Ross (1977) and Bhattacharya (1979).

5.2   Residual Claimant Interests and Agency Problems with Managers

Contract structures of organizations limit risks undertaken by most agents through contractual specification of payoffs that are either fixed or vary with specific measures of performance. Residual claims are claims to net cash flows that result from differences between inflows and promised payments to other claim holders. The risks of residual claims are restricted only by limited-liability provisions, but even these provisions are not universal.

Conflicts of interest generate agency problems between managers and residual claimants when risk bearing is separated from management—in the language of Berle and Means (1932), when "ownership" is separated from "control." Such agency costs can be reduced by the multitude of control procedures discussed in the accounting and control literatures. Fama and Jensen (1983a) analyze ways of controlling these costs by imposing restrictions on residual claims—for example, restricting their ownership to one or more of the major decision agents. This restriction ensures that decision agents bear the wealth effects of their decisions and thereby reduces the agency costs associated with outside ownership of residual claims.

Fama and Jensen (1983a) also emphasize that such restrictions on residual claims are the distinguishing characteristic among alternative organizational forms. A proprietorship is characterized by 100% ownership of the residual claims by the top-level decision agent, whereas partnerships and closed corporations generally restrict residual-claim ownership to major internal decision agents. In contrast, mutuals restrict residual-claim ownership to customers, nonprofits have no residual claims, and open corporations place no restrictions on ownership of their residual claims.

In the extreme, agency problems in the open corporation between managers and common stockholders can be eliminated by combining the two functions—that is, by abandoning the open corporate form. Thus it is useful to begin our analysis of corporations by analyzing the reasons why this organizational form survives.

Advantages of Common Stock Residual Claims:
Risk-Bearing Efficiencies

Fama and Jensen (1983a) emphasize that common stock residual claims of open corporations are unrestricted in the sense that (1) stockholders are not required to have any other role in the organization, (2) their residual claims are freely tradable, and (3) the residual claims are rights in net cash flows for the life of the organization. The unrestricted nature of the residual claims of open corporations allows almost complete separation and specialization of decision functions and residual risk bearing.

Activities of large, open, nonfinancial corporations are typically complicated. They involve contractually specified payments to many agents in the production process. Contracting costs with these agents increase if there is significant variation over time in the probability of contract default because such variation makes it necessary to reprice contracts. Concentrating much of this risk on a specific group of claimants can create efficiencies by reducing substantially the duplication of information costs incurred by all other contracting parties in the organization. However, specialized risk bearing by common stockholders is effective only if they bond their contractual risk-bearing obligation. This is accomplished by having common stockholders put up wealth used to purchase assets to bond payments promised to other agents. When the wealth required to bond promised payments exceeds the value of inputs optimally purchased rather than leased, common stock proceeds can be used to purchase liquid assets that have no function except to bond specialization of risk bearing by common stockholders.

In addition, the common stock of open corporations allows more efficient risk sharing among individuals than residual claims that are not separable from other roles in the enterprise. Nonseparable residual claims characterize financial mutuals, where the customers are the residual risk bearers, and proprietorships and partnerships, where the primary decision makers are the residual risk bearers. Since employees and managers develop firm-specific human capital, risk aversion generally causes them to charge more for the risk they bear compared to that charged by common stockholders. Unrestricted common stock allows residual risk to be spread across many residual claimants, each of whom can choose the extent to which he bears risk and can diversify across organizations offering such claims. The separability and tradability of common stock allows for the realization of risk-bearing efficiencies through diversification in the capital markets. Other things being equal, portfolio theory tells us that such unrestricted risk sharing lowers the price of risk-bearing services. (See, e.g., Arrow 1964a.) Thus, efficient large-scale specialized risk bearing by residual claimants is the major advantage of corporate common stock.

To summarize, the efficiencies in risk bearing offered by common stock residual claims imply that corporations will tend to survive and dominate in activities where the gains from specialization of risk bearing are large. This tends to occur in activities involving economies of scale where there are large aggregate risks to be borne.

Although complete markets for state-contingent claims as envisioned by Arrow (1964a) and Debreu (1959) would allow more specialization in risk bearing than common stock residual claims, it would be too expensive to prespecify all future states and payoffs in those states. However, it does pay to define a partial set of contingent claims such as insurance contracts, forward contracts, and futures contracts that permit additional specialization of risk bearing. They facilitate the shifting of risk in specified dimensions from stockholders. (See Mayers and Smith 1982; Smith and Stulz 1983.)

Disadvantages of Common Stock Residual Claims: Agency Costs

The unrestricted nature of the common stock residual claims of open corporations leads to an important agency problem between residual claimants and the agents in the decision process—the professional managers—whose interests are not identical to those of residual claimants. This problem of separation of "ownership" from "control"—more precisely, the separation of residual risk bearing from decision functions—has long troubled students of open corporations. (See, e.g., Berle and Means 1932; Smith 1776.) Fama and Jensen (1983b) argue that this agency problem is controlled by decision systems that separate the management (initiation and implementation) and control (ratification and monitoring) of important decisions at all levels of the organization. Effective separation means that no manager has control rights over decisions for which he has management rights.

Devices for separating management and control include

1. hierarchical structures in which the decision initiatives of lower-level agents are passed on to agents above them in the hierarchy, first for ratification and then for monitoring;
2. boards of directors that ratify and monitor the organization's most important decisions and hire, fire, and compensate top-level decision managers; and
3. incentive structures that encourage mutual monitoring among decision agents.

The cost of such mechanisms to separate decision management from decision control is the price that open corporations pay for the benefits of unrestricted common stock residual claims.

The Implications of Specific Knowledge

Specific knowledge is knowledge that can be transmitted between agents only at high cost. When an organization's activities are such that specific knowledge relevant for decisions is widely diffused among agents, efficiencies in decision making are accomplished by delegating decision-management rights to the agents with the specific knowledge valuable to those decisions. When such decision rights are diffused among agents throughout the organization, control of agency problems requires the separation of decision-management and decision-control rights. In this situation the net additional cost of achieving the separation of management and control rights required to realize the benefits of specialized risk bearing through common stock is smaller. Thus the value of the corporation is higher and the survival of corporations tends to be encouraged in activities where specific knowledge relevant for decisions is widely diffused among agents. Activities that are complex and subject to large economies of scale tend to satisfy these conditions and therefore tend to be dominated by the corporate form.

Control of the Conflict between Managers and Stockholders

The use of hierarchical control mechanisms in corporations is commonly recognized. Less generally recognized, however, is the use of mutual monitoring or "bottom up" monitoring in corporations. Many aspects of the administration of the corporation and the structures for monitoring managerial decisions are consistent with recognition and use of mutual monitoring to control conflicts between managers and the firm's other claim holders. For example, managers other than the president or chief executive officer (CEO) often serve on the board of directors. Competition among vice presidents for recognition and advancement provides an important source of information to the board-level control mechanism and reduces the likelihood that top-level managers will take actions in conflict with maximization of firm value.

The general administration of executive compensation plans reflects the separation of decision management and decision control, thereby enhancing the corporation's chances of survival. Executive compensation plans are administered by the compensation committee of the board of directors. Membership on this committee is typically restricted to outside members of the board and inside members not covered by the plan. This committee's primary function is to monitor and evaluate the inside board members' performance and determine inside board members' compensation.

Monitoring by the compensation committee is augmented by incentives for managers to monitor other managers, not only from the top of the organization to the bottom, but also at the same level and from below (see Alchian and Demsetz 1972; Fama 1980; Fama and Jensen 1983b; Zimmerman 1979). Lower-level managers have an incentive to monitor managers above them because of the interdependence of their productivities, as well as the direct gains from successfully stepping over less competent managers.

Management Compensation Contracts and Conflict Resolution

Sources of conflict. Managers make significant investments in firm-specific capital that must be amortized over their careers. As a result, their interests conflict with the interest of the firm's claim holders over three issues:

1. Choice of effort—additional effort by managers generally increases the value of the firm, but to managers effort is bad. (See Ross 1973.)
2. Differential risk exposure—managers typically have a nontrivial fraction of their wealth in firm-specific human capital and thus

are concerned about the variability of total firm value, including that portion of firm risk that can be eliminated through diversification by the firm's stockholders. (See Reagan and Stulz 1986 for a detailed discussion of risk-bearing incentives between residual claimants and employees, and references to the related literature.)

3. Differential horizons—managers' claims on the corporation are generally limited to their tenure with the firm. The corporation, on the other hand, has an indefinite life, and stockholder claims are tradable claims on the entire future stream of residual cash flows. Managers therefore have incentives to place lower values on cash flows occurring beyond their horizon than is implied by the market values of these cash flows. (See Chapter 6 of this volume and Furubotn and Pejovich 1973 for a detailed discussion of this problem.)

Control mechanisms in compensation plans. Smith and Watts (1982, 1983) offer detailed descriptions of typical provisions of compensation plans and analyze ways these provisions help control costs arising from conflicts of interest between managers and other claim holders. They group observed components of compensation plans into three categories: (1) compensation that does not depend on firm performance (salary, pensions, and insurance), (2) compensation that depends on market measures of firm performance (restricted and phantom stock, stock options, and stock appreciation rights), and (3) compensation that depends on accounting measures of performance (bonus, performance units, and performance shares).

Compensation in the form of salary payments fixed at the beginning of the period controls the major sources of conflict, primarily through future adjustments in salary. Salary renegotiation will be most effective in controlling younger managers where the present value of future salary subject to renegotiation is large. However, for managers closer to retirement, the control afforded by adjustment in future salary is less; in the extreme case, for managers less than a year from planned retirement, future salary changes provide no control of the effort problem.

Compensation by salaries fixed at the beginning of the period leads to three additional sources of conflict of interest with residual claimants because of the structure of the payoffs:

1. Asset substitution—when compensated with fixed claims that depend only on corporate solvency, managers will want to reduce the variance of cash flows because the expected payoff increases as cash-flow risk and the probability of default decline.
2. Overretention—managers compensated with fixed claims on the corporation have incentives to retain funds within the firm to increase the coverage on their fixed claims.
3. Underleverage—managers compensated with fixed claims have incentives to reduce debt and other fixed claims on the firm, even when such reductions adversely affect firm value.

Market-based compensation provisions are well suited to control the effort and horizon problems, since the market value of the stock reflects the present value of the entire future stream of expected cash flows. Market-based compensation provisions include stock options, stock appreciation rights (similar to stock options but upon exercise the holder receives cash rather than shares), restricted stock (common stock that carries restrictions on transferability for a stated period of time), and phantom stock (like restricted stock, but at expiration of the restrictions the manager receives the cash value of shares rather than common stock). Because the expected payoff to stock options increases with stock price variance, options provide the manager with incentives to invest in projects that increase the riskiness of the firm's cash flows. Options thus help to control the managers' incentives to take too little risk. Stock options also help control the underleverage problem. Higher leverage becomes more attractive to the manager since it increases the variance of the equity and thus the value of the options. Unless options are adjusted for dividends paid, however, they reinforce the overretention incentive associated with fixed claims.

Because use of accounting-based performance measures allows disaggregation of the firm's total performance among divisions, accounting-based compensation provisions will be relatively more important in compensating middle managers than market-based measures of performance. Bonus plans explicitly tie managers' compensation to an accounting measure of the change in the value of the firm. This formal tie to performance reduces the costs resulting from conflicts over the effort and horizon problems. Since bonus plans are tied to the previous year's performance, they motivate near-retirement managers to care about performance in their last year. Finally, part of the compensation can be deferred to the retirement period in a nonvested program that makes receipt of the deferred compensation contingent on satisfactory current and future performance. (See Becker and Stigler 1974 for a detailed discussion of this solution.)

Stock price effects of compensation plan announcements. Larcker (1983) and Brickley, Bhagat, and Lease (1985a, 1985b) examine stock price changes associated with the announcement of the initiation of compensation schemes. Brickley, Bhagat, and Lease (1985a) focus on the announcement of stock option, stock appreciation right, restricted stock, phantom stock, and performance plans. They find statistically significant abnormal returns of approximately 3.5% over the period between the board of directors' approval date and the stockholder meeting date, a period of approximately sixty trading days. Larcker (1983) finds a statistically significant two-day abnormal stock return of 0.8% associated with the announcement of the adoption of performance plans. Finally, Brickley, Bhagat, and Lease (1985b) examine returns at the announcement of stock purchase plans. They find two-day abnormal returns associated with the announcement date of these plans (which they take to be the proxy mailing date) of 3.4%. These stock price increases appear to be due to expected productivity increases rather than tax effects because these plans do not affect tax payments.

Management compensation and corporate accounting policy. Using accounting measures of performance to determine payments to managers gives managers a direct interest in the choice among alternative accounting techniques, since such choices can affect the bonus calculation. This means that compensation policy will affect the choice of accounting policy. The evidence of Healy and Kaplan (1985) indicates that the firm's choice of accounting-accrual policy is influenced by the effects of those policies on bonuses awarded to managers. Other studies (Dhaliwal, Salamon, and Smith 1982; Hagerman and Zmijewski 1981; Zmijewski and Hagerman 1981) find that bonus plans increase the probability of selecting corporate accounting procedures that shift accounting earnings from future periods to current periods.

Market control mechanisms. The degree to which top management's behavior can diverge from value-maximizing behavior is limited by the managerial-labor market and the capital markets (see Chapter 4 of this volume; Fama 1980). Competition in the labor market tends to ensure that managers receive only a competitive level of compensation. Reputation effects cause the value of managers' human capital to depend on their performance. In addition, investors try to anticipate managerial behavior that diverges from the interests of shareholders, and take such judgments into account when pricing the firm's traded claims. All of these forces provide incentives for the parties to construct procedures to reduce managers' divergence from value-maximizing behavior, but they seldom eliminate the problem.

Another factor contributing to the success of the corporation is the constraint imposed on managerial investment, financing, and dividend decisions by what Manne (1965) calls the "market for corporate control." Jensen and Ruback (1983) argue that this market is the arena in which alternative management teams compete for the rights to manage corporate resources, with stockholders playing the relatively passive role of accepting or rejecting offers from competing management teams.

Unrestricted transferability of common stock residual claims of open corporations makes possible a stock market that provides low-cost transfer and accurate valuation of claims. Low-cost transferability makes it possible for competing outside managers to bypass the current management and board of directors to acquire the rights to manage the corporation's resources. These rights can be acquired by direct solicitation of stockholders, either through tender offers or proxy solicitation. Alternatively, outside management teams can also acquire the management rights by merger negotiations with the target's management and board, subject to ratification by vote of the stockholders.

The corporation's internal control system has its foundation in the corporate charter. The effectiveness of this control system depends on operating practices and procedures and the quality of the individuals who hold board seats and management positions. Competition from alternative management teams in the market for corporate control serves as a source of external checks on the internal control system of the corporation. Thus the conflict in the control market is not between powerful entrenched managers and weak stockholders, as it is often characterized. Rather, it is between internal managers and the managers of other corporations that wish to take over the company and perhaps replace them.

When a breakdown of the corporation's internal control system imposes large costs on shareholders from incompetent, lazy, or dishonest managers, takeover bids in the market for corporate control provide a vehicle for replacing the entire internal control system. Competing managers who perceive the opportunity to eliminate the inefficiencies can offer target shareholders a higher-valued alternative than current management while benefiting their own shareholders and themselves. Similar incentives come into play when the acquisition of substantial synergy gains requires displacement of an efficient current management team.

Other institutional forms such as partnerships, nonprofit organizations, and mutuals do not receive the benefits of competition from alternative management teams in an external control market. Fama and Jensen (1983a, 1983b, Chapter 7 of this volume) provide an analysis of these alternative organizational forms and their survival properties. Wolfson (1983) provides analysis and empirical evidence on the agency problems in various forms of oil and gas limited partnerships and how the resulting agency costs are reduced. Mayers and Smith (1981, 1986) and Smith (1982) analyze the choice of organizational form in the insurance and thrift industries. Of course, internal competition in each of these organizations and the external regulatory environment (such as in insurance or banking) contribute to the control function. But because of their structure, only corporations benefit from the augmentation of their internal-control mechanisms by the private external control market.

Evidence from the Market for Corporate Control

Numerous studies estimate the effects of mergers on the stock prices of the participating firms. Table 5.1 presents a summary of stock price changes (measured net of marketwide price movements) for successful and unsuccessful takeovers in these studies. The returns reported in the table are the Jensen and Ruback (1983, tables 1 and 2) synthesis of the evidence reported in the thirteen studies noted in the footnotes to the table.

Table 5.1 shows that target firms in successful takeovers experience statistically significant abnormal stock price increases of 20% in merg-

Table 5.1 Abnormal percentage stock price changes associated with successful and unsuccessful corporate takeovers found by thirteen studies of such transactions as summarized by Jensen and Ruback (1983, tables 1 and 2)

Takeover technique	Targets		Bidders	
	Successful	Unsuccessful	Successful	Unsuccessful
Tender offers[a]	30%	−3%[d]	4%	−1%
Mergers[b]	20	−3	0	−5
Proxy contests[c]	8	8	NA	NA

Notes: Abnormal price changes are price changes adjusted for the effects of marketwide price changes. NA = not applicable.

a. Sources: Dodd and Ruback (1977), Kummer and Hoffmeister (1978), Bradley (1980), Jarrell and Bradley (1980), Bradley, Desai, and Kim (1983), Ruback (1983).

b. Sources: Dodd (1980), Asquith (1983), Eckbo (1983), Asquith, Brunner, and Mullins (1983), Malatesta (1983), Wier (1983).

c. Source: Dodd and Warner (1983).

d. Not statistically significantly different from zero.

ers and 30% in tender offers. Bidding firms realize statistically significant abnormal gains of 4% in tender offers and zero in mergers. Both bidders and targets suffer small negative abnormal stock price changes in unsuccessful mergers and tender offers, although only the −5% return to unsuccessful bidders in mergers is significantly different from zero. Stockholders in companies that experience control-related proxy contests earn statistically significant average abnormal returns of about 8%. These returns are not substantially lower when the insurgent group loses the contest.

The contrast between the large stock price increases for successful targets and insignificant stock price changes for unsuccessful targets indicates that the benefits of mergers and tender offers are realized only when control of the target firm's assets is transferred. This suggests that stockholders of potential target firms are harmed when target managers oppose takeover bids or take other actions that reduce the probability of successful acquisition. Moreover, since target managers are frequently replaced after takeovers, they have incentives to oppose takeover bids even though, if they were successful, shareholders might benefit substantially. On the other hand, management opposition to a bid can benefit stockholders if it leads to a higher takeover price. Thus the effect of management opposition on shareholder wealth is an empirical matter. Management opposition can be mitigated with "golden parachutes"—special termination agreements in executive compensation contracts that provide substantial compensation to executives if they leave the corporation subsequent to a control change. Interestingly, in their study of the effects of the announcements of such provisions, Lambert and Larcker (1985) find statistically significant positive abnormal returns to shareholders of 2.4%, an indication of their effectiveness.

The evidence indicates that the effect of unsuccessful takeover attempts varies depending on the technique used. In unsuccessful mergers, the target's stock price falls to about its preoffer level. In unsuccessful tender offers, the target's stock price remains substantially above its preoffer level unless a subsequent bid does not occur in the two years following the initial offer. If such a subsequent bid does not occur, the target's stock price reverts to its preoffer level. Finally, in proxy contests, the 8% increase in equity values does not depend on the outcome of the contest.

While the numbers in Table 5.1 suggest that merger bids are, on average, unprofitable for bidding firms, estimation of the appropriate return measure is more difficult for bidders than targets. Since stock price changes reflect changes in expectations, a merger announcement will not affect prices if it is fully anticipated. Since bidders can engage in prolonged acquisition programs, the present value of the expected benefits will be incorporated in the share price when the program is announced or becomes apparent. (See Schipper and Thompson 1983.) The returns reported in Table 5.1 measure only the incremental value change of each acquisition and are thus potentially incomplete measures of merger gains to bidders.

Spin-offs and divestitures. In a spin-off, corporate assets are divested and shares in the newly created entity are distributed to the original shareholders of the divesting firm. These transactions are in many ways the mirror image of a merger. The empirical studies of spin-offs (Hite and Owers 1983; Miles and Rosenfeld 1983; Schipper and Smith 1983) indicate that stockholders of the firms receive a statistically significant 3% return on the announcement of the event and that senior, nonconvertible security holders receive returns that appear to be positive but are insignificantly different from zero. This indicates that stockholder gains from spin-offs are not due to wealth transfers from senior security holders.

In a divestiture, assets of one firm are sold to another firm. Klein (1983) examines price effects of voluntary divestitures and finds 1% abnormal returns to shareholders of divesting firms. In the cases where returns to divesting and acquiring firms are both available, she finds positive but statistically insignificant gains to both divesting and acquiring firm stockholders. Wier (1983) examines price effects of involuntary divestitures ordered by the Federal Trade Commission and the Justice Department for violations of Section 7 of the Clayton Act. For firms that are subsequently convicted, she finds a 2% abnormal loss associated with the announcement of the complaint, followed by an additional 2% loss on the announcement of the conviction. These losses appear to eliminate the gains from the original acquisition.

Corporate charter changes. Corporate charters specify governance rules for corporations. They contain, for example, rules that establish conditions for mergers—such as the percentage of stockholders that must vote approval for a merger to take effect. Individual states specify constraints on charter rules that differ from state to state. This variation across states means that changing the state of incorporation affects the constraints on contractual arrangements among shareholders that are imposed through the corporate charter. Differences in state rules can affect the probability that a firm will become a takeover target. It is alleged that some states, desiring to increase their corporate charter revenues, compete to make their statutes appealing to corporate management. In doing so, it is argued, they provide management with great freedom from stockholder control and little shareholder protection. Delaware, for example, provides few constraints on corporate charter rules and therefore great corporate contractual freedom. William Cary (1974), the former chairman of the Securities and Exchange Commission (SEC), criticizes Delaware, arguing that it is leading a "movement towards the least common denominator" and "winning" a "race for the bottom." In a sample of 140 firms that switched their state of incorporation, most of them to Delaware, Dodd and Leftwich (1980) find no evidence of stock price declines at the time of the switch and some indication of small abnormal price increases. This is inconsistent with the notion that changes in the state of incorporation are motivated by managerial exploitation of shareholders.

Firms can amend their charters to make the conditions for shareholder approval of mergers more stringent. Such antitakeover amendments include supermajority provisions and provisions for the staggered election of board members. By increasing the stringency of takeover conditions, these amendments can reduce the probability of being a takeover target and therefore reduce shareholder wealth. However, by increasing the plurality required for takeover approval, the amendments could benefit shareholders by enabling target management to better represent their common interests in the merger negotiations. Studies by DeAngelo and Rice (1983) and Linn and McConnell (1983) of the stock price effects associated with the passage of antitakeover amendments indicate no negative effect on shareholder wealth, although it is possible that when new supermajority provisions grant a manager-stockholder effective blocking power there are negative effects. This can happen, for example, if a manager holds 21% of the stock when an 80% supermajority provision is enacted.

Corporate charters also specify voting rights of the firm's shareholders in elections to determine the board of directors. Some firms provide cumulative voting, which allows a group of minority shareholders to elect directors even if the majority of shareholders oppose their election. Bhagat and Brickley (1984) examine abnormal returns to stockholders around management-sponsored proposals that either eliminate cumulative voting or provide for staggered election of the members of the board of directors, thus reducing the effect of cumulative voting rights of shareholders. They find statistically significant negative returns of approximately −1% associated with proposals to reduce the effect of cumulative voting. Bhagat (1983) also examines the effects of elimination of the preemptive right in the corporate charter. This provision gives existing shareholders the prior right to purchase new equity offered by the firm in proportion to their current holdings. For a sample of 211 firms that eliminated the preemptive right from the corporate charter, he finds statistically significant negative abnormal returns to stockholders of approximately −0.5%. The results of both of these studies are inconsistent with the hypothesis that these management proposals are in the shareholders' best interests.

5.3   Creditor Interests and Agency Problems

Bondholder-Stockholder Conflict

A number of authors have discussed the conflict of interest between the firm's bondholders and stockholders.[1] An extreme example of this conflict is offered by Black (1976), who points out that "there is no easier way for a company to escape the burden of a debt than to pay out all of its assets in the form of a dividend, and leave the creditors holding an empty shell."

Some corporate decisions increase the wealth of stockholders while reducing the wealth of bondholders and, in cases where the wealth transfers are large enough, stock prices can rise from decisions that reduce the value of the firm. Smith and Warner (1979) identify four major sources of conflict between bondholders and stockholders:

1. Dividend payout—if bonds are priced assuming that the firm will maintain its dividend policy, their value is reduced by unexpected dividend increases financed either by reductions in investments or by the sale of debt (see Kalay 1982).
2. Claim dilution—if bonds are priced assuming that additional debt of the same or higher priority will not be issued, the value of the bondholders' claims is reduced by issuing such additional debt.
3. Asset substitution—the value of the stockholders' equity rises and the value of the bondholders' claim is reduced when the firm substitutes high-risk for low-risk projects (see Chapter 4 of this volume; Green 1984).
4. Underinvestment—when a substantial portion of the value of the firm is composed of future investment opportunities, a firm with outstanding risky bonds can have incentives to reject positive net present value projects if the benefit from accepting the project accrues to the bondholders (see Myers 1977).

Rational bondholders recognize incentives faced by stockholders in each of these four dimensions. When bonds are sold, bondholders forecast the value effects of future decisions. They understand that, after issuance, any action that increases the wealth of the stockholders will be taken. Therefore, on average, bondholders will not suffer losses unless they systematically underestimate effects of such future actions. But the firm (and hence its stockholders) suffers losses—agency costs—from all nonoptimal decisions motivated by wealth transfers from debtholders. Therefore, by reducing these agency costs, contractual control of the bondholder-stockholder conflict can increase the value of the firm.

Bond covenants constraining activities such as asset sales or mergers are examples of voluntary contracts that can reduce agency costs generated when stockholders of a levered firm follow a policy that deviates from firm-value maximization. The cost-reducing benefits of the covenants accrue to the firm's owners through the higher price the bond issue commands at the time the bonds are issued. Furthermore, if covenants lower the costs that bondholders incur in monitoring stockholders, these reductions in agency costs are also passed on to stockholders through higher bond prices at issuance. For example, Asquith and Kim (1982) examine bond returns around the announcement dates of merger bids for a sample of conglomerate mergers. They find that abnormal returns to bondholders are insignificantly different from zero at times of merger bids. This suggests that bondholders on average are effectively protected from potential wealth transfers in mergers.

Note that the bondholder-stockholder conflict would not be solved by giving the bondholders control of the firm; bondholders would have incentives to pay too few dividends, issue too little debt, and choose projects with too little risk. Moreover, the degree of control that can be given to bondholders is limited by Rule 10b-5 of Section 10 of the Securities Exchange Act of 1934 and by the Trust Indenture Act of 1939. See Smith and Warner (1979, section 3) for a discussion of these legal constraints.

Empirical Evidence from Financial Restructuring

Financial restructuring can be accomplished in many ways, for example, through issues of new securities, through retirement of securities by exercising call provisions, or through exchange offers. Table 5.2 summarizes the evidence from thirteen studies of the abnormal stock price changes associated with the announcement of various transactions that change corporate capital structure. The upper panel of Table 5.2 summarizes leverage-increasing transactions, for example, new issues of debt and convertible debt, common stock repurchases, and exchange offers in which debt is issued and common stock is retired, debt issued and preferred retired, preferred issued and common retired, and income bonds issued and preferred retired. Leverage-reducing transactions such as new issues of common stock, calls of convertible bonds, and preferred stock forcing conversion into common stock and the reverse of the exchanges listed in the upper panel of the table are grouped together in the lower panel of the table.

Examination of the upper and lower panels of Table 5.2 indicates that leverage-increasing capital market transactions are generally asso-

Table 5.2 Summary of common stock price effects associated with various leverage-increasing and leverage-decreasing capital market transactions found by thirteen studies

Type of transaction	Security issued	Security retired	Average sample size	Two-day announcement period return
Leverage-increasing transactions				
Exchange offer[a]	Debt	Common	52	14.0%
Exchange offer[a]	Preferred	Common	9	8.3
Exchange offer[a]	Debt	Preferred	24	3.5
Exchange offer[b]	Income bonds	Preferred	24	2.2
Repurchase[c]	None	Common	413	6.4
Security issue[d]	Debt	None	150	−0.4[g]
Security issue[d]	Convertible debt	None	132	−2.3
Leverage-reducing transactions				
Exchange offer[a]	Common	Debt	20	−9.9
Exchange offer[a]	Common	Preferred	30	−2.6
Exchange offer[a]	Preferred	Debt	9	−7.7
Security issue[e]	Common	None	408	−2.1
Conversion-forcing call[f]	Common	Convertible bond	113	−2.1
Conversion-forcing call[f]	Common	Convertible preferred	57	−0.4[g]

a. Source: Masulis (1983). (*Note:* These returns include announcement days of both the original offer and, for about 40% of the sample, a second announcement of specific terms of the exchange.)

b. Source: McConnell and Schlarbaum (1981).

c. Source: Weighted average (by sample size) of the returns reported in the seven studies summarized in column 5 of Table 5.3.

d. Source: Dann and Mikkelson (1984).

e. Source: Korwar (1983), examined 424 firms; Asquith and Mullins (1985), examined 128 industrials and 264 utilities. (*Note:* The reported sample size and returns are averages of the two studies, with no attempt to correct for overlap in observations.)

f. Source: Mikkelson (1981).

g. Not statistically different from zero.

ciated with significantly positive abnormal returns to common stockholders, and leverage-reducing transactions are associated with significantly negative abnormal returns to common stockholders. The exceptions are new debt issues and convertible debt issues that are leverage-increasing and yet are associated with, respectively, insignificantly negative returns of −0.4% and significantly negative returns of −2.3%. The interpretation of the significantly negative returns associated with the issuance of convertible debt is problematic because, while they initially increase leverage, their eventual conversion into common stock reduces leverage.

Masulis (1980, 1983) argues that, since exchange offers are simply a swap of one class of securities for another, the transaction has no effect on the firm's investment policy and, thus, if the Modigliani-Miller (1958) capital structure irrelevance proposition is applicable, they should have no effect on firm value. As Table 5.2 shows, the evidence from each of the exchange offers studied by Masulis is inconsistent with the Modigliani-Miller financial structure irrelevance propositions. In fact, the evidence presented in all thirteen studies summarized in Table 5.2 is inconsistent with the irrelevance propositions. Each of the studies documents statistically significant equity value changes associated with changes in corporate leverage, and only two of the events examined are associated with insignificant equity value changes.

Masulis (1980, 1983) attempts to separate value effects attributable to wealth redistribution among classes of security holders, bankruptcy cost effects, and the effects of corporate and personal taxes. His data provide evidence of tax shields from corporate debt around the date of announcement of exchange offers. As Table 5.2 shows, average common stock returns are 14% in debt-for-common exchanges, where tax-deductible interest expense is increased, but only 8.3% in preferred-for-common exchanges, where there should be no corporate tax effect for the issuing corporation. Masulis (1980) finds evidence of wealth transfers from debtholders to stockholders. For example, in exchange offers where debt is issued and common is retired, stockholders gain and bondholders lose; common stock returns are significantly positive at 9.8%, and straight debt returns are significantly negative at -0.3% (not shown in Table 5.2). However, Mikkelson (1981) finds no such evidence of wealth transfers in his examination of calls of convertible bonds.

The generally significant negative stock price effects associated with the six leverage-reducing transactions shown in the lower panel of Table 5.2 and the issuance of convertible debt shown in the upper panel present a puzzle. There is no convincing explanation for why firms voluntarily take such actions that consistently harm stockholders. These transactions might represent agency problems between stockholders and managers but, given the costs to stockholders, it is difficult to believe that managers gain enough from them to make the transactions worth the effort. In addition, it is possible that leverage-decreasing transactions are optimal responses to negative changes in the firm's fortunes and that the negative stock price changes are due to the factors causing the hard times. The leverage reduction, while beneficial itself, might well signal information to market participants that the firm has received bad news. In this situation the incremental value effects of the leverage reduction could be positive but our empirical methods do not allow separation of this component from the value decrease caused by the bad news.

In the upper panel of Table 5.2 we have aggregated the results associated with repurchases of common stock reported by seven studies. Because corporations repurchase their own shares in a number of different ways, however, it is worthwhile to examine the stock price effects associated with different forms of repurchase. The different forms include tender offers, simple repurchases in the open market, negotiated repurchases of large blocks, targeted repurchases of small holdings, repurchase of all publicly held shares in going-private transactions, and repurchase of all shares in mutualization transactions. Table 5.3 summarizes the evidence from nine studies of these various methods of repurchasing the firm's stock. The table reports by method of repurchase the premium offered, the fraction of shares repurchased, the predicted stock price change for the remaining shares given no change in firm value, and the actual stock price change for the remaining shares. As Table 5.3 shows, evidence on the stock price changes associated with common stock repurchases is consistent with that from exchange offers; leverage-increasing events are generally associated with positive stockholder returns.

In tender-offer repurchases of corporate stock, the average premium above the preoffer market price of the stock offered to selling shareholders is approximately 23% (column 3). If there is no change in overall firm value, the premium paid to selling shareholders represents a loss to the remaining shareholders, and this predicted loss is on average −4% in tender offers (column 5). Thus the 15% actual average stock price increase for the remaining shares (column 6) indicates that tender-offer repurchases of common stock are associated with positive changes in total firm value. These figures for intra-firm tender offers should be contrasted with those that occur when a corporation buys its stock through open-market purchases at a zero premium; remaining

Table 5.3 Summary of average repurchase premiums and price effects of common stock repurchases for various repurchase methods found by nine studies

Repurchase method (1)	Average sample size (2)	Premium offered (3)	Fraction of shares repurchased (4)	Predicted stock price change for remaining shares[a] (5)	Actual stock price change for remaining shares[b] (6)
Tender offer[c]	148	23%	15%	−4%	15%
Open market repurchase[d]	182	0	4	0	4
Negotiated large blocks[e]	68	10	11	−2	−5
Targeted small holdings[f]	15	13	Under 1	Slightly negative	2
Going private[g]	81	56	54	−35	NA
Mutualization[h]	29	54[i]	100	NA	NA

NA = not applicable.

a. This assumes no change in firm value and is calculated as minus the premium times the fraction of shares repurchased divided by one minus the fraction of shares repurchased.

b. Abnormal price changes are price changes adjusted for marketwide price changes.

c. Sources: Dann (1981), Masulis (1980a), Vermaelen (1981), Rosenfeld (1982).

d. Sources: Dann (1980), Vermaelen (1981).

e. Sources: Dann and DeAngelo (1983), Bradley and Wakeman (1983).

f. Source: Bradley and Wakeman (1983).

g. Source: DeAngelo, DeAngelo, and Rice (1984). *Note:* The abnormal stock price change on announcement of the going-private transaction is 30%.

h. Source: Mayers and Smith (1983).

i. Measured by abnormal stock price change, not the premium offered to selling shareholders.

stockholders earn average abnormal returns of approximately 4% (column 6).

In a negotiated large-block repurchase, a firm buys a block of its common stock from an individual holder at an average 10% premium over market price (column 3). Remaining stockholders of the repurchasing firm realize statistically significant losses of approximately 5% (column 6) on the announcement of such privately negotiated large-block repurchases. Since large-block sellers in negotiated repurchases are frequently actual or potential takeover bidders, the premium can be interpreted as payment to the holder to cease takeover activity. Moreover, takeover offers are frequently canceled at the time of negotiated repurchases. Therefore, one explanation for the losses to remaining stockholders in negotiated repurchases, in contrast to the gains in tender-offer and open-market repurchases, is that they reflect the loss of expected benefits of takeovers to the repurchasing firm.

In repurchase offers targeted only for small shareholdings (generally odd lots), the average premium paid to sellers is about 13% (column 3), and remaining stockholders earn average abnormal returns of approximately 2%. This value increase apparently reflects the savings in administrative expenses associated with servicing small accounts.

Going-private transactions represent an extreme case of stock repurchases. In these transactions public stock ownership is replaced with full equity ownership by an incumbent management group and the stock is delisted. In some cases, generally called "leveraged buyouts" (LBOs), management shares the equity with private outside investors. On average, 54% of the total shares are held by the public and repurchased in these transactions (column 4). It is often argued that conflicts of interest between incumbent managers as buyers of the stock and outside shareholders as sellers of the stock result in exploitation of outside shareholders. Hence, these transactions are frequently labeled "minority freezeouts." There is, however, no evidence that outside shareholders are harmed in these minority freezeouts. In fact the announcement by management of the going-private repurchase offer at an average premium of 56% (column 3) is associated with a 30% average abnormal stock price increase. DeAngelo, DeAngelo, and Rice (1984a) conjecture that the gains are due to improved incentives for corporate decision makers under private ownership, as well as savings of registration and other public-ownership expenses.

The average premium received by stockholders' life insurance companies when their shares were repurchased in order to switch to a mutual ownership structure was 54% (column 3). Mayers and Smith (1986) conclude that the premium arises from the increased efficiency of the mutual ownership form for this group of life insurance firms.

The Structure of Creditor Contracts

Smith and Warner (1979) analyze the role of bond covenants in the control of bondholder-stockholder conflicts. They group covenants into four categories: production-investment covenants, dividend covenants, financing covenants, and bonding covenants. The fact that investment equals net cash flow plus net proceeds from new financing minus dividends means that investment, financing, and dividend policies are interrelated. This implies that covenants restricting dividend and financing policies also restrict investment policy. Smith and Warner argue that bond contracts are structured to maximize the value of the firm. This analysis yields a substantial body of theory describing the contracting incentives associated with the choice of provisions in corporate bond contracts.

A convertible bond gives the holder the right to exchange the bond for the firm's common stock. Chapter 4 of this volume, as well as Smith and Warner (1979), Mikkelson (1981), and Green (1984), discuss the use of convertible debt to control the asset substitution problem, that is, the stockholders' incentive to have the firm take some unprofitable but variance-increasing projects. With convertible debt, risk-increasing activities increase the value of the conversion option, and thus reduce the gains to stockholders from taking high-risk projects by transferring part of the gains to convertible bondholders. This lowers agency costs by reducing incentives for the firm to take highly risky negative net-present-value projects. Issuance of warrants also has some of these effects.

Secured debt gives the bondholders title to pledged assets until the bonds are paid in full. Smith and Warner (1979) argue that security provisions control the asset substitution problem and lower administrative and enforcement costs by ensuring that the lender has clear title to the assets and by restricting the firm's disposition of assets. Stulz and Johnson (1985) suggest that the option to issue secured debt controls the underinvestment problem. They show that secured debt allows stockholders to sell claims to the payoffs of a new project that otherwise would accrue as a windfall to holders of previously issued debt. Thus, some new positive net-present-value projects can increase the value of equity if financed with secured debt, but not with unsecured debt.

Myers (1977) argues that a corporation's future investment opportunities can be viewed as call options. The value of such options depends on whether the firm is expected to optimally exercise them. But, with risky debt outstanding, situations can arise in which stockholders do not benefit from even highly profitable investment decisions because the benefits go primarily to the debtholders. In these cases the value of the investment options is zero because they are unlikely to be exercised and this lowers the value of the firm. With longer-lived debt claims in a firm's capital structure, the conflict between debtholders and stockholders over the exercise of investment options is greater, and without resolution the value of the firm is lower. Myers argues that firms can control these incentive problems by matching effective maturities of assets and liabilities. Mayers and Smith (1981) note that the incentive to match maturities of assets and liabilities is easily observable in the insurance industry and is consistent with Myers' proposition. Life insurance companies purchase more long-lived assets, such as privately placed loans and mortgages, than casualty insurers that have much shorter effective maturities of their outstanding liabilities.

The standard bond covenant restricting the payment of dividends specifies that the maximum allowable dividend payment is a positive function of both accounting earnings and the proceeds from the sale of new equity. Since dividend and investment policy are interdependent, specification of a maximum on dividends imposes a minimum on the fraction of earnings retained in the firm. Increased earnings retention generated by lower dividend constraints, however, imposes overinvestment costs in a firm that expects few profitable projects over the life of the bonds. Thus, the theory predicts that an unregulated firm that expects recurring profitable future investment projects will set a low maximum on dividends, and therefore a high minimum on retentions. This reduces both the requirements for externally raised equity capital and the associated equity flotation costs, as well as the present value of agency costs.

Rozeff (1982) and Easterbrook (1984) note that a policy of paying dividends increases the frequency with which the corporation's managers go to the capital markets to obtain new equity. This policy subjects the firm more frequently to the intensive capital market monitoring and discipline that occurs at the time new funds are raised and lowers agency costs. They also argue that dividend payments to stockholders allow the firm to raise its debt-equity ratio without requiring the firm to increase its assets by issuing debt. Their arguments predict that firms with high growth rates and high demand for new capital will have less reason to pay high dividends because they are going to the capital markets frequently anyway. Consistent with this prediction, such firms generally have low dividends.

In contrast, utilities historically have had high demands for new capital and high dividend payout rates. Smith (1983) argues that utility stockholders are likely to fare less well in the rate-regulation process if the dividend rate is lowered to reduce the frequency and costs of floating new equity in the capital markets. By paying high dividends, the regulated firm subjects both itself and its regulatory body to the discipline of the marketplace more frequently. Stockholders are less likely to suffer expropriation through low rates set in the adversarial regulatory setting when the regulatory body is more frequently policed by the capital markets. Giving suppliers of debt and equity capital an opportunity to signal their dissatisfaction with confiscatorily low rates through low prices, or perhaps through denial of funds required to maintain service, accomplishes this. Thus, high dividends are a way of bonding to stockholders that they will receive a normal rate of return on the capital invested in the corporation.

Kalay (1982) examines corporate dividend covenants and finds that firms do not pay all dividends allowed under the contract. If firms are behaving optimally, this implies that there are benefits from maintaining a reservoir that gives the firm the right to pay dividends. These benefits could come from avoiding forced investment at low returns when no profitable projects are available.

Handjinicolaou and Kalay (1984) examine returns to both stockholders and bondholders to distinguish between two potential explanations of positive stockholder returns associated with the announcement of dividend changes. One hypothesis is that dividend increases are associated with higher expected cash flows and thus higher firm value; the other is that higher dividends transfer wealth from bondholders to stockholders. They find that bonds of firms with low leverage show no significant reaction to announcements of dividend changes and that stockholders of such firms receive statistically significant abnormal returns of the same sign as the dividend change. However, for high-leverage firms, dividend increases are associated with significantly positive stockholder returns and insignificant bondholder returns; but for dividend decreases, bondholders receive significant negative returns while stockholders' returns are insignificantly different from zero. Handjinicolaou and Kalay suggest that this asymmetry in response is due to the structure of the typical dividend constraint that allows the stockholders to capture the value implications of positive information through higher dividends. Interestingly, their evidence indicates that stockholders of high-leverage firms do not share the losses that bondholders experience in association with unexpected dividend decreases.

The major weakness in all of the agency hypotheses about dividend policy is that they only explain distributions to stockholders; they do not explain why they take the form of cash dividends. Bond dividend covenants reflect an understanding of the availability of substitute forms of distributions. They universally restrict "all distributions on account of or in respect of capital stock . . . whether they be dividends, redemptions, purchases, retirements, partial liquidations or capital reductions, and whether in cash, in kind, or in the form of debt obligations of the company" (American Bar Foundation 1971, p. 405). Stock repurchases and exchange offers accomplish many of the same ends as cash dividend payments and do so at potentially lower tax costs. Thus we still do not have a satisfactory explanation of why firms pay cash dividends.

Section 4(2) of the Securities Act of 1933 provides that a sale of securities not involving a public offering is exempt from registration. Such exempt issues are referred to as "private placements" or "direct placements" and represent an alternative to publicly placed debt. Because of the legal limitations on the discretion allowed a trustee, the modification of tightly restrictive covenants for a public debt issue requires a supplemental indenture approved by a majority of the bondholders. Therefore, the benefit from private rather than public placement of the firm's debt can be substantial when it is anticipated that such renegotiations will be desirable in the future. This implies that riskier debt issues are more likely to be privately placed because they require modification more frequently. The argument also implies that private placements will include more detailed restrictions on the firm's behavior than do public issues because change is less costly.

Leftwich (1981) compares the specification of covenants in public versus privately placed bond issues. He finds that privately placed bonds include more frequent use of constraints on investment and financing policy as well as more frequent specification of the accounting methods to be used. He also finds that the accounting procedures required for use in calculating constraints on financing, dividend, and investment policies usually differs from generally accepted accounting principles (GAAP) by eliminating noncash items.

Other covenants specify that various bonding activities be performed by the firm to help control the bondholder-stockholder conflict. These activities include requirements for the provision of audited financial statements, the use of specified accounting techniques, and periodic provision of a statement, signed by the firm's officers, indicating compliance with the covenants.

Covenant-imposed constraints are typically specified in terms of accounting numbers. Since different accounting techniques imply different accounting numbers, firms have incentives to relax onerous constraints through the choice of accounting techniques. Bowen, Noreen, and Lacey (1981), Deakin (1979), Dhaliwal (1980), Dhaliwal, Salamon, and Smith (1982), Lilien and Pastena (1982), and Zmijewski and Hagerman (1981) have examined corporations' accounting choices. All find that the structure of corporate bond contracts establishes incentives that are consistent with the evidence on choices of accounting techniques by corporations.

We have discussed the bondholder-stockholder conflict as if there were only two homogeneous classes of capital claims on the corporation. In fact, the typical corporation has multiple classes of debt claims outstanding that can differ in dimensions such as coupon, maturity, and priority. Intra-debtholder conflicts over wealth transfers are highly visible in bankruptcy proceedings. The conflict is exacerbated by the deviations from absolute priority in court decisions documented by Warner (1977). He shows that junior claim holders systematically receive higher-valued claims in corporate reorganizations under the bankruptcy code than a literal application of absolute priority would imply. Smith and Warner (1979) note that bond covenants frequently restrict the issuance of new debt, not just of the same and higher priority, but the issuance of debt of any priority. The analysis by Ho and Singer (1982) of the risk of corporate debt helps explain such puzzling restrictions. Restriction of the issuance of junior debt is consistent with the fact that junior debt that matures earlier than a senior debt issue has effective priority in payment as long as the firm is not in bankruptcy.

A lease is a substitute for secured debt. It is a contractual arrangement in which a firm acquires the services of an asset for a specified time period as an alternative to purchasing the asset. In a secured debt contract, the user owns the asset but the bondholder has a lien that allows seizure of the asset if the borrower defaults. In a lease contract, the lessor keeps title to the asset and the lessee (borrower) uses the asset as long as he does not default on the lease. Thus leases help control the asset substitution and underinvestment problems in the same ways as secured debt.

Leasing, however, also generates conflicts of interest and therefore agency costs. For example, consider organization-specific assets. They are assets that are more highly valued within the organization than in their best alternative use; for example, crude-oil-gathering pipelines have little alternative-use value and are therefore specific to the oil fields they serve. Lease of organization-specific assets generates agency costs in the form of significant additional negotiation, administration, and contract enforcement costs due to conflicts between lessor and lessee. These conflicts arise over the division of the value in excess of the alternative-use value of the asset. Klein, Crawford, and Alchian (1978) argue that agency costs are reduced when such organization-specific assets are owned rather than leased.

In addition, since lessees do not have claim to the residual value of the asset at the end of the lease, they have limited incentives to maintain the asset or to limit abuse in other ways, and this generates agency costs. Damage from inappropriate asset use and maintenance will be reflected in the lease price. Smith, Wakeman, and Hawkins (1985) argue that this leads to a tendency to lease assets whose value is less sensitive to abuse. (For example, the furnishings in a rental unit will generally be more durable and less sensitive to abuse than furnishings in owner-occupied dwellings.) The additional abuse problems in lease contracts mean that, if they are leased at all, assets whose use is difficult to monitor but that are easily abused will have rental rates for short periods that are a high fraction of the purchase price. Lessee bonding through large damage deposits should also be more frequently observed in these situations. Service leases that include prepaid maintenance contracts are a way for lessees to bond a promise not to abuse the asset by failing to maintain it. These arguments imply that financial leases will generally be used only for assets where the costs of under-maintenance are low.

Smith, Wakeman, and Hawkins also argue that the higher the ratio of the term of the lease to the asset's usable life, the less severe are the perverse use and maintenance incentives. Thus long-term leases, options to extend the life of the lease, and options to purchase the asset at the end of the lease are contractual mechanisms that can reduce the agency costs of leasing. They all give the lessee a greater financial interest in the future value of the asset. In contrast, Flath (1980) analyzes situations where there are advantages to leasing because the useful life of the asset is significantly longer than the period over which a particular company or individual expects to use the asset. He analyzes arrangements that reduce contracting costs of short-term leases, focusing on reductions in monitoring costs and the costs of transferring ownership that are available through specialized leasing contracts rather than ownership. (Thus, for a week at the beach, one is more likely to rent a room than to buy a condominium.)

Bond indentures frequently contain covenants requiring the firm to maintain certain types of insurance coverage. These provisions reduce the firm's incentives to reject certain variance-reducing positive net-present-value safety projects. For example, if an uninsured firm invests in an unanticipated safety project, such as a sprinkler system, that reduces the variance of corporate cash flows, wealth is transferred to bondholders. If the firm has previously purchased full-coverage fire insurance, however, the risk of corporate cash flows—including indemnity payments from the policy—is unchanged. In this situation there are no wealth transfers to bondholders and the firm need only compare the cost of the safety project with the present value of the reduction in insurance premiums. In addition, insurance companies, because of economies of scale and specialization, develop a comparative advantage in claims administration. In fact, claims-only contracts exist wherein the insurance company provides only claim management services, and the corporation pays the claims. These contracts reduce the administrative costs of self-insurance programs.

5.4   Conclusions

Agency theory has provided a useful tool for detailed analysis of the determinants of the complex contractual arrangement called the modern corporation. Our purpose in this chapter has been to survey the applications of this theory to the conflicts of interest between corporate managers, stockholders, and creditors. The analysis of these conflicts and their resolution increases our understanding of the survival of many contractual practices that heretofore have either been taken for granted or viewed with great suspicion. It also illustrates the often close relation between financial and organizational practices. Future work promises even greater increases in our knowledge of organizational and contracting practices.

6 | Rights and Production Functions: An Application to Labor-Managed Firms and Codetermination

6.1   Introduction

It is traditional in the theory of the firm to define the production opportunity set available to the firm in terms of its boundary—the maximum attainable set of output quantities for various input quantities, given the state of technology and knowledge. This boundary is the production function of the firm. One of our purposes in this chapter is to point up the dependence of such production functions on the structure of property rights and contracting rights within which the firm exists. We redefine the production function in order to recognize the dependence of output on the structure of property and contracting rights. That expanded framework is then used to discuss a concrete set of problems surrounding the role of labor in the firm ranging from the "labor-managed firm" system (in which tradable capital value residual claims—common stock—are legally prohibited) and the codetermination and industrial democracy movements (in which management participation by labor is required by law), to cooperatives and professional partnerships (i.e., quasi-labor-managed firms that arise out of the voluntary contracting process) and the capitalist corporation.

6.2   The Production Function Redefined

In Jensen and Meckling (1976, p. 310) and Chapter 4 of this volume, we argue that most organizations such as the corporation are simply legal fictions that serve as a nexus for a complex set of contracts among

By Michael C. Jensen and William H. Meckling; originally published in *Journal of Business* 52 (October 1979), pp. 469–506. © 1979 by The University of Chicago. All rights reserved.

individuals. Suppliers of inputs (labor, raw materials, capital, and so forth) along with consumers of the product implicitly or explicitly enter into a set of contracts that delineates the rights and obligations of the respective participants in the activities of the organization. Moreover, the very notion that inputs are "supplied" already implies the existence of a system of "rights" in resources. In most cases the police powers of the state are available to enforce the rights and the contracts or impose penalties for violation of rights or noncompliance with contracts. Since such sets of contracts specify the disposition of rewards and costs arising out of the organization's activities, they are important in determining the behavior of the participants and thereby the behavior of the organization as a whole. In particular, in the case of the firm, the nature of the rights and the contracts affects output. This in turn means that the production function of the firm depends on the specification of rights and the laws or rules of the game governing contracting. The maximum attainable output of a firm is then *not* purely a matter of "physical" possibilities given the technology and knowledge; the production function depends on the contracting and property-rights system within which the firm operates. In a world in which the rules of the game prohibit certain kinds of contracts—for example, limited liability for investors or the issuance of tradable residual claims on cash flows—production functions will reflect those prohibitions.[1]

All of this can be summarized more formally by representing the production function of the firms as $Q = F_\Theta (L, K, M, \phi:T)$, where Q is the quantity of output; L, K, and M are, respectively, the labor, capital, and material inputs; T is a vector describing the state of knowledge and physical technology relevant to production; ϕ is a generalized index describing the range of choice of "organizational forms" or internal rules of the game available to the firm given Θ; and Θ is a vector of parameters or characteristics describing the relevant aspects of the contracting and property-rights systems within which the firm exists. The symbol F denotes a family of production functions whose members differ according to the characteristics of Θ of the rights system, and F_Θ denotes a particular member of this set. Ignoring uncertainty, $Q = F_\Theta(L, K, M, \phi:T)$ represents the boundary of the actual output opportunity set of the firm in a rights system described by Θ that has available to it technology denoted by T, chooses an organizational structure ϕ, and utilizes inputs of labor, capital, and materials of L, K, and M.

The rights structure, Θ, is taken to be exogenously given to the firm by the political, social, and legal system within which it exists. It summarizes the external rules of the game, specifying not only illegal actions (both statutory and regulatory) and the penalties associated with committing illegal acts, but also the types of voluntary contracts and organizational forms that the powers of the state will be used to enforce. This exogenous rights structure, Θ, defines the set of potential organizational structures, ϕ, available to the firm. The characteristics of the organizational structure or internal rules of the game that define the elements of ϕ include such parameters as partnership or corporate form, divisionalized cost or profit centers, the degree of decentralization, whether to own or lease equipment, the nature of compensation plans (including profit-sharing and incentive systems), unionization, conditions of employment, the nature of contracts with suppliers and customers, and so on.

Formally defining the production function in terms of Θ is a way to recognize through ϕ (the internal rules of the game) the effects of the external rights structure on output. It is of little importance to know that it is *physically* possible to produce 100 units of a good with some given level of factor inputs if no one in the system has an incentive to do so (that is, no one can make himself better off by doing so). The rights and organizational structures, Θ and ϕ, play an important role in motivating self-interested and maximizing individuals to achieve the physically possible output. For some purposes, such as the analysis of socialized firms, nonprofit organizations, and cooperatives, this characterization of the organization and its production function is a useful analytic framework.

The dependence of firm production functions on the organizational and rights structures is also important in the discussion of labor-managed firms, the codetermination movement in Europe, and the "industrial democracy" movement in the United States. In Section 6.3, we define these terms and summarize the major policy issues involved. Section 6.4 contains a detailed and critical discussion of much of the literature on the economic theory of the labor-managed firm. That discussion applies a subset of the general organizational issues raised above. Section 6.5 discusses the major operational example of the labor-managed firm—the Yugoslav labor-managed firm. Section 6.6 discusses a more general set of organizational forms in the context of the theory developed earlier. Here, we give attention to some characterizations of prototype organizational forms such as the Soviet-type firm, cooperatives, professional partnerships, and, finally, the codetermined firm. Our aim in Section 6.6 is (1) to provide a somewhat wider perspective on alternative organizational forms to help us better understand the traditional capitalist firm; (2) to provide some qualitative evidence (from the nature of cooperatives and professional partnerships) on the theory developed in Section 6.4; and (3) to stimulate others to view these organizations in a somewhat different light and to motivate additional work aimed at increasing our understanding of them.

6.3 The Codetermination and Industrial Democracy Movements

In Western Europe, the movement toward so-called industrial democracy has received much attention. Legal developments there are institutionalizing industrial democracy in two forms. First, firms are being required to seat voting labor representatives on their policy-making boards—a movement hereinafter referred to as "codetermination." Second, various new legal constraints are being imposed on the rights of management and owners of firms to make decisions: for example, on their right to dismiss or lay off employees, their right to modify production processes, and their right to close plants. These "management rights" that are being constrained (as well as the right to organize corporations without labor representation on the boards of directors) are all specific examples of the general right of individuals to voluntarily enter into contracts. Before turning to an analysis of the effects of the contractual environment imposed on firms by the state (which is what industrial democracy is all about), we discuss some often ignored facts about organizations that have relevance for codetermination. We believe these facts constitute important evidence to be reckoned with in any discussion of this subject.

In most Western nations there is no prohibition against the development of firms that have labor representation on the boards of directors. Indeed, labor can start, and in rare cases has started, firms of their own. Moreover, firms are free to write any kind of contracts they wish with their employees. If they choose to, they can offer no-dismissal, no-layoff contracts (tenure at universities). If they choose to, they can establish worker councils and agree not to change production methods without worker approval. Moreover, employers would establish such practices if the benefits exceeded the costs.

Furthermore, if laborers value the security and "self-realization" that such participatory contract arrangements afford them at more than their costs to the employer, they are in a position to offer voluntary exchanges it will pay the employer to take. Again, one would expect to see such arrangements emerge voluntarily unless the contracts are forbidden by law. Since (with minor exceptions) these arrangements are not observed,[2] we infer that workers do not value the security, management participation, "self-realization," and so forth at more than the costs of providing them.

Indeed, we infer from what is going on in Europe that industrial democracy can only be brought into being by fiat. We observe there the enactment of laws specifying that stock companies cannot exist unless 50% of their supervisory boards are labor representatives, or laws saying that such firms cannot lay off workers without the approval of workers' organizations, and so on. A striking fact about industrial democracy is that it cannot be effected on any significant scale voluntarily. Without fiat, codetermination would be virtually nonexistent. Given a choice, potential investors will not voluntarily put their wealth in the hands of codetermined firms; and this includes labor itself, even though many unions in the United States could easily do just that by buying entire companies with their pension funds.

The fact that this system seldom arises out of voluntary arrangements among individuals strongly suggests that codetermination or industrial democracy is less efficient than the alternatives that grow up and survive in a competitive environment (i.e., an environment in which no possible organizational alternatives are restricted). Of course, it is always possible that the frailty of industrial democracy is due to some "deficiency" that arises when individuals are given broader freedom in choosing organizational forms, but it seems reasonable to place the burden of proof on proponents of codetermination in this exercise.[3] This is especially important in view of the simple alternative hypothesis that can be advanced for codetermination, namely, that it is another case of a powerful special interest group using the political system to effect a wealth transfer from others to themselves (see Jensen and Meckling 1978 for a general exposition of this view of the political system).

The proponents of codetermination (including the official commissions nominally set up to study the question) have a delicate problem with the case they present. On the one hand, they want to reassure those who worry about the impact of codetermination on the rights of stockholders; on the other hand, they want to argue that codetermination bestows substantial benefits on labor. It is difficult to be on both sides of that fence simultaneously. If codetermination is beneficial to both stockholders and labor, why do we need laws to force firms to engage in it? Surely they would do so voluntarily. The fact that stockholders must be forced by law to accept codetermination is the best evidence we have that they are adversely affected by it. But the evidence is not limited to this fact. Firms in the "Montan" industries[4] in Germany tried to escape the more extreme codetermination requirements that applied there after World War II by changing their organizational structure and activities. The practice was widespread enough to induce the government to enact a series of special laws (the so-called Codetermination Protection Acts) to prevent avoidance. There is also evidence that under the less-than-parity[5] codetermination laws that prevailed outside the Montan industries in Germany prior to 1976, firms often created "executive" committees with review and decision-making responsibilities from which labor was deliberately excluded. This evidence suggests that those who argue that codetermination either benefits stockholders or is innocuous have a difficult task in making their case.

6.4   The Economics of the Labor-Managed and "Pure-Rental" Firm

Overview

Research on the "theory of the labor-managed firm" relevant to the codetermination issue has received attention in the economics profession. Labor-managed and codetermined firms are two very different types of organizations. But if we can explain the behavior of the labor-managed firm it will help us to say something about codetermination. Along the spectrum of potential firm organizational structures, the private corporation lies on one side of codetermination and the labor-managed firm lies on the other. Understanding how those two function allows us to bound the performance of the firm under codetermination. Unfortunately, with the exception of the work of a few individuals— like Pejovich and Furubotn—this "theory of the labor-managed firm" is not very helpful. Much of the economic literature on the labor-managed firm suffers from failure to specify clearly the institutional arrangements the authors have in mind. The use of the modifier "labor-managed" to describe whatever it is they have in mind itself raises semantic problems because it focuses attention on only one aspect of the institutional milieu. Labor-managed cannot mean that labor owns the firm in the traditional sense; that is, it cannot mean that tradable residual claims on the firm are held by employees. If that is all it means we are back to the traditional profit-maximizing firm. What the term "labor-managed" really means is that the models being used presume there are *legal prohibitions* against the existence of tradable residual claims on the entire sequence of future cash flows generated by the firm (what we usually think of as common equity).

Economists' attempts to analyze labor-managed firms have generally taken the form of comparisons between the behavior of labor-managed firms and traditional firms.[6] These are not comparisons of the empirical results of alternative structures of the firm; instead they are comparisons of alternative theoretical models. What renders most of these efforts unproductive is the almost universal tendency in the modeling to ignore precisely those institutional factors that are most crucial for the comparisons.

In our analyses of the labor-managed firm below we criticize the claim that labor-managed systems are efficient. Many of our criticisms revolve around the fallacious assumption that the actual outcomes of the system are solely a function of physical production functions, and that these production functions are independent of the contracting and property-rights structure within which the firm exists. The analysis leading to the efficiency claim ignores the importance of the organizational arrangements and the structure of rights in providing the appropriate incentives for people to realize the productive opportunities offered by the purely physical laws of production. In the analysis to follow we focus on what we believe are the crucial factors that determine incentives and thereby govern human behavior under alternative economic systems.

Pure-Rental Firms

The economics literature dealing with the so-called labor-managed firm has generated a special kind of firm (or more accurately, a kind of economy) for which there is no real-world counterpart. Meade (1972,

p. 402) provides what is perhaps the best definition of a labor-managed firm when he summarizes Vanek's (1970) structure as

> a system in which workers get together and form collectives or partnerships to run firms; they hire capital and purchase other inputs and they sell the products of the firm at the best prices they can obtain in the markets for inputs and outputs; they themselves bear the risk of any unexpected gain or loss and distribute the resulting surplus among themselves, all workers of any one given grade or skill receiving an equal share of the surplus; their basic objective is assumed to be to maximize the return per worker . . . the workers may be hiring their capital resources either in a competitive capital market fed by private earnings or else from a central governmental organization which lends out the State's capital resources at rentals which will clear the market.[7]

Although the term is ours and not one common to the literature, we think it better to describe this structure as a "pure-rental" system to emphasize its crucial nature. Individual firms in this economy are the product of private initiative. Individuals are permitted to own full rights in durable productive assets, that is, to have claims on the revenue from productive resources and to have rights in deciding how those resources are to be used. Moreover, such rights are transferable in whole or in part to other individuals. What is unique about the pure-rental economy is that *firms* are forbidden to hold claims or rights in durable productive resources like those held by individuals.[8] Firms can, however, secure temporary use rights in such resources by renting them from the individuals who hold the "full" claims on them. All claims on the firms themselves are held by employees, but there is no market for these claims; that is, employees have claims on current net revenues that they cannot sell to anyone else because eligibility for claims is conditional on employment, and the right to become an employee is not legally for sale. In effect, this arrangement bans the existence of common stock claims on the firm as we know them in the traditional capitalist firm. In the pure-rental firm, hiring is controlled by management, somehow in the interest of the workers as a group (e.g., by maximizing net revenue per worker).

The rather particular institutional construct of the pure-rental firm has been generated in order to satisfy two conflicting objectives: on the one hand to create an analytical model that countenances private claims, private initiative in the creation of firms, and private markets, but on the other hand to restrict decision-making authority in the firms to the employees. The latter, of course, is the sense in which such firms are labor managed.

Within the context of this pure-rental firm Ward (1958), Domar (1966), Vanek (1970), Maurice and Ferguson (1972), and Meade (1972) purport to demonstrate a number of propositions, the more important of which are[9]

Proposition 1. Given costless entry and exit of new firms, perfect competition, perfect mobility of factors, and constant returns to scale, the long-run equilibrium of the pure-rental or labor-managed firm and industry is Pareto-optimal in the same sense as the traditional firm and industry.

Proposition 2. In the short run when capital is fixed and the firm is not constrained by the supply of labor, an increase in industry demand leads the labor-managed firm to reduce its output and employment.[10]

Proposition 3. In any given monopolistic situation the labor-managed firm will restrict output more than a comparable traditional firm.[11]

If true, Proposition 1, the Pareto optimality of the pure-rental or labor-managed system, is a surprising result. However, it is incorrect for a number of reasons, and we discuss the major ones in the remainder of this section.

The Importance of Free Entry

As Meade (1972) emphasizes, Proposition 1 above depends in a crucial way on the assumption of costless formation of new firms and a smoothly running system of free entry into any endeavor. Proposition 2 says that all single-product labor-managed firms will have negatively sloped short-run supply curves. A price-increasing shift in demand will cause firms to *contract* their output and release labor rather than the usual expansion predicted for the traditional firm. In the short run this moves the labor-managed firm away from a Pareto optimum.

Suppose we start from an initial long-run equilibrium in which the value of the marginal product of labor is equal to the average earnings in each of the firms and equal across firms in industry *A* and all other industries. An increase in demand for the product of *A* leading to an increase in the price of *A*'s product raises the value of the marginal product of labor and capital in each firm and the average earnings per worker. Since every firm is assumed to be maximizing the average earnings per worker, their reaction is to cut back on employment to raise the value of the marginal product of labor up to the average earnings per worker and thus increase the average earnings even further.[12] Furthermore, the value of the marginal product and average earnings per worker in industry A are now greater than in all other industries. This situation is nonoptimal and can be corrected only by the formation and entry of new industry A firms.

It is argued that new firms will be made up of the unemployed from industry A (who were laid off because of the increased demand) and workers from other industries who now earn less than those in industry A. Entry continues until all released labor in industry A is employed and until the average earnings (and therefore value of the marginal product) of labor is again equalized across all industries. The result is a Pareto-optimal solution that satisfies all the marginal conditions familiar to the perfectly competitive capitalist industry.

Thus the competitive adjustment process through entry plays a vital role in bringing about optimality in the labor-managed economy. Given this, it is noteworthy that its advocates have spent little effort analyzing or developing a theory of entry within the labor-managed structure. We return to this issue below after discussing a number of basic issues associated with the labor-managed structure that imply that there is considerable difficulty with entry in this system.

Optimal Contracting and Rental versus Ownership

Dreze (1976) provides an even more recent example of analysis of the pure-rental version of a labor-managed economy (one in which all capital goods are rented):

> For our purposes here a labor-managed economy is an economy where production is carried out in firms organized by workers who get together and form collectives or partnerships. These firms hire nonlabor inputs, including capital, and sell outputs, under the assumed objective of maximizing the welfare of the members, for which a simple proxy is sometimes found in the return (value added) per worker. The capital can be either publicly or privately owned. To permit easier comparison, I will base this presentation on private ownership. (p. 1125)

Again, we have a system in which firms are implicitly prevented by law from having "ownership" of durable productive assets, but individuals (in Dreze's "private ownership" case) are allowed complete ownership rights in capital assets.

There are many reasons why the rental of durable productive assets is not a universally observed practice in systems where both ownership and rental are allowed. Alchian and Demsetz (1972) discuss some of the conditions under which the rental of such assets will be dominated by outright ownership. We prefer to think of these problems in the framework of the agency problem as discussed in Chapter 4. In those cases where the agency costs (defined as the sum of the monitoring and bonding expenditures plus the residual loss) engendered by the rental arrangement are greater than the costs of outright ownership, the asset will be purchased (if the law allows it). The obvious agency costs of the rental arrangement are those associated with the reduced incentives for the user to maintain the asset properly, to guard it from theft, and the increased incentives for misuse. Users who do not bear the cost of improper maintenance, etc., and who cannot be costlessly monitored will have less incentive to care optimally for rented property. The magnitude of these costs along with the monitoring and bonding costs that would be incurred in an effort to control them explains why rental or leasing of most durable production goods is not observed. It is simply a more costly contracting arrangement. Ignoring the agency costs of alternative contractual forms in comparing two systems where the only difference between the two is the contractual form allowed is unlikely to shed light on the major issues. But Dreze as well as most others writing on the topic does exactly this. In his summary paper on the subject he states:

> On the assumption that production possibilities are the same under profit maximization and under labor management, the following propositions are readily established (Dreze 1974): (i) With every labor-management equilibrium, one can associate a vector of salaries such that the given allocation, the given prices, and these salaries, together, define a competitive equilibrium. (ii) The set of allocations that can be sustained, under suitable redistribution of initial resources, as competitive equilibria and as labor-management equilibria, are identical and coincide with the set of Pareto optima.

In other words, maximizing average value added gross of wages, or maximizing total value added net of competitive wages, leads to the same general equilibrium solutions . . .

The propositions are useful in establishing the compatibility of labor management with efficiency. Conditionally on equilibrium, they establish compatibility of labor management with profit maximization, within a given economy or even within a single firm. The propositions also permit reliance upon the more developed theory of competitive economies to study such questions as existence, uniqueness, stability, and continuity of labor-management equilibria. (Dreze 1976, p. 1127)

These conclusions (which are just Proposition 1 in the general equilibrium form) cannot hold unless the optimal form of the voluntary contract in the free contracting traditional system is always rental and never ownership—an empirical conjecture easily rejected by observation of the world.

Major Flaws in the Pure-Rental and Labor-Managed Firm Structure

The special characteristics of the claims that individuals and firms have on producer assets in the pure-rental or labor-managed firm economy are the keystone to analyzing how those economies would function. We concentrate here on five major flaws induced by particular aspects of the rights structure in these economies and their implication for Pareto optimality. In brief, they are

- The impossibility of pure rental: induced by the necessity for any firm to acquire intangible assets that by their nature cannot be rented.
- The horizon problem: induced by the truncated (nonperpetual) claims on firm cash flows.
- The common-property problem: induced by equal sharing of firm cash flows among all employees.
- The nontransferability problem: induced by the fact that workers' claims on firm cash flows are contingent on employment with the firm and are nonmarketable.
- The control problem: induced by the specification of the political procedures within the firm by which the workers arrive at decisions and control the managers.

The impossibility of pure rental. Suppose for the moment that a group of workers decide to form a new firm. Advocates such as Dreze and Vanek have never made clear how this group is to obtain the funds for rental of the equipment, the design and engineering of products, the establishment of distribution systems and inventories, advertising of the product, training of the labor force, and so on. Reviewing this list the reader will notice that many of these things, unlike a production line or a blast furnace, are intangible and yet essential to the success of any enterprise. Economists like Dreze and Vanek who claim efficiency for the mandatory pure-rental system have never explained just how a group of workers can go about "renting" these intangible organizational factors that often represent a major component of what is generally called "capital."

It is literally impossible to effect period-by-period renegotiable price contracts to "rent" intangible items. Since by their very nature intangible assets cannot be rented, if these assets are to be obtained they have to be financed either through the personal contributions of the workers or through a pure financial claim (such as a "bond" or "stock" issue). But if they are obtained in either of these ways, the claims of the workers or the claims of the bondholders or stockholders represent investments. As investments, they run head-on into the "horizon" problem (discussed below) pointed out by Pejovich (1969), Furubotn and Pejovich (1973), and Furubotn (1976), and the horizon problem ensures that the system will not in fact arrive at a Pareto-optimal allocation.

The horizon problem and the reduced demand for capital. Once we recognize that it is in principle impossible to have a pure-rental firm we are left with analyzing labor-managed firms—those with the following organizational characteristics: (1) workers have the option of investing in the firm; (2) the firm can issue debt claims; (3) workers have nontradable claims on the year-by-year residual cash flows contingent on employment.[13]

Consider the case in which resources are obtained from the workers either through direct contributions or through retention of earnings in the firm. Since by law there are no ownership claims on the pure-rental firm, the workers have no claim on the principal amount they "lend" ("give" is the appropriate word) to the firm as they would if they were to lend the same amount to a savings bank. Employees have claims on cash flows that are contingent on employment. The horizon employees want used in the investment decisions of the firm is their expected employment termination date. To the extent that this date falls short of the productive life of potential assets, employees will use truncated flows in choosing investment projects including, for example, the investments in intangibles at start-up. Only those projects for which the present value of the truncated flows exceeds the present value of the outlays will be taken. This reduces the number of projects the firm takes; it rules out some projects for which the present value of the total stream of expected cash flow is positive.[14]

If the interest rate obtainable at a savings bank[15] (or through personal lending) is i, workers will require a rate of return on the firm's investments that is higher than i before they will "loan" to it as long as they perceive their tenure in the firm to be shorter than the life of the investment project. Suppose all individuals in the firm have identical horizons of N years, and let us restrict consideration for the moment to projects that have infinite lives with risks equivalent to the savings-bank investment and constant returns. In this situation the perpetual annual rate of return on the investment, r^*, that leaves the workers indifferent between investing in the firm and investing in the savings bank at the annual rate is given by

$$r^* = \frac{i(1+i)^N}{(1+i)^N - 1} \tag{1}$$

where the right-hand side of (1) is just the reciprocal of the present value of an annuity factor at the rate of i, for N years (see Pejovich 1969). Thus for $i = 5\%$ and horizons of 1, 5, 10, or 15 years, the workers' required return on investment in the firm, r^*, is, respectively, 105%, 23%, 13%, and 10%. Furthermore, the problem is more general than this since projects as a rule do not yield uniform flows, and for equivalent-return projects those that pay off relatively more quickly will be most favored. Those projects that require long investment and development periods and whose payoffs occur far into the future are less likely to be taken. These effects are due to the absence of marketable claims on the future cash-flow streams, and they imply a reduction in the use of capital as compared with the traditional firm.[16]

It is worthwhile here to point out the full generality of this horizon problem. Economists who have analyzed these problems have never faced up to the fact that the real constraint on what the workers in a pure-rental or labor-managed firm can pay themselves as wages or perquisites (or more generally consume) at any point in time is the *net cash balance* available at that time. Therefore, the workers have strong incentives to behave in ways that maximize the near-term net cash flows of the firm. The tendency of economists to deal with a world in which all flows are uniform and perpetual masks this issue and along with it a set of serious problems. "Depreciation," for instance, is not a cash flow. In fact the maintenance of capital equipment or buildings is an investment decision itself. To the extent that today's workers can pay themselves higher salaries by reducing, postponing, or eliminating maintenance where the major negative effects on cash flows will occur in the future beyond their own horizons, they will be more likely to do so.

But there are many other ways in which workers can increase the near-term flows to the firm. They will prefer to borrow under conditions that place the repayment burden on future generations of workers; for example, by the issuance of long-term bonds with low coupons and on sinking-fund provisions. The cash proceeds from such borrowings can be paid out in wages or increased fringe benefits and therefore can be consumed directly. Alternatively, to accomplish the same end the funds might be invested in projects whose near-term cash flows are high. In a similar vein, current workers have incentives to vote themselves large pension benefits that carry no funding provisions.[17] Current cash flows (and therefore worker payments) would not be reduced, and the full burden of the payment of the pensions would be shifted to future generations of the firm's workers. To overcome many of these difficulties we expect a myriad of legal constraints to be imposed by the political sector in a labor-managed system. In fact, as we discuss below, it is exactly these kinds of laws that have arisen in Yugoslavia—laws to control the aberrant behavior of the Yugoslav labor-managed firm.

The common-property problem. In an important respect employee claims suffer from a common-property defect. New employees acquire the same claims on cash flows as those already employed by the firm. This means that whenever investment is accompanied by additional labor old workers have to share with new workers the anticipated cash flows from past investments. Thus the expectation that a new project will generate cash flows that have a positive present value to the *firm* will not be sufficient to induce the current workers to undertake that project.

Consider a one-period investment-decision model. Let C be the cash flow that would be generated at presently planned investment levels. If employment is E, each worker will receive C/E as his share of the flows. Let C^* be the cash flow that will be generated if the firm takes a new investment project involving employment of E^* workers. The project will be taken by the present workers only if

$$\frac{C^*}{E^*} > \frac{C}{E},$$

that is, if the cash flow per worker rises.[18] This simple example illustrates the common-property defect and also points up the symmetry of that problem. A subset of workers (those who do not lose their jobs) can make themselves better off by having the firm take a project that adds nothing to cash flows but simply decreases the number of workers. Indeed, they can also be made better off by "unprofitable" projects that decrease cash flows, so long as there is a proportionately larger decline in employment. Again, these incentives will tend to reduce aggregate welfare and prevent attainment of Pareto optimality.

The nontransferability problem: monitoring and the efficient allocation of risk. The claims that workers have are not transferable, that is, they cannot sell their jobs. This fact has two important consequences for the operation of the firm: the monitoring of management will be far less efficiently performed, and employees will have serious "portfolio" problems that reduce their ability to diversify and therefore reduce their demand for capital.

THE MONITORING PROBLEM. There will be no market in which the value of the employees' (common-property, truncated-flow) claims get capitalized and traded. Where such markets exist there are large potential gains to be made from ferreting out firms that are undervalued or overvalued. The mere existence of these potential gains leads to the development of specialists who make a business of analyzing the prospects for individual firms. One of their main interests will be in evaluating the management of the firms, and their management evaluations will be reflected in an impartial published measure—security prices. The existence of a well-organized market in which corporate claims are continuously assessed is perhaps the single most important control mechanism affecting managerial behavior in modern industrial economies.

Employees of the pure-rental firm will also have an interest in monitoring the performance of management, but no one in the pure-rental economy will have the same incentive to specialize in performance evaluation (monitoring) as exists in a corporate economy, because there is no way for any individual employee to capture more than a small fraction of the potential gains from such activities. It is therefore naive to believe that pure-rental managers will take the same pains as would corporate executives to seek out high-payoff new projects, to weed out projects that have negative payoffs, to control waste and shirking, and so on.[19]

A similar argument is made by Alchian and Demsetz (1972), who argue, for these reasons and others, that in order to reduce the costs of shirking, the monitor (i.e., manager) must be the residual claimant on the firm's cash flows. They argue therefore that this provides the incentive that leads the parties involved to adopt the entrepreneurial and corporate organizational forms we observe. We agree with their analysis and recommend it to the reader.

PORTFOLIO PROBLEMS AND EFFICIENT RISK BEARING. When uncertainty is explicitly introduced into the discussion of the behavior of the pure-rental or labor-managed economy, great difficulties ensue. The nontransferability of employees' claims also means that employees face a serious constraint on diversifying their "portfolio." Vanek (1970) never mentions these issues in his book. Meade (1972, pp. 426–427) briefly points out the basic problem and hypothesizes that this is one of the reasons why voluntary labor partnerships occur primarily in occupations involving such labor-intensive services as lawyers, accountants, and doctors. Dreze (1976) summarizes the issues clearly and concisely, but arrives at some peculiar conclusions. We return to this below.

The basic problem with uncertainty in the pure-rental firm is that the workers' shares in the firm's cash flows would in fact be similar to nonmarketable finite-lived shares of common stock.[20] The nonmarketability feature means that the workers cannot diversify their holdings across many different firms and assets. This leads to a non-Pareto-optimal solution for two reasons:

1. There is no opportunity for specialization in risk bearing across individuals with different degrees of risk aversion and wealth, and therefore the resulting distribution of risk is inefficient.
2. The worker-investors are forced in the aggregate to bear risks that are in fact "insurable" by diversification. Therefore, there is an additional net deadweight welfare loss.[21]

The inefficiencies introduced by this nonmarketability problem do not end with these allocation effects. Both of these effects lead the participants to demand higher rates of return on potential investments, and this must result in a reduction in the demand for capital as compared with the traditional system[22]—again violating Pareto optimality. In addition, these misallocations of risk will also affect the types of projects undertaken by the labor-managed firm. Those projects whose total variance of returns is large but whose "social risk" or "covariance risk" is small or zero (because they are independent of returns elsewhere in the economy) will tend not to be taken even though their expected returns are above the riskless rate. This also is non-Pareto-optimal.

Dreze (1976) clearly understands these issues. He comments on a suggestion by Vanek (1974) that labor-managed firms be financed by a combination of bonds, negotiable shares of stock issued on the market, and nonnegotiable shares of stock issued to workers.[23] Considering the case where worker shares are identical (but nonnegotiable) with those issued on the market, Dreze states (and we agree) that

> [e]fficiency analysis of [this] case is straightforward. It is always desirable for a labor-managed firm to issue on the market shares representing 100 per cent of future output and to divide the proceeds of the sale among the workers, who may then allocate freely their income between current consumption and a diversified portfolio acquired on the stock market. The workers cannot gain from tying up part of their income in a risky asset that cannot be traded (p. 1134).

Furthermore, Dreze also mentions the implications of this for the management control issue:

In this simple model, where asset diversification by firms and future labor inputs are ignored, an efficient allocation of risk-bearing in private ownership labor-managed economies requires the organization of a stock market, so as to permit portfolio diversification. Given the existence of a stock market, efficiency of production decisions requires that control rights be vested with the shareholders (p. 1134).

It is worth emphasizing this last point regarding control. What Dreze does not mention is that, efficiency aside, it is highly unlikely that potential investor demands for the residual claims on a labor-managed firm would be large without some sacrifice of the control right by the workers. It seems to us unlikely that outside investors would voluntarily entrust their funds to a labor-managed enterprise in which the workers maintained complete control and the investors were allowed to hope that the worker-managers would behave in such a way as to leave something for them, the residual claimants.

Dreze (1976, pp. 1136–1137) goes on to point out that in fact there is a basic and unavoidable problem associated with the "solution" that accomplishes an "efficient" allocation of risk between labor and capital. This "solution" is not compatible with appropriate production incentives in a decentralized environment. This is nothing more than the agency problem, which we have written about extensively (Jensen and Meckling 1976 and Chapter 4 of this volume). There, we define the concept of "agency costs" and use it to show how the conflict of interest between management and outside owners (a special case of the problem raised by Dreze) of the firm is resolved. When we take account of the fact that such costs are an inevitable by-product of joint activity by more than one person, both parties to the effort have the incentive to reduce these costs by the formation of the optimal form of contracts and the establishment of the socially (and privately) optimal amount of monitoring, bonding, and other control activities. To speak of the resulting solution as inefficient is to commit the Nirvana fallacy, and it is comparable with saying that a world in which iron ore does not jump out of the ground at zero resource cost is "inefficient."

What is surprising is that after pointing out this "agency" problem (and without any analysis) Dreze (1976) concludes that there is a need to reconcile the interests of both groups through some form of participatory decision making (p. 1137) "[in which] both capital and labor [define] criteria for managerial decisions affecting the future incomes of both groups" (p. 1136). Tentative as this conclusion may still be, we regard it as providing theoretical justification for the participation of both labor and capital—whether it be publicly or privately owned—in decisions affecting the future of the firm and hence of its workers and capital owners (p. 1137).

Ignoring the fact that Dreze is appealing to an unexamined alternative for a solution, we emphasize that neither he nor any other advocate of the labor-managed or codetermined system has provided any justification for why this participation does not arise as a result of voluntary contracting and why it must in fact be imposed on the respective parties by the force of law.

The control problem. Other than vague suggestions about the establishment of "workers' councils" elected (somehow) by the workers, none of the advocates (or analysts) of the pure-rental or labor-managed firm have suggested just how the workers can or should solve the control problem. No one has specified a well-defined set of procedures for solving the decision-making problem within the firm when the preferences of the workers are not all identical. It is usually simply assumed that the workers will have a common set of preferences and that no conflicts will arise in translating these into operational policies at the firm level. For some purposes of analysis this can be a useful simplification, but if we are ever to develop a positive model of the behavior of a pure-rental or labor-managed firm and economy this is a crucial element. Unfortunately, this is essentially a political problem, and no one today has a viable theory of such political processes. We postpone further discussion of this issue to Section 6.5, where we discuss the general problem in the context of the behavior of the Yugoslav-type firm.

The Difficulty with Entry in the Pure-Rental System

Recall the crucial role of entry in the establishment of Pareto optimality in the pure-rental system. In the short run the pure-rental firm will respond to an increase in demand with a *reduction* of output and employment (Proposition 2). The increase in output and employment of the affected industry is accomplished in the long run by the costless formation and entry of new firms into the industry. Thus, as discussed earlier, Proposition 1 depends in a crucial way on free entry.

In considering the entry problem it seems clear that, if the equal sharing of income provision among all workers is enforced,[24] the incentive for any potential entrepreneur to incur the necessary effort to start a new firm is substantially reduced. In the capitalist system the entrepreneur can capture all or a substantial part of the *present value* of the entire future stream of profits. This constitutes the reward for entrepreneurship and thereby creates the incentive for prospective entrepreneurs to incur the costs involved in building a new enterprise.

But what is true in the labor-managed environment? Most clear is that entrepreneurs do not legally obtain claim to the present value of the stream of earnings they create for two reasons. First there is the common-property problem: the fruits of the enterprise must be shared with all the firm's labor, so an entrepreneur obtains roughly only 1/Nth of the total increment in earnings his creation makes possible (where N is the average number of employees over his tenure).[25] Second there is the horizon problem: entrepreneurs have no legal claim whatsoever to the enterprise's incremental earnings stream that continues beyond their own tenure with the firm. This reduction in the reward to entrepreneurial activity tends to reduce substantially the quantity of entrepreneurial effort supplied, and for any given level of social benefits to entry this tends to reduce the rate of formation of new firms in the labor-managed economy. In effect, the prohibition of private ownership of the capital value claims on the future streams of cash flows to the firm drives a wedge between the social and private benefits of entrepreneurial activity and therefore drives the pure-rental and labor-managed economies away from a Pareto-optimal solution.

Vanek (1970) is the only advocate of the labor-managed economy who has attempted to face this issue. He devotes an entire chapter in his book to the "Entry, Expansion, and Exit of Labor-Managed Firms," arguing at one point that the "government" will start new firms and turn their management and control over to the workers. He provides no analysis showing why bureaucrats or elected officials would (1) choose to start only those new firms where the expected risk-adjusted benefits exceed the costs, and (2) why if they start *any* firm they would find it in their interest to relinquish control of it. Vanek presumes, as do so many economists, that upon taking office politicians or bureaucrats go through a metamorphosis—setting aside their own tastes and preferences and concerns for their own welfare, adopting the "public welfare" as their objective function, and choosing among alternatives solely on the basis of the "public good." We know of no empirical evidence supporting this model of political behavior.[26]

Jaroslav Vanek also argues that existing firms will foster, finance, and nurture the formation and entry of new firms—again ignoring the workers' own self-interest when it suffices to help solve a problem. Several chapters earlier he rigorously derives the negatively sloped supply condition of Proposition 2 based upon the self-interest of the firm's participants. He then passes off all of that analysis based on self-interest with the following assertion: ". . . the resistance to the creation of competing firms, which is so natural to the capitalist system, is mitigated in the labor-managed environment by the fact that the 'new competition,' socially, is nothing but part of the old working collective. As between parents and children, resentment of competition may turn into the pride in good performance" (Vanek 1970, p. 236). He goes on to argue that yet another force bringing about entry is the "bee-swarm effect" (pp. 286ff.). Apparently, this is meant to refer to the spontaneous collection of unemployed workers into firms after the fashion of a bee swarm in nature. We say "apparently" because after promising at several points in the book to "explain . . . more thoroughly" (p. 4) and to "substantiate" (p. 12) the "bee-swarm effect," Vanek gives the reader nothing more in his chapter on the topic than the repetition of the phrase (p. 286).

The Choice of Working Conditions

Dreze argues that "competitive profit maximization does not imply an efficient choice of working conditions" (1976, p. 1130). His analysis leading to this conclusion treats the problem as one of "choosing a vector of semi-public goods." However, the only limitation in the traditional competitive environment that prevents laborers from obtaining the exact working environment they prefer is whether there are enough workers with identical tastes to make it profitable for some firm to specialize in producing its product with the preferred working conditions. Suppose enough workers value any particular set of working conditions so much that they would accept a wage reduction with a present value large enough to more than cover the costs of providing this set of working conditions. Given these circumstances, some profit-maximizing employer will discover the opportunity to make both the firm and potential laborers better off by offering them the "optimal" set of working conditions and a correspondingly lower wage.

Of course, if the homogeneous groups are individually so small that it does not pay employers to provide a complete variety of conditions, we are back in the usual public-good situation. But to call this inefficient is to simply ignore the costs associated with increasingly finer specification of the goods.[27] The competitive capitalist firm has the correct incentives to take account of these costs and thus generate an efficient solution. The labor-managed system might accomplish this same thing, it might do even better (if the costs were lower), or it might do worse. We do not know, and Dreze provides no analysis to eliminate our ignorance. Instead, he commits the classic Nirvana fallacy. He deduces that some system does not perform ideally (because some costs are not zero) and, proclaiming failure, appeals to an unexamined alternative as a superior solution.

6.5. The Yugoslav-Type Firm: An Alternative Specification of the Labor-Managed Firm

A Spectrum of Organizational Forms

We concentrated in the previous section on a detailed analysis of the pure-rental firm that forms the basis for most of the analysis in the economics literature. In this section we analyze in some detail the characteristics of the Yugoslav version of the labor-managed firm—the major operational example of this phenomenon. The Yugoslav system differs in important ways from the pure-rental construct of the literature and an analysis of the differences is instructive. Before proceeding to this task, however, it is useful to point out that a number of interesting structures for firms exist, ranging from the Soviet firm to the private corporation. Six of them, arranged according to the degree to which the residual claims on the firm can be capitalized and sold by the claimants, are

- the Soviet firm,
- the Yugoslav firm,
- the pure-rental firm,
- the cooperative firm,
- the professional partnership, and
- the private corporation.

Except for the pure-rental firm, which is purely hypothetical, we use these as titles to characterize idealized firms or structures that roughly correspond to their popular prototypes (without attempting to be faithful in every respect to the actual complexities). We concentrate on the Yugoslav-type firm next and then go on to discuss in Section 6.6 the Soviet-type firm, the cooperative firm, the professional partnership firm, and, finally, the codetermined firm.

Definition of the Yugoslav-Type Firm

The major difference between a Yugoslav-type firm and a pure-rental firm is that in the Yugoslav economy neither firms *nor individuals* are allowed to possess full ownership claims on productive assets. Each Yugoslav-type firm is permitted to set output prices and to decide what quantity it will produce. Existing firms, the state, and individuals can create new firms. Decisions within the firm are made in accord with legally prescribed political procedures. Workers elect a workers' council which appoints a manager. The authority to decide output level, output prices, and the organization of production is delegated to the manager.

While individuals are prohibited from having personal claims on the assets of any firm, the employees of firms are given a "communal" claim on current period "net revenues" that are determined by a set of accounting rules. Roughly speaking, net revenues are sales minus outlays minus depreciation. The workers' claims on net revenues are contingent on continued employment and are not transferable. Compensation plans are subject to state-set maxima and minima and are submitted each period (year) to a referendum of the workers. Net revenues can be retained in the firm and invested. Firms face a legal prohibition against consuming their capital assets, that is, they cannot generate net revenues for workers by using up the assets. The firm also cannot sell its assets and distribute the proceeds to workers. The state lends money to firms at prescribed interest rates.

Problems with the Yugoslav-Type Firm

The Yugoslav-type labor-managed firm has all the defects of the pure-rental and labor-managed systems discussed in the last section plus some more. It is subject to all the difficulties associated with the horizon problem, the common-property problem, the nontransferability problem, the control problem, and the entry problem—and for all the same reasons. Except for the control problem, which we shall discuss in more detail here, there is little to be gained from repeating any of the discussion of the other problems.

The discussion of the Yugoslav-type system proceeds in three sections: (1) the control problem (or the worker vs. the worker), (2) the definition of net revenues (or the worker vs. the state), and (3) the savings-investment problem.

The control problem (or the worker vs. the worker). The Yugoslav-type rules assign a major role to a one-vote-per-employee political process for decision making within the firm. Unfortunately, there is no generally accepted theory about how such political processes operate. Simple majority-rule models do not predict very well in the political sector at large. They cannot explain the mass of minority-interest legislation that gets enacted in Western democratic societies. Vote trading or log-rolling (the formation of coalitions that constitute majorities) helps explain how some of this legislation can come about, but leaves us with the question of why particular coalitions are formed and are viable while others are not. The same problem arises in economics in a different guise, namely, our inability to explain what it is that determines union behavior. What is it that unions maximize?

Without a theory of political processes, it is difficult to put together a fully satisfactory theory of the Yugoslav-type firm. We have no good theoretical or empirical reasons for believing that the firm will actually behave as though it were maximizing the average income per worker. We know there are divergences of interests among employees of the firm—for example, that employees aged sixty and over will have a different time horizon from those under thirty. When investment decisions are made, how are these conflicts of interest resolved? Such conflicts will be the rule rather than the exception. They will also be present in decisions about the nonpecuniary aspects of employment. If it is possible (as it actually is in Yugoslavia) to use part of the wage fund each year for community facilities—housing, sports arenas, hospitals, and so on—those decisions will also be a source of conflict.

It is worthwhile to reflect for a moment on why we do not expect these "political" factors to be such an important matter for concern when predicting the behavior of the large capitalist corporation. The first is purely empirical—in fact, we observe private corporations behaving in ways that are consistent with value maximization and in very different ways from nonprofit organizations like universities and government agencies such as the post office. Although we (Jensen and Meckling 1976 and Chapter 4 of this volume) and others (especially Alchian and Demsetz 1972; Fama 1978; Myers 1977; Smith and Warner 1979) have begun to develop a positive theory of the corporation, there is much we do not understand about the workings of the corporate form of organization. The unexplained problem, however, is not why the corporate form is so inefficient, but exactly the opposite: why is it as efficient and robust as it is?

We believe that one of the reasons for the enormous success of the corporation with investors and workers and one of the major reasons it can be treated as a black box for many purposes in economics is because it severely restricts the opportunities for any individual shareholder or group of shareholders to reallocate wealth away from other shareholders to themselves. The proportional sharing rules that govern distributions and the fact that the nonpecuniary aspects of share ownership are usually either zero or small make it difficult to benefit some shareholders at the expense of others. If the manager decides to take an investment project that has positive net value, all shareholders benefit, and the extent to which an individual benefits depends solely on how many shares he or she owns. There is, in other words, a clear-cut rule outside of the control of the manager or anyone else for determining how benefits are to be distributed.[28]

When managers of Yugoslav-type firms decide on investment projects, however, they will consider how their decisions will affect the election outcome—reelection presumably being in their personal interest. Managers certainly cannot be presumed to maximize net revenue per employee;[29] they will be led to consider the distribution effects that any investment will have on the welfare of workers. While we cannot with any confidence specify a model that yields an equilibrium for this process, we can say some things about the impact it will have. However the conflicts are resolved, it would be very surprising indeed if they brought the firm close to Pareto-optimal performance.

Meanwhile, the process is certain to impose costs. Workers will find it in their interest to organize and engage in various political activities within the firm. When new hires are to be made, those in control will want to see that the new employees conform to their tastes, or at least can be induced to vote for their side. They will similarly want to force nonconformist employees out of the firm.

The definition of net revenues (or the worker vs. the state). The desire on the part of the Yugoslav state to limit the kind of claims that individuals can have on producer assets leads to the flaws outlined above, and these in turn lead to a labyrinth of other problems. If the state grants the firms unlimited authority to decide the total compensation package each year, it will in effect be giving authority to the workers to "eat up the assets of the firm."[30] Employees would (with state blessings) be able to convert firm wealth into personal wealth via the annual vote on compensation.[31]

In an effort to prevent this practice the state lays down rules for computing the amount that will be available each year for distribution among employees and ordains that the firm must "maintain its capital." These rules define what we have called "net revenues."

Unfortunately, where the resourceful, evaluative, maximizing models (REMMs) of human behavior (Jensen 1994; Jensen and Meckling 1994; Meckling 1976) are involved, invoking rules is no guarantee that the intended purpose will be approximated. Workers will still have the incentive to convert firm wealth into personal wealth. This incentive, of course, exists in private corporations as well. The difference lies in the opportunity set facing workers in the two cases. In the private corporation, stockholders and bondholders, who bear the wealth effects of changes in firm value, have incentives to monitor managers to prevent them from making transfers of corporate assets to workers or permitting workers to make such transfers. To the extent that managers fail, their failure will be reflected in stock prices for all to see. Since the management of the Yugoslav firm is responsible to and elected by workers, however, the management will have less incentive to prevent such transfers and it will be very difficult to tell whether they are doing so.

The dependence on accounting rules for limiting the annual wage package is particularly susceptible to manipulation. Accountants in the United States have struggled in vain for years to develop acceptable rules for computing income. This is the same problem faced by the Yugoslav state. Depreciation, for example, is a completely artificial and unreliable way to impute the cost of using assets. Moreover, insofar as accepted depreciation practices depend on experience, the depreciation rules for the Yugoslav firm will in time simply reflect the fact that workers have an incentive to "consume" more of their equipment.

The opportunities for Yugoslav-type workers to avoid the constraints the state tries to impose, however, go far beyond simply running down inventories, failing to maintain machinery, and so forth. Real difficulties arise over the opportunities they have to transfer cash flows from the future to the present—opportunities to take actions that expand current cash flows in exchange for reducing future ones. Investment projects, for example, that yield cash flows that decline over time but can be financed by borrowing where the loan is repaid in level amounts will be attractive to the current Yugoslav-type workers. For the same reasons Yugoslav-type workers will welcome inflation, and they will not be interested in adopting LIFO (last in first out) for valuing inventories or in replacement costs for valuing fixed assets.[32] Neither will they find it desirable to capitalize research and development (R&D) expenditures, or for that matter any cash outlay that can be construed as an expense. If they capitalize any items such as R&D, the law requires that they depreciate them *and* maintain their book value, and this would limit further potential withdrawals from the firm. Given the demonstrated ability of American accountants to get around many of the IRS, SEC, and various accounting-principles boards' rulings, one can only presume that the Yugoslav worker accountants will prove to be similarly ingenious at mitigating the efforts of the state to constrain the workers' current consumption proclivities.[33] In brief, models of the Yugoslav-type firm that simply assume that all of the constraints imposed by the state are effective will not be very successful in predicting actual behavior.[34]

The savings-investment problem. Because there are no private rights in productive assets, however, the Yugoslav-type system will have a much lower level of voluntary saving and investment.[35] Investment opportunities available to individuals will consist primarily of durable consumer assets such as art, automobiles, housing (unless socialized), antiques, precious stones, jewelry, fine china and tableware, and assets used in home production. Interpersonal lending (perhaps through the medium of a savings bank) provides the only alternative investment or savings alternative for the individual. Such "investments," of course, do little to increase the productive capacity of the economy and in general offer lower yields than producer assets.

In this situation the state must provide the productive assets if they are to exist at all. There are only three sources of resources to finance these assets: taxes (on both consumers and firms), borrowing (through debt issues and the establishment of a state bank), and the printing press (money). There are no forces based in the self-interest of the decision makers to determine the correct amount of savings and investment as in the pure-rental economy. The state must set the level of interest rates, and it will have very little information for use in doing so. In addition to all these problems, the most difficult problem faced by the state is the establishment of the incentives to cause those demanding capital goods to reveal the correct information regarding the expected payoff and risk of each project and to cause those granting the requests to fund only the most desirable projects. The experience with state-financed activities throughout the world leaves us with little hope that these incentive problems are likely to be solved.[36] The result is that not only does the state have enormous problems in arriving at the appropriate level of investment, but it is also highly likely to misallocate it among projects.

6.6 The Soviet Firm, Cooperatives, Professional Partnerships, and the Codetermined Firm

The Soviet-Type Firm

In this section we discuss the remaining organizational firms outlined above. The Soviet firm is of interest here mainly because it occupies one end of the spectrum of possible firms. It is an example of the extreme in eliminating individual rights in productive assets, and we briefly summarize the implications of that aspect of the Soviet institutional structure.

In the Soviet economy neither individuals nor firms are permitted to have claims on returns generated by nonhuman productive resources or rights in deciding how such resources will be used. Even individual rights in human resources are severely restricted. Compensation policy is decided by the state; individuals are required to work and the state has the authority to assign individuals to particular occupations, firms, or locations. Each Soviet firm is a creature of the state responsible for carrying out some part of the central plan, much like an operating division of an independent firm. In the Soviet economy, production and distribution (what, how, how much, and so on) are centrally directed (Gosplan and the Central Committee). The terms of trade are fixed by the state. All decisions regarding the organization of firms (vertical and horizontal integration) and involving the creation, expansion, contraction, or dissolution of firms or enterprises are made by the state.

Once the Soviet state has denied individuals and firms the right to claims in producer assets, it must, if it wants to avoid social chaos, take responsibility for the operation of the entire economy. It is a physical fact of life that uses of resources conflict with one another. The same axe cannot be used simultaneously to cut down two different trees; the same piece of land cannot simultaneously support the Empire State Building and serve as a pasture. Somehow, one or the other use must prevail. The social function of systems of individual rights is precisely to resolve these conflicts. The system of private rights specifies which individuals can do what, with what.

The Soviet alternative to individual rights is centralized decision making. Even if we ignore the overwhelming information requirements that must be satisfied if central authorities are to set prices and output at Pareto-optimal levels in a Soviet economy,[37] we are left with a staggering problem of divergence between private and social costs. Since no one in the entire system, including the central authorities, has a claim on the capitalized value of productive resources, changes in the value of those resources brought about by "better" or "worse" uses of them are simply dissipated throughout the economy.

If the Soviet state literally limits rewards for productive activity to more or less egalitarian wages with a guaranteed minimum, workers and managers will be supremely indifferent about producing. This is why authorities in the Soviet-type state end up instituting "bonus schemes" (e.g., bonuses based on output) or, in cases like Yugoslavia, attempting to emulate the private firm with schemes like the labor-managed firm. In brief, even if the central authorities in the Soviet economy set all the "correct" (i.e., Pareto-optimal) prices (which they cannot), the system would not produce the corresponding optimal quantities of goods and services because individuals would not have the appropriate incentives. Thus the Soviet-type system has all the problems of the pure-rental and Yugoslav systems plus many more.

The Cooperative Firm

The cooperative is an institutional form that is a close relative of the pure-rental firm but is in certain respects distinctly different. The cooperative is of interest because it survives in societies where choice of organizational form is largely voluntary. It holds full claims on productive assets; unlike the pure-rental firm it has transferable use rights in assets. Like the pure-rental firm, the members of the co-op hold the claims on the cash flows, claims that are conditional on membership. Each member of the co-op usually has an equal claim in the assets and cash flows. In contrast to the Yugoslav-type firm, however, co-op members can if they wish sell off the assets of the firm and divide the proceeds among the membership. The co-op also differs from the private corporation in that it will admit new members without charge. In addition, the claims that co-op members hold are not individually marketable. The members elect a manager who hires the employees.

If membership in the co-op is open to anyone at a zero price, the cooperative suffers from the common-property problem just like the pure-rental and Yugoslav-type firms. It also suffers from the horizon problem, but this effect is to some extent mitigated by the fact that members can sell the firm either in whole or in part and distribute the proceeds among themselves.

The co-op also suffers from the nontransferability problem—but not to the same extent as do the pure-rental or Yugoslav-type firms. While the lack of a market for claims in the co-op creates some difficulty for workers in evaluating the performance of management as in the pure-rental case (the monitoring problem), this effect is mitigated by the opportunity for competitors to set up private firms in competition with the co-op. That is, competition in the establishment of organizational forms coupled with voluntary choice on the part of workers and capital suppliers regarding which organization they "join" will ensure that neither organizational form will be significantly less productive than the other—otherwise it would be driven out of existence.

While cooperatives arise and persist in societies characterized by freedom of choice in organizational form, they have never been a significant factor on the economic scene. Moreover, in the United States, at least, they are not labor managed. Members of the co-op are generally not employees; they are customers (consumer co-ops) or suppliers (producer co-ops). We hypothesize that one of the reasons these forms of organization have arisen rather than the employee co-op (i.e., labor managed) is closely related to the second difficulty associated with the nontransferability problem—the portfolio diversification problem. Producer- or consumer-managed co-ops do not as a condition of membership directly tie the individual's labor income to a risky proportional claim on the residual flows of the firm. Thus the individual's portfolio diversification opportunities are not limited to the same extent as they are in a labor-managed organization.

The list of organizations that generally fit under the rubric "cooperative" is diverse and itself a separate subject for study. It includes mutual savings banks and mutual insurance companies, retail cooperatives, agricultural marketing cooperatives, and private clubs (e.g., golf, tennis, athletic, dining). The success of some of these is clearly due to the special legal and tax treatment they receive (or received at the onset). In other cooperatives, like the mutual savings banks and mutual insurance companies, the members' "claims" on the cash flows of the firm are related to the size of the member's interest in the firm, that is, the claims are not equal across members. Others, like the private clubs, charge rather large initiation fees, and where memberships are limited, members can sometimes sell their memberships to new members with the approval of the club.

Professional Partnerships

While little attention has been paid to them as a specialized organizational form, professional law, accounting, brokerage, and consulting partnerships in the United States are in important respects labor-managed firms. Partners generally hold claims on annual residual flows. These claims are usually nonmarketable, though some firms offer to repurchase them at stipulated prices upon retirement or death. Partnership is generally by invitation, and many of the employees, professional as well as nonprofessional, are not partners. The initiation of new partners is usually accompanied by a redistribution of claims, and new partners sometimes are required to pay a price for entrance into the partnership. Often, shares in net flows are decided on a year-to-year basis, taking into account the performance of each partner during the year in question.

The existence of these professional partnerships is interesting for a number of reasons. First, of course, is that they have survived the test of competition from alternative organizational forms in an environment where choice is possible. Therefore, they perhaps can provide us with some ideas and evidence regarding situations in which some variant on the labor-managed or participatory form of organization in fact dominates not only the corporate form but other alternatives as well.

The professional partnerships have many of the defects of the pure-rental system. To the extent that there is no charge for entry to the partnership and to the extent that the partnership shares are equal for each member, they are subject to the common-property problem. However, these problems can be reduced somewhat by charging for entry to the partnership (as is done in some instances), by giving "newer" partners smaller shares than "older" partners, and by not giving partnership to all employees. Large law firms, for instance, not only do not grant partnership standing to all lawyers employed by the firm but generally do not grant partnership rights to any other employee—such as secretary, legal assistant, or other office help—and the same is true of accounting and consulting firms.

The professional partnership is also subject to the horizon problem. The difficulties arising from this defect can be mitigated to some extent by agreements to repurchase the partner's share upon his retirement from the firm at prices that reflect to some extent his share of the accumulated "capital stock." This apparently is done in some circumstances.

The control problem poses difficulties for the professional partnership for exactly the same reasons as for the pure-rental and Yugoslav firms. Close study of these partnership organizations can potentially lead to a much better understanding of how alternative internal structures help to reduce or amplify the costs from this source of conflict.

The nontransferability problem in principle also poses difficulties for the professional partnerships, although we argue below that the monitoring and diversification problems in some industries can be such that these aspects in fact provide a strong positive advantage for the partnership form. Meade argues that we will find labor-managed cooperative

structures only in lines of activity in which the risk is not too great, and this means in lines of activity in which two conditions are fulfilled: first, the risk of fluctuations in the demand for the product must not be too great; and, secondly, the activity must be a labor-intensive activity in which the surplus accruing to labor does not constitute a small difference between two large quantities, the revenue from the sale of the product and the hire of capital plus the purchase of raw materials. This may help to explain why such labor partnerships as do exist are usually to be found in labor-intensive services, such as lawyers, accountants, doctors, etc. (Meade 1972, pp. 426–427)

Meade's argument makes sense if we believe that the standard deviations of percentage changes in revenues and costs are not strongly negatively related to the levels of these quantities. If the standard deviations do not show strong negative relations to their levels, and if they are not highly positively correlated with each other, then as the labor value added as a percent of total cost falls the standard deviation of percentage changes in labor value added will increase—thus the portfolio problems will become more severe.

We also expect to find professional partnerships (or modified labor-managed systems) to be more successful in situations where the optimal production technology involves very little capital relative to labor. In these situations the inefficiencies arising from the horizon problem will be much smaller and so, too, will those from the common-property problem (although to a lesser extent). Casual observation seems to be consistent with this implication of the theory.

What are the possible advantages of the professional partnership organizational form? Alchian and Demsetz (1972) in their insightful paper on organization argue that "profit sharing" (as in our professional partnership) is appropriate in "team" (joint) production when the size of the team is smaller and when the cost of monitoring to prevent shirking among team members is larger. They argue that the monitoring issue becomes an even stronger force encouraging profit sharing in artistic or professional situations where an individual team member's productivity is difficult to relate to observable behavior. Profit sharing will also tend to be more efficient when the team members themselves have a comparative advantage over an outsider in monitoring the behavior of other team members; profit sharing will increase each member's incentive to monitor the productivity of colleagues.

Finally, in circumstances in which a disproportionately large fraction of an individual's wealth is represented by his or her human capital and when the cash flows on that human capital are highly uncertain from period to period we also expect to see profit-sharing partnerships arise. In such a situation it will be difficult for the individual to capitalize (sell off) a portion of his or her future labor income because of the effect such a sale would have on the incentives to produce in the future.[38] This itself is not sufficient to prevent such a sale. It is the combination of these incentive effects and the difficulty of devising monitoring or bonding arrangements to limit it that makes the sale uneconomic.[39] Under such circumstances it is conceivable that some of the diversification effects could be achieved by a group of such individuals with less than perfectly correlated labor income banding together in a partnership-sharing arrangement. The desirability of such arrangements would clearly be enhanced if they were able to monitor each other at less cost than an outsider and if there were any economies of scale to be gained from cooperation.

In summary, then, it appears that the professional partnership form of labor-managed firms is more likely to dominate other organizational forms when

- the capital-labor ratio is small,
- the ratio of labor value added to all nonlabor costs is high,
- there are economies of scale to team production,
- external monitoring costs are high or the monitoring of the productivity of team members is more cheaply performed internally,
- the size of the team is small,
- the returns to the human capital of the individual team members are farther from perfectly positively correlated, and
- the agency costs associated with the capitalization of future labor income are high.

The Codetermined Firm

Efforts to analyze the behavior of the codetermined firm face a serious problem just getting off the ground. We do not have a theory that will tell us how supervisory boards will behave, or at least none in which we have any confidence. Even in the "parity" representation case the supervisory boards could end up behaving as if they represented only the stockholders. Given the German law, for example, where the chairman, who is elected by stockholders, has the deciding vote in case of ties and where one of the labor representatives is from the salaried ranks, it is possible that the stockholders will have complete control over the affairs of the firm. Certainly in the short run this is a reasonable prediction of how codetermination will work. In the long run, however, it is possible that codetermination will lead to the other end of the spectrum—that is, codetermination could end up effectively turning the firm over to labor.

If labor gets complete control of supervisory boards, what will happen? Our prediction: it will likely turn into the Yugoslav-type system with state ownership of productive resources and all the problems of the pure-rental and Yugoslav firms. In brief, they will have (1) the horizon problem, induced by the truncated (nonperpetual) claims on firm cash flows; (2) the common-property problem, induced by the equal sharing of firm cash flows among employees; (3) the nontransferability problem, induced by the fact that workers' claims on firm cash flows are contingent on employment with the firm and are nonmarketable; (4) the voting problem, induced by the rule requiring one vote per employee in the political process for decision making within the firm; and (5) the savings-investment problem, induced by the illegality of personal investment in productive capital goods and the necessity for the state to set interest rates, choose projects, and supply all producer capital.

If the workers were to get complete control of the codetermined firm, the scenario leading to the Yugoslav-type firm is likely to come about in the following way. Upon gaining control of the firm the workers will begin "eating it up" by transforming the assets of the firm into consumption or personal assets through many of the procedures we discussed above in the context of the Yugoslav-type firm. As this continues and the process becomes clear to the capital markets, the value of the stock will go to zero. It will become difficult for the firm to obtain capital in the private capital markets. Eventually some firms will simply go out of business and others will reach the point where the returns on investment are so high that, even given the horizon bias, further reduction in the capital of the firm makes the workers worse off. The result of this process will be a significant reduction in the country's capital stock, increased unemployment, reduced labor income, and an overall reduction in output and welfare. This state of affairs will lead to unfavorable international comparison, outcries of outdated technology, foreign exchange problems, and a general clamor for state subsidies to capital accumulation to augment the "failures" of the private markets. As the state provides capital loans to firms it will impose additional controls to prevent the workers from simply transforming the new resources into consumption. These controls will take many of the forms discussed in the Yugoslav case: requirements for maintenance of the capital stock, maximum possible wage payments, and so on. The final result will be fairly complete, if not total, state ownership of the productive assets in the economy. If there is a minimum size below which firms are not subject to the codetermination laws (2,000 employees in the case of Germany), many firms will simply shrink through dissolution or spin-offs to sizes below this level to avoid the laws. If the laws are not changed to include these firms in the codetermined sector the process will end there, with those firms for which economies of scale are very large being socialized and most of the rest of the economy remaining private but incurring the inefficiencies resulting from the diseconomies of small-scale operation.

7 | Organizational Forms and Investment Decisions

7.1 Introduction

Different organizational forms are distinguished by the characteristics of their residual claims on net cash flows—for example, restrictions on the extent to which residual claimant status is separable from decision roles, or restrictions on the alienability of the residual claims. Different restrictions on residual claims imply different rules for optimal investment decisions. This chapter analyzes the relations between characteristics of residual claims and investment decision rules in open and closed corporations, partnerships, proprietorships, financial mutuals and nonprofits. Our purpose is to determine whether the decisions of each of these organizations can be modeled as if they come from the maximization of an objective function—for example, the value maximization rule of the financial economics literature. We focus on investment decisions, but the rules are applicable to all decisions. We ignore the effects of taxes.

We first analyze the investment decision rule implied by the common stock residual claims of open corporations. We compare this rule to the decision rules implied by the more restricted residual claims of proprietorships, partnerships, and closed corporations, and we discuss aspects of the choice of organizational form. Finally, we analyze the investment decision rules implied by the even more specialized residual claims of financial mutuals and nonprofits.

7.2 The Decision Rule Implied by the Common Stock of Open Corporations

The least restricted residual claims in common use are the common stocks of large corporations. These residual claims have property rights

By Eugene F. Fama and Michael C. Jensen; originally published in *Journal of Financial Economics* 14 (March 1985), pp. 101–119.

in net cash flows for an indefinite horizon. They are separable in that stockholders are not required to have any other role in the organization. The residual claims of open corporations are also alienable without restriction. We call these organizations "open corporations" to distinguish them from closed corporations that are generally smaller and have residual claims that are largely restricted to decision agents.

The unrestricted nature of the residual claims of open corporations fosters the development of a capital market that specializes in pricing such claims and transferring them among investors at low cost. Suppose the capital market is perfectly competitive; that is, suppose there are perfect substitutes for the unrestricted residual claims of any open corporation, and both investors and open corporations are price takers in the capital market. Suppose also that unrestricted residual claims can be traded costlessly among investors, and that the capital market is efficient or rational in the sense that the prices of residual claims correctly reflect available information. In this situation, a corporation's stockholders all agree that all decisions, including investments with payoffs in future periods, should be evaluated according to their contribution to the current market value of their residual claims. (See, for example, Fama 1978.)

The logic of the market value or maximum wealth rule is straightforward. The existence of perfect substitute securities that are always correctly priced and can be traded without transactions costs in a perfectly competitive market means the consumption streams that an investor can realize in future periods are constrained only by current wealth, that is, the market value of current and future resources. When the stream of payoffs implied by the wealth or value-maximizing investment decisions of an open corporation does not correspond to an investor's optimal consumption stream, the capital market can be used to exchange residual claims in the corporation for other claims with the same market value but with a stream of payoffs that better matches the investor's desired consumption stream.

Because most residual claimants in open corporations have no direct role in the decision process, and because there are conflicts of interest with managers, there are agency problems between managers and residual claimants. As a consequence, an important investment choice in open corporations is the decision control process. As for other investment decisions, maximizing market value involves extending decision control mechanisms to the point where the incremental market value of improved decisions is just offset by the market value of the cost of improved decision control. This means some decisions that nominally reduce value will be taken when the cost of preventing them exceeds the value reduction they cause. It is obvious, but worth emphasizing, that market value reflects all costs, including agency costs—the costs incurred because contracts with decision agents are not costlessly written and enforced. These issues are discussed in detail in Jensen and Meckling (1976 and Chapter 4 in this volume) and in Fama and Jensen (1983a, 1983b).

One can quarrel with the perfect capital market assumptions needed to obtain the conclusion that all investors prefer the market value rule for investment decisions by open corporations. However, this case is a useful point of reference for judging the effects of restrictions on residual claims on rules for investment decisions.

7.3 Decision Rules Implied by the Restricted Residual Claims of Proprietorships, Partnerships, and Closed Corporations

Unlike the unrestricted common stock of open corporations, the residual claims of proprietorships, partnerships, and closed corporations are generally restricted to the organization's important decision agents. We are concerned with the effects of this restriction on investment decisions.

Proprietorship Investment Decisions under Certainty

Many issues central to the analysis of investment decisions involve risk bearing and agency problems that are somewhat artificial in a world of certainty. We begin the analysis with the certainty case because it allows simple derivation of many major results.

Consider a proprietorship faced with a two-period perfectly certain world and the investment opportunities summarized in Figure 7.1 by the function $F(K;P)$, where K is the amount of resources invested in the venture in period 1, and P indicates that the organizational form is a proprietorship. A proprietorship is an organization in which the primary decision agent holds 100% of the residual claim on net cash flows. Open corporations are distinguished from proprietorships by the outside ownership of residual claims.

Proprietorships and open corporations can finance with debt as well

Resources at time 2

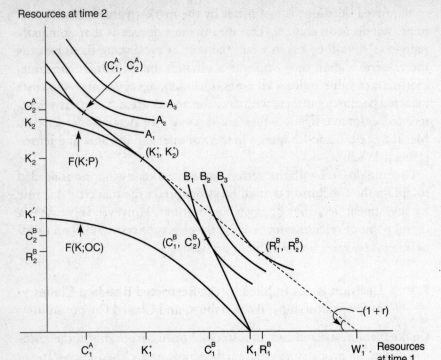

Figure 7.1 Investment decisions under certainty for two unleveraged proprietorships. Consumption preferences on resources at times 1 and 2 for proprietors A and B are denoted by indifference curves A_j and B_j, respectively. $F(K;P)$ is the transformation function relating investment at time 1 to payoffs at time 2 for the venture when organized as an unleveraged proprietorship, P. Investment, K, is measured from K_1. $F(K;OC)$ is the transformation function for the same venture when undertaken by an open corporation, OC. C_1^A and C_1^B are the resources consumed at time i by proprietors A and B. The dashed line denotes that an unleveraged proprietorship does not issue outside debt or residual claims. The proprietorship is the optimal choice of organizational form for this venture.

as residual claims. For the moment, we only consider unleveraged proprietorships, which means the organization is financed entirely from the proprietor's wealth. This restriction is dropped shortly, without major effects, when we extend the analysis to partnerships and closed corporations in which there are multiple residual claimants. The certainty assumption is relaxed below, when the capital structure issue is addressed.

At time 1 the proprietor puts up K_1 units of resources. His opportunities for transforming current resources into future resources through investment in plant, equipment, and the like are given by the function $F(K;P)$. The proprietor can also acquire resources at time 2 by buying the securities of open corporations. The capital market interest rate for such claims is r, and we continue to assume that they are traded without cost in a perfectly competitive capital market.

Suppose the indifference curves A_j, $j = 1, 2$ represent the proprietor's tastes for combinations of resources consumed at time 1 and time 2. The proprietor optimally invests K_1^* K_2^* within the proprietorship and C_1^A K_1^* in the securities of open corporations. He then consumes C_1^A at time 1 and C_2^A at time 2. The proprietor stops investment within the proprietorship at K_1^* K_1 because further investment has a marginal return less than the rate of interest available on the securities of open corporations. An open corporation with investment opportunities summarized by the same function $F(K;P)$ would also invest K_1^* K_1 since this decision produces the maximum possible current wealth, W_1^*.

Although proprietor A in Figure 7.1 makes the same investment decision as an open corporation with the same opportunity set, a proprietor with tastes summarized by the indifference curves, B_j, $j = 1, 2, \ldots$, chooses to invest less. The essence of an unleveraged proprietorship is that the proprietor is sole residual claimant. Thus, if proprietor B invests K_1^* K_1 internally at time 1, she cannot sell off part of the resulting claim to the payoff K_2^* generated at time 2. As a result, proprietor B maximizes utility by investing only the amount $C_1^B K_1$ that generates the resource combination $(C_1^B C_2^B)$ for consumption at time 1 and time 2.

Proprietor B's welfare would improve if she could borrow $K_1^* K_1^B$, or if she could reorganize as an open corporation, invest $K_1^* K_1$ internally, and then sell her residual claim for $K_1^* W_1^*$. However, as Jensen and Meckling (1979) and Fama and Jensen (1983a, 1983b) emphasize, differences in the contract structures of different organizational forms are likely to affect the costs of delivering products. Because alternative organizational forms involve different costs and thus different net payoffs for the same level of investment, the production or transformation function for a venture depends on organizational form. In Figure 7.1, the function $F(K;P)$ shows the maximum payoffs net of all costs that can be generated by an unleveraged proprietorship at time 2 with different amounts of wealth invested internally at time 1. If the unleveraged proprietorship is the optimal form of organization for the investment activities underlying Figure 7.1, the transformation function for the same venture undertaken by an open corporation, OC, might be $F(K;OC)$, which lies below the proprietorship transformation function.[1] Similarly, if proprietor B issues debt, conflicts of interest with debtholders lead to contracting and other agency costs that also cause the transformation function (not shown in Figure 7.1) to shift downward by an amount that depends on the amount of debt issued. We compare here only open corporations and unleveraged proprietorships.

In our certain world the dominance of the proprietorship transformation function for the venture in Figure 7.1 can be thought of as due to higher contracting costs in open corporations associated with writing and administering contracts with external residual claimants and internal decision agents. In a world of uncertainty these costs would be balanced against the efficiencies in risk sharing allowed by the open corporate form. A realistic situation where the analysis in Figure 7.1 is relevant occurs when the personal human capital of the primary decision agent is the important resource in an organization. Because human capital is difficult to sell, the decision maker is in a situation like that of proprietor B, who cannot sell residual claims on the project.

Proprietors like A evaluate investment opportunities according to the maximum wealth or market value rule because they also purchase claims for resources to be delivered at time 2 in the open capital market. The restriction of the proprietorship residual claim to an investor like proprietor A is not a binding constraint on his portfolio decisions. Thus, the market interest rate r on external investments provides the relevant opportunity cost for internal investments. On the other hand, a proprietor like B is not also a net investor in the outside capital market. The marginal rate of time preference implied by the slope of her indifference curve at (C_1^B, C_2^B) is higher than the market interest rate, r. Thus, it is rational for proprietor B to assign lower value to future resources generated from internal investment than is implied by the market interest rate on the unrestricted common stocks of open corporations.

If "diversified" proprietors like A are sufficient to absorb all the proprietorships that exist in a general equilibrium, the market price for the rights to the transformation function $F(K;P)$ is $K_1 W_1^*$ and B sells her rights to the venture to an A-type proprietor. After purchasing residual claims on open corporations in the amount $R_1^B W_1^*$, B then consumes R_1^B at time 1 and R_2^B at time 2 and achieves utility $B_3 > B_1$.

If "diversified" proprietors like A are not sufficient to absorb all the proprietorships that will exist in a general equilibrium, that is, if, like B, the marginal proprietor in the activity only invests internally, the market price for the transformation function $F(K;P)$ is less than $K_1 W_1^*$. Proprietors like B do not use the market value rule for decisions and they invest less than open corporations faced with the same investment opportunities.

Partnerships and Closed Corporations

The analysis extends to partnerships and closed corporations in which residual claims are again generally restricted to decision agents. If all residual claimants in these organizations also invest in the residual claims of open corporations, that is, if they have tastes similar to proprietor A in Figure 7.1, then in a world of certainty partnerships and closed corporations make the same decisions as open corporations faced with the same investment opportunities. However, partnerships or closed corporations whose residual claimants have consumption preferences like proprietor B do not use the market value decision rule and invest less than an open corporation with the same opportunity set. A partnership or closed corporation with a mix of As and Bs, with differing demands for current vs. future resources, faces a difficult contracting problem in making investment decisions. Such conflicts over investment and payout policies are common, for example, in family corporations and partnerships. Unlike open corporations, where all residual claimants agree on the maximum wealth or market value rule for investment decisions, in partnerships and closed corporations investment decision rules that satisfy the interests of all residual claimants require either that all residual claimants are "diversified" (like proprietor A in Figure 7.1) or that they have identical tastes.

The residual claims in partnerships and closed corporations are generally restricted to important decision agents and to outsiders acceptable to the important decision agents. The residual claims of these organizations generally specify rules for compensating residual claimants when they retire or otherwise leave the organization. The difficulties in designing valuation processes to substitute for the capital market that continuously revalues the unrestricted residual claims of open corporations means that partnerships and closed corporations will not generally follow the value-maximizing decision rule. They will tend to underinvest in assets with long-term payoffs whose current values are not easily established.

We do not expect to see voluntary contractual restrictions on the alienability of residual claims in activities where the capital value problem described above is important, that is, where decisions present major opportunities to substitute between present and future cash flows. This occurs in activities optimally carried out with large quantities of long-term assets that are difficult to value and that are more efficiently purchased by residual claimants rather than rented, for example, plant and equipment, and reputation and goodwill that can be transferred from one generation of residual claimants to the next. For example, organizations in business and financial consulting, like brokerage houses and underwriters that were partnerships with restricted residual claims, are tending to reorganize as open corporations. We hypothesize that this is largely due to changes in the nature of these activities that increase capital value problems—for example, increased demand for wealth from residual claimants to purchase risky assets that are difficult to value, and pressure to transfer the rights to the net cash flows from such assets from one generation of residual claimants to the next.

In contrast, we hypothesize that when the important asset in an activity is the human capital of existing decision agents, the activity can be efficiently supplied by partnerships with restricted residual claims. This will be true when there are no important patents, specialized assets, or technologies to be passed from one generation of partners to the next. It will also be true when the reputation and goodwill that are important in some professional service activities, such as law, public accounting, and business consulting, are tied to the human capital currently in the organization. In such cases rather extreme restrictions on residual claims can survive. For example, professional partnership residual claims often limit a partner's rights in net cash flows to period of service in the organization. (See Fama and Jensen 1983a.)

Choice of Organizational Form

Figure 7.2 shows a situation in which the contracting costs of the open corporate form are low enough relative to its advantages that it pays

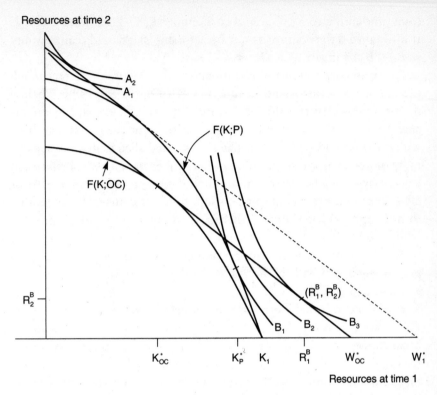

Resources at time 2

A_2
A_1

$F(K;P)$

$F(K;OC)$

(R_1^B, R_2^B)

R_2^B

B_1 B_2 B_3

$\overset{*}{K}_{OC}$ $\overset{*}{K}_P$ K_1 R_1^B $\overset{*}{W}_{OC}$ $\overset{*}{W}_1$

Resources at time 1

Figure 7.2   Choice of organizational form and investment under certainty when the consumption preferences of the marginal proprietor make it desirable to incur the costs of the open corporate form of organization. The transformation function for the venture as an unleveraged proprietorship is $F(K;P)$ and as an open corporation it is $F(K;OC)$. The dashed line indicates that an unleveraged proprietorship does not issue outside debt on residual claims. $\overset{*}{K}_P K_1$ is the optimal investment when undertaken by B as a proprietorship, and $\overset{*}{K}_{OC} K_1$ is the optimal investment when undertaken by an open corporation. $K_1 \overset{*}{W}_{OC}$ and B_3 are respectively the value of the rights to the venture and B's welfare level when the venture is undertaken by an open corporation. $B_1 < B_3$ is B's welfare level when the venture is undertaken as a proprietorship. $K_1 \overset{*}{W}_1$ is the value of the venture when the marginal proprietor in general equilibrium is of type A.

the proprietor, B, to organize the venture as an open corporation. In Figure 7.2, $F(K;OC)$ is the transformation function for an open corporation undertaking the venture. Proprietor B realizes the amount $K_1 \overset{*}{W}_{OC}$ from sale to the corporation of her rights to the venture and $\overset{*}{K}_{OC} K_1$ is the value-maximizing level of investment by the corporation. B achieves welfare level B_3 by purchasing shares of other open corporations amounting to $R_1^B W_{OC}^*$ and consuming (R_1^B, R_2^B) at times 1 and 2. If B organized the venture as a proprietorship she would realize utility of $B_1 < B_3$ by investing $K_P^* K_1 < K_{OC}^* K_1$.[2]

The open corporate form is optimal for B in Figure 7.2 even though the corporate transformation function $F(K;OC)$ is everywhere below the proprietorship transformation function $F(K;P)$. B's strong preference for current consumption causes her to incur the costs associated with the open corporate form. The unrestricted alienability and separability of open corporate claims allow her to rearrange her consumption pattern by selling her claims in the capital market and devoting part or all of the proceeds to current consumption. Of course, the corporate form is optimal for B only if there are no other potential proprietors willing to purchase her rights to the venture for more than $K_1 W_{OC}^*$. In particular, if the marginal proprietorship is "well diversified" like proprietor A, then B will sell her rights to the venture to A for $K_1 W_1^* > K_1 W_{OC}^*$.

While the optimal corporate investment level $K_{OC}^* K_1$ in Figure 7.2 maximizes value, $K_1 W_{OC}^*$, conditional on choice of the corporate organizational form, this is obviously not equivalent to the value, $K_1 W_1^*$, that could be obtained (at investment level $K_P^* K_1$) if the transformation function $F(K;P)$ applied to open corporations as well as to proprietorships. The distance $W_{OC}^* W_1^*$ is what Jensen and Meckling (1976, p. 320, and in Chapter 4 of this volume) define to be the gross agency costs of the corporate form: the difference between the maximum value attainable if the proprietorship production function were available to the open corporation and the maximum value attainable from the production function actually available to the corporation.

The transformation function for a proprietorship does not always dominate that for an open corporation. This is illustrated in Figure 7.3, where scale economies cause the transformation function for the open corporation to cross that for the proprietorship. Moreover, in an uncertain world the gains from specialization of risk bearing and decision functions discussed in Fama and Jensen (1983b) can become so large with increasing scale that the open corporate form dominates the proprietorship. In general at each point in time there is a set of transformation functions for each venture, one for each possible organizational form.

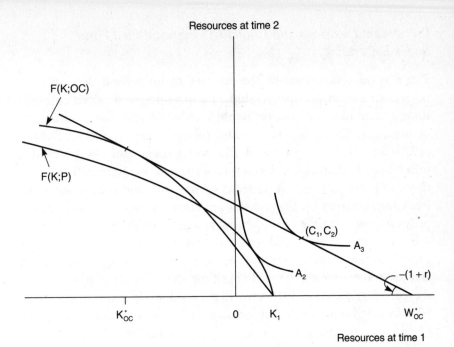

Figure 7.3 Example of a case in which gains from economies of scale cause the transformation function for a venture when undertaken by an open corporation, *F(K;OC)*, to cross that for the proprietorship, *F(K;P)*. Maximum wealth and utility are obtained by undertaking the venture through the open corporate form and selling outside residual claims to make the value-maximizing investment, $K^*_{OC}K_1$. In this case the proprietor's total initial wealth, OK_1, is less than the value-maximizing investment level, $K^*_{OC}K_1$. He cannot make the value-maximizing investment even by reducing period 1 consumption to zero. Thus his personal wealth constraint also pushes him to the open corporate form.

At various stages in the life of a venture it may be best carried out under different organizational forms. For example, it might first be organized as a proprietorship and then, with increasing demands for financing risky investments, converted to a partnership or a closed corporation, and then to an open corporation. At a later time, conditions can indicate reconversion to a closed corporation, partnership, or even proprietorship form. (See DeAngelo, DeAngelo, and Rice 1984a for an analysis of "going private" transactions in which open corporations are transformed into closed corporations or proprietorships; see also DeAngelo, DeAngelo, and Rice 1984b.)

Investment Decisions and Choice of Organizational Form under Uncertainty

The general conclusions of the analysis of investment decisions for open corporations, proprietorships, partnerships, and closed corporations extend to a multiperiod world in which future payoffs from investment are uncertain. The "states of the world" model of Debreu (1959) and Arrow (1964b) is an illustrative framework. In this model, uncertainty is characterized in terms of the possible states of the world that can occur at $t + \tau$. A perfectly competitive and transaction-cost-free capital market for the securities of open corporations fixes a set of prices $p^s_t, t + \tau$ at time t for a unit of resources to be delivered at time $t + \tau$ if the state of the world realized at $t + \tau$ is s. With the appropriate capital market transactions, any set of payoffs across states that has a given market value can be exchanged for any other set of payoffs with the same market value. In this world the residual claimants of open corporations again prefer that investment decisions are evaluated in terms of effects on the market values of their residual claims.

Moreover, graphs like Figures 7.1 to 7.3 can be used to describe the tradeoffs of current resources for future resources conditional on a given future state and on organizational form. As in the perfect certainty model, when all the residual-claimant decision makers of a proprietorship, partnership, or closed corporation are also net purchasers of contingent claims for all possible future states of the world, these organizations then make the same investment decisions as open corporations faced with the same investment opportunities. However, if there are future states in which some residual claimants receive only the resources generated by internal investment, then proprietorships, partnerships, and closed corporations tend to invest less than open corporations.

More generally, proprietorships, partnerships, and closed corporations tend to invest less than would be implied by the market value rule when the restriction of residual claims to decision agents is binding—that is, when residual-claimant decision makers hold more residual claims of an organization than would be implied by portfolio considerations alone. More specific implications of this conclusion require more specific models for determining market values of investment net cash flows.

For example, in the context of the Sharpe (1964)–Lintner (1965b) model of capital market equilibrium, a proprietor would generally prefer to sell part of her residual claim to achieve the risk reduction offered by a better diversified portfolio. Such sales imply an alternative organizational form and higher agency costs for delivering outputs. When the costs of an alternative organizational form exceed the benefits from better diversification, the proprietor will tend to hold the scale of investment below that implied by the market value rule. Moreover, the implicit price of risk applied by the proprietor in evaluating investments will tend to exceed the market price of risk used by open corporations, causing the proprietor to invest less in risky projects. In addition, the contribution of a project to the risks of the proprietor's imperfectly diversified portfolio will tend to be greater than the contribution of the same project to the risks of the diversified portfolios of capital market participants. This also causes proprietorships to undertake less investment than open corporations and to choose technologies that reduce project risks measured from the viewpoint of undiversified portfolios. These conclusions also hold for partnerships and closed corporations when the restriction of residual claims to decision makers is a binding constraint on personal portfolio diversification.

On the other hand, suppose a proprietorship's opportunities for risky investment are so good that the proprietor's personal wealth constraint is binding on investment decisions but the scale of the profitable projects is not large enough to warrant the higher costs of the open corporate form. In this case, the proprietor invests all his wealth in the organization, and he can end up with "too little" risk: the proprietor can desire to invest more in risky projects, but his wealth constraint prevents him from doing so. As a consequence, his implicit marginal price for risk bearing can be less than that charged by the market.[3] In this case as well, however, a proprietorship invests less than an open corporation faced with the same investment opportunities. This conclusion also holds for partnerships and closed corporations in which the personal wealth of residual-claimant decision makers is a binding constraint on decisions.

We can, however, construct situations in which proprietorships invest more than open corporations with the same investment opportunities. For example, suppose technological trade-offs make it possible for a proprietor to reduce the variance of her undiversified portfolio return by moving to more capital-intensive production procedures. Reducing variance that arises because of lack of diversification may then cause the proprietor to undertake more investment than an open corporation that follows the market value rule.

Debt and Related Issues

Proprietorships, partnerships, and corporations can finance with debt as well as equity. Like other kinds of decisions, different decisions with respect to capital structure (the mix of debt, equity, and other kinds of claims) imply different contracting, monitoring, and bonding costs that affect the total costs of delivering outputs with a particular organizational form (Jensen and Meckling 1976 and Chapter 4 of this volume). The competition for survival among organizational forms pushes each toward capital structures that minimize the total costs of outputs at different levels of activity.

We are concerned here, however, with the effects of capital structure on investment decisions. It is well known that the market value rule for investment decisions is ambiguous when organizations finance in part with debt. (See, e.g., Chapter 4 of this volume, or Fama and Miller 1972, chap. 4.) Is it the wealth of residual claimants, or bondholder wealth, or the combined wealth of bondholders and residual claimants that is to be maximized?

A rational bond market prices bonds to reflect the effects of organizational decision rules and the possibility of future changes in rules. In this case, ignoring contracting, monitoring, and bonding costs, the current wealth of an open corporation's residual claimants is maximized when they can guarantee that the rule for future decisions is maximization of the combined wealth of bondholders and stockholders (Fama 1978). However, as emphasized by Jensen and Meckling (1976 and Chapter 4 of this volume), contracting, monitoring, and bonding costs generally cause the costs of a perfect guarantee to exceed the benefits. As a result, deviations from combined wealth maximization can be predicted in some future states. In the terms of this chapter, contracts without perfect guarantees are optimal because they maximize value on an ex ante basis even though in some ex post states combined value is not maximized.

There are related issues that warrant mention. Like the debtholders and unlike residual claimants, most agents (labor, raw material suppliers, managers, and so on) contract for fixed promised payoffs or incentive payoffs tied to specific measures of performance. Thus there are conflicts of interest between these agents and residual claimants that are similar to those between debtholders and residual claimants and that raise the same conflict of interest issues for decision rules.

Moreover, the observation that most organizational forms settle on contract structures characterized by multiple fixed payoff contracts with varying degrees of default risk and a single residual risk-bearing contract can help explain a common role for debt. In the event of default, debtholders are typically last in the line of priority among agents with fixed payoff contracts. Thus credible periodic signals from debtholders about the status of the default risks on their contracts can save duplication of monitoring activities by agents with higher priority contracts. Incentives to lower the total monitoring costs imposed on an organization's outputs by its fixed payoff contracts can also explain why organizations purchase and publish signals from outside specialists about the default risks of their debt. Examples are payments for bond rating services and for lines of credit that involve periodic monitoring by banks and other financial intermediaries that specialize in evaluating default risks on fixed payoff contracts.[4]

Finally, it is well to point out that a theory of optimal capital structure (debt vs. equity) would be part of a more general theory of the optimal risk structure of contracts in organizations. Such a theory would explain the allocation of risk among agents in an organization given the agency costs imposed on the organization's activities by the writing, monitoring, and bonding of alternative risk structures.

7.4   Special Forms of Residual Claims

Limited alienability and limited separability of residual claims from roles in the decision process distinguish the restricted residual claims of proprietorships, partnerships, and closed corporations from those of open corporations. There are, however, other organizational forms like financial mutuals and nonprofits that offer more unique residual claims. In Fama and Jensen (1983a) we explain the special characteristics of the residual claims of these organizations as responses to special characteristics of the activities in which they survive. Now we are more interested in the implications of special characteristics of residual claims for investment decisions.

Financial Mutuals

A common form of organization in financial activities is the mutual. An unusual characteristic of mutuals is that the residual claimants are customers—for example, the policyholders of mutual insurance companies, the depositors of mutual savings banks, and the shareholders of mutual funds. However, the important differentiating characteristic of the residual claims of mutuals is that they are redeemable. The decision of the redeemable claim holder to withdraw resources is a form of partial takeover and liquidation that deprives management of control over assets. This control right can be exercised independently by each claim holder. It does not require a proxy fight, a tender offer, or any other concerted takeover bid.[5]

It is reasonable to assume that no individual financial mutual provides its customers—residual claimants—with access to investments that are not available elsewhere. Under these conditions, as in open corporations, the residual claimants of a financial mutual can agree on the maximum wealth or market value rule for decisions.

The redeemable feature of the residual claims, however, limits the kinds of activities in which the mutual format is efficient. In mutuals, assets must be expanded and contracted at low cost in response to purchase or redemption of residual claims. Moreover, redeemability generally means there is no secondary market for residual claims. As a consequence, the assets of mutuals must have easily determined values. Thus mutuals with redeemable residual claims tend to survive in financial activities where the assets held are primarily the securities of other organizations that are themselves traded at low cost in secondary markets (see Fama and Jensen 1983a).

In contrast, the capital markets that have evolved for the common stock residual claims of open corporations specialize in establishing market values for uncertain future net cash flows. Thus common stockholders forgo the direct control rights inherent in redeemable residual claims. But active capital markets for common stocks make them more appropriate as residual claims in activities that involve large amounts of assets that are difficult to price, have high transaction costs, and are more efficiently owned within the organization rather than rented.

Nonprofits

Nonprofit organizations are characterized by the absence of residual claims. For example, the ABA-ALI Model Non-Profit Corporation Act used in many states prohibits nonprofits from issuing shares or paying dividends.

When the activities of an organization are financed in part through donations, net cash flows are in part due to the resources provided by donors. Contracts that define the share of residual claimants in net cash flows are unlikely to assure donors that their resources are protected against expropriation by residual claimants. We hypothesize that the absence of residual claims in nonprofits avoids the donor–residual claimant agency problem and explains the dominance of nonprofits in donor-financed activities (see Fama and Jensen 1983a).

Given that there are no residual claimants in nonprofits, there seems to be a puzzle about whose interests are to be satisfied in resource allocation decisions. From the broader viewpoint of organizational survival, however, the investment problem is part of the general problem of combining available technologies, characteristics of residual claims (including the absence thereof), and techniques for controlling agency problems so as to allow a given type of organization to deliver an activity's outputs at lower prices. Without the analytical crutch provided by residual claimants, criteria for optimal investment decisions in nonprofits must be viewed in terms of the more general competition for survival among nonprofits and between nonprofits and other organizational forms that could engage in the same activities. The key to the analysis is in the economics of donations.

Donations can substitute for the resources provided by residual claimants to bond fixed payoff contracts and to purchase assets that are optimally owned rather than rented. From a survival viewpoint the advantage of donations over resources provided by residual claimants is that donors forgo claims on the monetary returns earned on their donations. This tends to allow the organization to deliver its products at lower prices. Donations can mean that a nonprofit can survive even when it is otherwise less cost effective than a for-profit organization in the production and delivery of the goods and services demanded by customers.

An individual nonprofit survives by competing successfully for customers and donations. In part this means developing internal control mechanisms to assure donors that the resources they provide are not easily expropriated by internal agents. Survival also means providing products that donors wish to subsidize and customers wish to buy or accept and internal rules for allocating resources that conform to the tastes of donors and customers. To a large extent, then, we look to the donors for the criteria for optimal investment decisions in nonprofits.

Consider first a nonprofit with donors that provide periodic subsidies. The organization's internal agents appeal to donors for increased current contributions for capital projects that will lower current and future costs and substitute for future donations. In effect, the nonprofit presents its donors with the option of paying now for the capital investments or paying the stream of costs that will be incurred later if the investments are not undertaken. If the donors have diversified portfolios, they evaluate the alternatives presented by the nonprofit in terms of the trade-offs of current for future resources available in the outside capital market. They choose the alternative with the lowest market value of costs since this minimizes the market value of the donations needed to carry out the nonprofit's activities and maximizes the market value of donor portfolio holdings available for other uses, including consumption in the form of increased current and future donations to this or other nonprofits.

For example, in an Arrow-Debreu "states of the world" model, donors with portfolios that provide payoffs in all future states price out the future cost savings of a nonprofit's capital projects with the relevant state contingent claim prices. When the market value of the cost savings exceeds the cost of the investments, the donors are willing to sell off portfolio assets to substitute current for future donations because this increases the value of wealth remaining for other uses. On the other hand, when the market value of future cost savings is less than the current cost of a nonprofit's capital projects, donors will advise internal agents that the capital projects are best forgone since equivalent current wealth invested in the outside capital market generates more resources for absorbing future costs than are saved with the projects.

The reasoning of the donors becomes clearer to the decision agents of a nonprofit when the donors prepay donations and the nonprofit itself acquires a diversified endowment portfolio. Then cost-saving capital projects should be substituted for endowment portfolio investments only when the future benefits of the capital projects are greater than the future returns promised by investing the resources for the capital projects in portfolio investments. In other words, the opportunity costs signaled by endowment portfolio investments lead the internal agents of nonprofits to evaluate cost-saving capital projects according to the same maximum wealth or market value rule that is optimal for open corporations and financial mutuals.

The market value rule for investment decisions also properly accounts for donor preferences for the types of activities they are willing to subsidize. The market value rule says that a nonprofit should engage in new activities, or expand the scale of existing activities, or lower product prices to elicit higher donations as long as the current market value of incremental current and future revenues, from both donations and the sale of products, exceeds the current market value of incremental current and future costs. Decisions made in this way properly balance the tastes of donors (i.e., equate marginal rates of substitution) for the resources donors provide to subsidize a nonprofit's activities with the generalized consumption opportunities provided by donor investments in diversified portfolios. Because of the incentives created by donations, application of the market value rule in donor nonprofits yields different decisions than application of the market value rule by an otherwise identical open corporation (which could not obtain donations) in the same activity.

7.5 Summary

This chapter analyzes the relations between the characteristics of the residual claims of different organizational forms and rules for investment decisions. The analysis indicates that decision rules for open corporations, financial mutuals, and nonprofits can be modeled with the market value rule popular in the financial economics literature. On the other hand, decision rules for proprietorships, partnerships, and closed corporations cannot in general be modeled by the market value rule.

Open Corporations

The least restricted residual claims in common use are the common stocks of open corporations. When common stock prices reflect relevant available information and when common stocks are traded without transaction costs in a perfectly competitive capital market, the consumption streams that a stockholder can realize in future periods are constrained only by current wealth. The interests of stockholders are then served by investment decisions that maximize the current market value of their wealth. Market value, of course, reflects all costs, including the agency costs in the decision process.

Financial Mutuals

It is reasonable to assume that no individual financial mutual provides access to investments that are not available elsewhere. Thus, as in open corporations, the residual claimants of a financial mutual agree on the maximum wealth or market value rule.

The redeemable feature of the residual claims, however, limits the kinds of assets that are easily accommodated within the mutual framework. Assets must be expanded and contracted at low cost in response to purchase and redemption of residual claims. Moreover, because redeemability preempts the development of a secondary market for residual claims, the assets that are varied in response to purchases and redemptions must have values that are easily determined. These considerations largely limit the assets of financial mutuals to the securities of other organizations that are themselves traded in secondary markets. In contrast, the common stockholders of open corporations forgo the direct control rights inherent in redeemable residual claims, but active capital markets for common stocks make them more appropriate as residual claims in activities that involve large amounts of assets that are difficult to price, have high transaction costs, and are more efficiently owned within the organization rather than rented.

Nonprofits

When donors hold diversified portfolios or when nonprofits hold diversified endowment portfolios, optimal decisions in nonprofits also conform to the market value rule. However, donations affect both the way the market value rule is applied and the decision opportunities available to nonprofits. In a nonprofit, the market value of revenues to be balanced against costs includes the marginal donations that are generated by an activity. Because the existence of residual claims chokes off any potential supply of donations, this source of revenue is irrelevant in open corporations. On the other hand, since a nonprofit cannot use residual claims to raise wealth to bond fixed payoff contracts or to finance the purchase of risky assets, nonprofits are limited to activities where the supply of donations or internally generated funds is sufficient to replace resources that would otherwise be provided by residual claimants.

Proprietorships, Partnerships, and Closed Corporations

The decision agents in open corporations, financial mutuals, and nonprofits are generally professionals whose interests are not identical to those of residual claimants or donors. We contend in Fama and Jensen (1983b) that the resulting agency problems are controlled in all these organizations by decision systems that separate the management (initiation and implementation) and control (ratification and monitoring) of important decisions.

The proprietorships, partnerships, and closed corporations observed in small-scale production and service activities take a more direct approach to controlling agency problems in the decision process. The residual claims of these organizations are implicitly or explicitly restricted to decision agents. This restriction avoids costs of controlling agency problems between decision agents and residual claimants, but at the cost of inefficiency in residual risk bearing and a tendency toward underinvestment. As a result proprietorships, partnerships, and closed corporations will not generally follow the market value decision rule.

The limited personal wealth of the residual claimants in proprietorships, partnerships, and closed corporations can cause these organizations to invest less in capital projects than open corporations faced with the same opportunities. Moreover, the residual claimants in proprietorships, partnerships, and closed corporations forgo optimal portfolio diversification so that residual claims and decision making can be combined in a small number of agents. With limited diversification, it is generally optimal for residual claimants to undervalue claims on future cash flows relative to the market value rule. Finally, the restricted alienability generates uncertainty about whether a residual claimant can capture the full value of his claims against future cash flows when he leaves the organization. As a consequence, the residual claimants—decision agents of proprietorships, partnerships, and closed corporations—tend to choose lower levels of investment in plant, equipment, and the like that reduce future production costs, and they choose different technology than when residual claims allow unrestricted risk-sharing arrangements. These organizations survive in the face of such inefficiency when the agency costs that are avoided by restricting residual claims to decision agents exceed the higher costs induced by forgone investments and inefficiency in residual risk bearing.

8 The Distribution of Power among Corporate Managers, Shareholders, and Directors

8.1 Introduction

Understanding the behavior of the corporate organization requires a deep knowledge of its governance and the factors that determine the distribution of power among corporate managers, shareholders, and directors. The papers summarized here add considerably to the scientific framework for analyzing issues of corporate governance that have arisen in the courts, the regulatory sector, and the deliberations of corporate boards. These issues include (1) the mix and ownership distribution of the firm's financial claims, (2) the effects of the capital and takeover markets on firm behavior and efficiency, (3) the voting rights of common shares, (4) antitakeover provisions such as poison pills, and (5) top management changes and internal controls. This work is both theoretical and empirical, and reflects the intense interest among financial economists in the inner workings of corporations. Several key points derive from these papers:

- Share ownership can be an important source of incentives for management, boards of directors, and outside blockholders. The pattern and amount of stock ownership influence managerial behavior, corporate performance, and stockholder voting patterns in election contests. In addition, a firm's characteristics can influence its ownership structure. The data suggest that for some firms the

By Michael C. Jensen and Jerold B. Warner. This article resulted from the Conference on the Distribution of Power among Corporate Managers, Shareholders, and Directors held at the University of Rochester on May 28–30, 1987. The conference was jointly sponsored by the Managerial Economics Research Center and the *Journal of Financial Economics,* and the seventeen papers presented at the conference were published in a special issue of the *Journal of Financial Economics,* vol. 20, issue 1–2, February 1988. This article highlights insights from the seventeen papers and other work in the area and suggests directions for future research.

amount of ownership by inside or outside stockholders is economically significant. The precise effects of stockholdings by managers, outside blockholders, and institutions are not well understood, however, and the interrelations between ownership, firm characteristics, and corporate performance require further investigation.

- Managerial share ownership and control of voting rights influence a firm's attractiveness as a takeover target, as does the debt-equity ratio. Managerial takeover resistance takes many forms, including changes in capital and ownership structure that decrease the probability of a successful takeover.

- How common stock voting rights are specified also influences corporate behavior and shareholder wealth. Theoretical analysis indicates that in certain situations departures from one share, one vote can increase firm value by enabling shareholders to capture the benefits of control from the winning bidder in a control contest. Under such governance rules, however, the best management team is less likely to win control, and this reduces economic efficiency. Empirical evidence from firms recently abandoning one share, one vote indicates such changes decrease value. Explanations of the conflicts between the theory and evidence await further research.

- Evidence on management actions taken to forestall takeovers is inconsistent with the view that management always acts in shareholders' interest. Share prices decline on target-manager announcements of defensive restructurings in response to hostile takeovers and on announcement of poison pill antitakeover measures.

- Top management turnover is negatively related to share-price performance. Turnover is not highly sensitive to share performance, however, and only performance that is extreme influences the likelihood of a management change. Several internal monitoring mechanisms appear to be at work, and the relation between turnover and performance is stronger if the board is dominated by the outsiders.

8.2   Corporate Ownership Structure

Background

The idea that general characteristics of a firm's ownership structure and financial claims can affect its performance is receiving increasing attention in the finance profession. Modigliani and Miller's classic paper (1958) demonstrated that the value of a firm with given cash flows is invariant to its debt-equity ratio in the absence of taxes. Extensions of their propositions (see Jensen and Smith 1984 for a survey) incorporating variables such as taxes, bankruptcy costs, and agency costs indicate that the mix of financial claims (including debt and equity) affects the value of the firm because changes in the mix change the firm's total cash flows.

In addition, both the distribution of financial claims and the distribution of votes can affect firm performance and therefore value. For example, Jensen and Meckling (1976 and Chapter 4 of this volume) argue that the greater management's ownership stake in the firm, the better managers perform. Managerial incentives are also affected by debt (Grossman and Hart 1982; and Jensen 1986a, 1986b), so firm value will depend on capital structure as well as inside stock ownership by managers. Ownership concentration is also the focus of work by Shleifer and Vishny (1986) and Wruck (1989); Demsetz (1983) and Demsetz and Lehn (1985) treat ownership concentration as an equilibrium response to a firm's operating characteristics. Carney (1987) analyzes how the agency costs associated with coordinating the actions of coinvestors are affected by the distribution of shareholdings, capital structure, and contracting devices such as supermajority rules. Voting rights are analyzed by Easterbrook and Fischel (1983), DeAngelo and DeAngelo (1985), Lease, McConnell, and Mikkelson (1983, 1984), and Bhagat and Brickley (1984). Furthermore, there is extensive empirical evidence already in the literature indicating that changes in leverage and ownership concentration are associated with substantial changes in shareholder wealth (see Smith 1986).

Evidence on Share Ownership

Table 8.1 summarizes recent evidence on ownership of corporate common stock from a variety of studies. For large—for example, Fortune 500 or New York Stock Exchange (NYSE)-listed—firms, on average the largest shareholder holds 15.4% of the shares. On average the board of directors holds 10.6%, the chairman and president between them hold 3.7%, the chief executive officer (CEO) holds 2.4%, institutions hold over 19.1%. For 25.7% of firms, the largest shareholder is an institution. Median ownership figures are typically lower, however, particularly for insider holdings. For example, Jensen and Murphy (1990b)

Table 8.1 Mean and median percentage ownership of firm's common stock by insiders and institutions from studies of various samples in different subperiods in the interval 1980–1985

Percentage of common stock held by:	Mean (%)	Median (%)
Largest shareholder[a]	15.4	NR
Five largest shareholders[b]	24.8	NR
Board of directors[c]	10.6	3.4
Board of directors plus officers[d]	10.1	4.4
Chairman and president[e]	3.7	NR
CEO[f]	2.4	0.2
All institutions		
Brickley, Lease, Smith[d]	32.9	33.9
Pound[g]	19.1	NR
Investment counsel firms[d]	6.2	4.7
Banks[d]	5.9	4.5
Mutual funds[d]	3.4	1.9

Identity of largest shareholder[a]	% of firms
Family represented on board	32.7
Pension and profit-sharing plans	19.7
Institution	25.7
Firm or family holding company	21.9

NR = not reported.

a. Shleifer and Vishny (1986, p. 462). Sample: 456 *Fortune* 500 firms based on the data from Corporate Data Exchange *Stock Ownership Directory: Fortune 500*, compiled for December 1980.

b. Demsetz and Lehn (1985). Sample: 511 firms from Corporate Data Exchange *Stock Ownership Directory: Energy* (1980), *Banking and Finance* (1980), and *Fortune 500* (1981).

c. Morck, Shleifer, and Vishny (1988). Sample: 371 *Fortune* 500 firms based on the data from Corporate Data Exchange *Stock Ownership Directory: Fortune 500*, compiled for December 1980.

d. Brickley, Lease, and Smith (1988, tables A.3, A.4). Sample: 191 firms proposing antitakeover ammendments in 1984.

e. Weisbach (1988, table 6). Sample: 208 New York Stock Exchange firms in 1980.

f. Jensen and Murphy (1990a, table 4). Sample: 746 CEO's in 1987 Forbes Compensation Survey. Ownership includes shares held by family members and includes options exercisable within sixty days.

g. Pound (1988, table 3). Sample: 95 firms with proxy contests in the years 1981–1985.

show that while the average CEO holding is 2.4% of his or her firm's stock, the median holding is only 0.2%, and 80% of CEOs hold less than 1.4%. Nevertheless, the data suggest that ownership in at least some firms is sufficiently concentrated to be important to our understanding of corporate behavior. Moreover, although the benchmark for gauging the importance of firm ownership is not obvious, managers' ownership stake represents the bulk of their wealth, and this affects their incentives (Benston 1985; Lewellen 1971; and Murphy 1985).

8.3 Management Ownership, Capital Structure, and Takeovers

Theoretical papers by Stulz (1988) and Harris and Raviv (1988a) examine the links between managerial control of voting rights, the firm's debt-equity ratio, and the takeover market. Both papers assume that managers who face a possible takeover bid act in their own interests. These interests can diverge from those of nonmanagement shareholders because of the assumed benefits from control. Stulz examines how, for an all-equity firm, managerial ownership and control of voting rights affect firm value by influencing the firm's attractiveness as a takeover target. Both the Stulz and the Harris and Raviv paper examine how leverage affects management's control of voting rights and serves as a takeover defense.

Takeovers and an All-Equity Firm

Stulz (1988) shows that the fraction of share votes owned by managers is an important variable for an all-equity firm because it influences both the likelihood of a tender offer and the magnitude of the offer premium. In Stulz's model, the higher the fraction of votes controlled by managers, the higher the premium rational bidders must offer to acquire shares, but the lower the probability that a hostile bid will occur. Given that the value of the firm will reflect the expected premium, Stulz demonstrates that firm value initially rises as managerial control of voting rights increases, but then falls. Firm value is generally maximized when management owns shares and hence controls a positive fraction of voting rights.

Leverage and Voting Rights

In both the Stulz (1988) and the Harris and Raviv (1988a) papers, managers are found to acquire voting rights by purchasing shares, but wealth limitations and restrictions on personal borrowing make control of a large fraction of votes difficult in large firms. For a given dollar investment in shares, the greater the amount of debt or other nonvoting securities, such as preferred stock or warrants in the firm's capital structure, the greater the managerial control of voting rights.

Recognition of the relation between capital structure and managerial control of voting rights leads to additional insights along several different dimensions. First, the firm's optimal (i.e., value-maximizing) capital structure is affected. Given his result that managerial voting rights affect firm value, and the link between financing and voting rights, Stulz also demonstrates there is a positive debt-equity ratio that maximizes the value of the firm. The basic argument is that debt makes it easier for managers with limited resources to control the optimal fraction of votes. Second, as Harris and Raviv emphasize, leverage is an important device that incumbent managers can use to defend against takeovers. The basic idea in Harris and Raviv is that incumbent management can strengthen its control of voting rights and its incumbency by issuing debt and using the proceeds to purchase equity from nonaligned shareholders. Managers can also issue new equity to dilute the holdings of a potential acquirer.

Empirical Tests

Stulz (1988) and Harris and Raviv (1988a) provide a rich set of empirical predictions. The predictions concern, for example, how capital structure affects the likelihood, form, and success of a takeover attempt, how share performance is affected by the various forms of takeover activity, and how takeover attempts will affect capital structure. Although many predictions in the Stulz and Harris and Raviv papers are yet untested, the theory is consistent with a number of known empirical regularities. For example, Stulz argues that the theory is consistent with empirical evidence indicating that increases in the debt-equity ratio reduce the likelihood of takeover (Palepu 1986) and reduce the value of the firm when the change leads to large concentrations of voting power by managers (Dann and DeAngelo 1988). He also argues that the theory is consistent with empirical evidence that calls of convertible debt decrease the value of the firm (Mikkelson 1981) and are systematically delayed beyond the optimal call date (Ingersoll 1977), and that shares with higher voting rights are usually held by managers (DeAngelo and DeAngelo 1985; Partch 1987).

The Dann and DeAngelo (1988) study of thirty-three targets of hostile bids whose managers resisted takeover in the period 1962–1983 provides strong evidence that a firm's financial structure is affected by managers' desire to avoid a takeover. In 48% of their cases, managers made changes in capital structure that created a consolidated voting bloc or increased the proportionate voting power of an existing bloc. In the remaining cases, managers used acquisitions or divestitures to inhibit a takeover attempt. Although in the authors' sample the contest results are approximately equally divided between cases in which the hostile bidder acquired control, another bidder acquired control, or the target firm remained independent, hostile bidders rarely prevailed when management's defensive restructurings were actually implemented.

The resistance of these target managers cannot be explained as being in the shareholders' interest. Target shareholders in the Dann and DeAngelo sample experienced statistically significant average wealth losses at the announcement of defensive corporate restructurings. The mean and median abnormal value changes are -2.2% $(t = 4.0)$ and -2.7%, respectively. Although shareholders gain if a takeover ultimately succeeds, loss of the large tender premiums and the substantial declines in share prices that occur when a sole bidder fails more than offset the gains to successful takeover targets. Dann and DeAngelo's evidence is also consistent with that of Ruback (1988b), who shows statistically significant losses to target firm shareholders when management defeats a takeover and the firm remains independent. (See also Bradley and Wakeman 1983; Easterbrook and Jarrell 1984; and Jarrell 1985.)

Dann and DeAngelo conclude that managers' defensive reactions to hostile takeovers are best explained by their desires to entrench themselves in office. Consistent with Stulz and Harris and Raviv, they also conclude that financial policy, including both capital structure and ownership structure, is affected by the market for corporate control. The combination of theoretical and empirical work in these papers provides a good start in understanding how managerial interests interact with voting rules, ownership structure, and the market for corporate control to affect corporate financial policy.

8.4   Voting Rights of Common Shares

Limited-voting stock distributes voting rights to shareholders in ways that are not proportional to their claims on corporate cash flows. The increased use of limited-voting common stock in the wake of relaxation of the NYSE prohibition on limited-voting shares has created a major controversy in the regulatory sector.

Jarrell and Poulsen (1988) examined the wealth effects on shareholders of ninety-four dual-class recapitalizations in the period 1976–1986 in which a new class of stock with limited voting rights is exchanged for old shares. They found significant negative average price effects of −0.64% at the announcement of such recapitalizations, with the negative effects concentrated primarily in the cases that have occurred since the NYSE relaxed its listing standards in June 1984; previous work by Partch (1987), who studied forty-four such dual-class recapitalizations in the period prior to the NYSE relaxation of listing standards, found no negative effects. The Jarrell and Poulsen evidence also indicates that firms recapitalizing after the NYSE relaxation of listing standards had substantially larger institutional ownership and insider holdings than those recapitalizing before the change in standards. The largest wealth losses occurred for those firms with insider holdings in the 30–55% range. This evidence is consistent with the hypothesis that post-1984 dual-class recapitalizations were by firms vulnerable to takeover and that such recapitalizations serve to entrench managers.

The negative wealth effects of such exchange offers pose a puzzle because the exchanges are approved voluntarily by corporate shareholders. Although, as Jarrell and Poulsen point out, the voting power of insiders is important in achieving shareholder approval, this cannot explain all approvals. Ruback (1988a) develops a model of the shareholder exchange decision that explains shareholders' behavior. He demonstrates how managers can entrench themselves by inducing shareholders to exchange their shares for limited voting right shares carrying higher dividends (as is frequently observed), even though such shareholders are harmed by the exchange. When individual shareholders cannot act jointly, the offer of shares with claim to a higher dividend places each shareholder in the classic prisoner's dilemma. The rational choice of each shareholder to acquire the higher dividend leads to a decline in all shareholders' wealth. The wealth decline occurs because such shareholders generally cannot collude to avoid the reduced probability of receiving a takeover bid caused by their aggregate exchange decision.

The Jarrell and Poulsen and Ruback results suggest that managers use dual-class exchange offers to expropriate wealth from existing shareholders. Protecting against this expropriation does not require the banishment of dual-class organizational forms, but can be achieved through limitations on the use of coercive exchange offers of the type analyzed by Ruback. The proposed SEC Rule 19c-4 restrictions on issuance of dual-class shares will make such exchanges more difficult.[1]

Gilson (1987) argues that dual-class reorganizations are substitutes for leveraged buyouts (LBOs) because both transactions transfer control of the company to managers. Because the dual-class reorganization allows the firm continuing access to the equity capital markets, he argues that managers of rapidly growing firms would rationally, and in the shareholders' interests, choose the dual-class reorganization over the LBO form. Similarly, he argues, following Jensen (1986a, 1986b), that managers of low-growth firms would rationally, and in the shareholders' interests, choose the LBO form.

Dual-class reorganizations and LBOs differ, however. Agency costs are higher for dual-class firms because for given voting power, insiders in dual-class firms have smaller claims on cash flows than LBO insiders. Also, the dual-class firm does not receive the control benefits of high leverage (Grossman and Hart 1982; Jensen 1986a, 1986b; and Stulz 1988). Consistent with these arguments, shareholders in LBO transactions earn premiums of 50% (DeAngelo, DeAngelo, and Rice 1984a; Kaplan 1989b), whereas those in dual-class recapitalizations experience small losses.

Grossman and Hart (1988) and Harris and Raviv (1988b) analyze the optimality of the one share, one vote rule for deciding corporate control contests. The issues are complex and difficult to model fully. Generally, the papers show that firm value is affected by voting rules and that under certain conditions firm value can be increased by moving away from one share, one vote. Grossman and Hart distinguish between the private benefits of control that a management team receives from running the corporation and the public benefits that accrue to security holders. They show that if only one party to a control contest obtains significant private benefits of control, one share, one vote maximizes firm value and is socially optimal. If more than one party obtains a significant private benefit, however, shareholders may choose to capture some of these private benefits by deviating from one share, one vote. They argue that the one party case is most likely to describe the usual situation and, therefore, that one share, one vote should be widely observed. Harris and Raviv show that a simple majority rule system with one share, one vote ensures that the better management team is always elected and is therefore the socially optimal system. Maximizing the value of the firm, however, requires issuing equity claims with no voting rights and voting rights with no cash flow claims. Moving away from one share, one vote allows shareholders to gain by capturing more benefits from the winner in a control contest. In contrast to one share, one vote, such a dual-class system does not ensure that the best management team will win control, and the result is a reduction in efficiency.

The two papers differ in several interesting respects. Grossman and Hart assume that each investor is negligible in the sense that he does not believe his action is pivotal in determining the outcome of the contest, and that votes cannot be traded separately from claims on the underlying cash flows. Harris and Raviv relax both of these assumptions, while assuming that no control candidate can purchase shares anonymously before the announcement of a takeover attempt. Their model implies, contrary to the evidence of Jarrell and Poulsen (1988), that share value will increase when a firm announces a switch from a one share, one vote rule to a dual-class system with differential voting rights.

8.5   Ownership, Voting Behavior, and Monitoring

Recent evidence indicates that ownership structure and shareholder voting in corporate election contests are related. Pound (1988) examines election contests in which a dissident faction either attempts to obtain seats on the firm's board of directors or opposes a management proposal (or offers its own proposal) for a change in corporate structure, such as an antitakeover proposal. He focuses on how the outcome of these proxy contests is related to ownership characteristics. Pound's cross-sectional evidence indicates that the probability of dissidents' success is higher (1) the lower is the number of shareholders and (2) the lower are ownership levels by either institutions (i.e., banks, mutual funds, insurance companies) or blockholders not affiliated with the contesting factions. He argues that a large number of shareholders makes dissident victory more difficult because it is less costly for management than for the dissidents to identify shareholders. Furthermore, incumbents have an advantage because dispersed public stockholders evaluate management performance by simple measures such as accounting earnings, which are subject to managerial manipulation (DeAngelo 1988). Pound also argues that institutional investors and unaffiliated blockholders are likely to side with management. Although institutional investors such as pension fund money managers and insurance companies have fiduciary responsibilities to their beneficiaries, they can be influenced by existing business relationships with management. Money managers are subject to pressure from corporate managers to vote shares they control in the interests of management rather than in the interests of fund beneficiaries. Corporate managers can deny noncooperating money managers the opportunity to manage the firm's pension plan.

Direct evidence that institutions can be influenced by existing business relations with the firm is presented by Brickley, Lease, and Smith (1988). They examine voting behavior on management-proposed antitakeover amendments. Their evidence indicates that institutions such as banks and insurance companies (both of which can benefit from existing business relationships with management) are significantly more likely to vote with management on antitakeover amendments than institutions such as college endowments and mutual funds (which seldom have other business relations with management). This evidence supports the reports in the popular press (see Heard and Sherman 1987, pp. 43–44) that managers of large corporations try to influence the votes of managers of pension and other funds where they have the ability to impose costs by withholding their business.

Brickley, Lease, and Smith also indicate that institutional investors and other blockholders vote more actively on antitakeover amendments than nonblockholders and that opposition by institutions is greater when the proposal appears to harm shareholders. In contrast to Pound's results, this suggests that blockholders serve a monitoring role. The importance of this role is unclear, however, because 95% of the proposed amendments in their study passed, and Brickley, Lease, and Smith argue that there is too little cross-sectional variation in their sample outcomes to detect the influence of blockholders on passage. The two papers' somewhat conflicting results on the role of blockholders could arise for several reasons. For example, the events the papers study are different. Proxy contests launched by a dissident faction represent a direct threat to management's continued tenure, whereas management typically does not propose antitakeover amendments unless their passage is likely. The incentives of institutions and other blockholders could differ in the two situations. In addition, the mix of institutions and blockholder types can systematically differ for firms having each type of event, and the different results would therefore not be surprising. Attempts to reconcile the apparent differences between the two studies appear to be a fruitful area for future research. At this point, however, the conclusion that stock ownership and voting patterns are related seems safe.

8.6 Ownership and Corporate Performance

Share ownership by management and the board of directors varies substantially across firms. This cross-sectional variation provides the basis for tests of the relation between ownership and firm behavior. Moreover, the tests raise important questions about the nature of the relation. Morck, Shleifer, and Vishny (1988) examine the cross-sectional relation between measures of firm performance and the ownership stake of the board of directors. The performance measures are (1) Tobin's Q, defined as the ratio of the market value of the firm's securities to the replacement cost of the firm's plant and inventories, and (2) the firm's accounting profit rate. Morck, Shleifer, and Vishny report a strong relation between performance measures and ownership stake, but the relation is not monotonic. In particular, as board ownership increases from zero to 5%, Q rises; as ownership increases from 5% to 25%, Q falls; as ownership rises beyond 25%, Q again increases. Although somewhat weaker results are obtained using profit rate as the measure of firm performance, the relation between performance and ownership applies both for ownership by managers and for ownership by outside board members.

The trade-offs between the alignment of manager-shareholder interests and managerial entrenchment imply a nonmonotonic relation between insider holdings and the value of a given firm. Managerial interests become more closely allied with shareholders' as inside stock ownership rises from zero. Thus, value should increase with ownership until inside stock ownership is large enough to begin to give managers control, at which point entrenchment begins to occur, and as this happens value declines with ownership. Managers usually have effective control at less than 50% ownership of the stock. From this point increases in managerial holdings cause firm value to rise because such increases cause managers' interests to be more closely aligned with those of shareholders. Morck, Shleifer, and Vishny's cross-sectional evidence, although consistent with this scenario, is surprising because it indicates that inside stock ownership of as little as 5% begins to give managers control powers important enough to cause firm value to fall. Their estimates imply that effective managerial control of the firm occurs by 25%, the point at which firm value begins to rise. This conclusion is inconsistent with the Jarrell and Poulsen (1988) evidence that the largest negative value effects in recent dual-class recapitalizations occur for those firms with insider holdings in the 30–55% range; if managers of these firms already had effective control at 25%, there would be no negative value effects from the additional concentration of voting power in insider hands.

A caveat to the alignment-entrenchment interpretation of the cross-sectional evidence, however, is that it treats ownership as exogenous, and does not address the issue of what determines ownership concentration for a given firm or why concentration would not be chosen to maximize firm value. Managers and stockholders have incentives to avoid inside ownership stakes in the range where their interests are not aligned, although managerial wealth constraints and benefits from entrenchment could make such holdings efficient for managers. As Morck, Shleifer, and Vishny discuss, there is an alternative interpretation. Suppose firms with high levels of intangible assets, for which measured Q is high, require greater management ownership if the value of the firm is to be maximized. Such considerations could induce a positive correlation between management ownership and Tobin's Q, even though the high Q causes high ownership rather than vice versa. This Q-causing-ownership explanation, however, does not predict the particular relation implied by the alignment-entrenchment trade-offs and the Morck, Shleifer, and Vishny evidence. In addition, recent work by Wruck (1989) adds considerable support to the alignment-entrenchment hypothesis; her time-series evidence on changes in firm value associated with changes in ownership concentration around private sales of equity yields regression coefficients very similar to that of Morck, Shleifer, and Vishny.

Nonetheless, the notion that firm characteristics can affect ownership is useful and is also suggested by other work. Demsetz and Lehn

(1985) and Brickley and Dark (1987) present evidence that variation in ownership structure is partly explained by variation in firm characteristics, such as size and location. In addition, using a variety of data, Holderness and Sheehan (1988) find no evidence that majority ownership by managers can be explained as an attempt to expropriate resources from shareholders. They examine 114 listed firms in the 1978–1984 period in which a shareholder has at least a 50% stake. They find average majority-shareholder positions of 62%. In over 90% of these firms the majority shareholder is either an officer or director (or employer of an officer or director). Holderness and Sheehan document that majority-shareholder firms survive over time, but the authors do not fully investigate the characteristics that would make it optimal for a firm to be majority controlled. In sum, the direction of causality between ownership concentration and firm characteristics is an important question raised, but not entirely resolved, by papers exploiting cross-sectional variation in ownership. Although the evidence indicates that firm characteristics and inside stock ownership are related, disentangling the causal relation between inside stock ownership and firm value requires additional investigation.

Time-series evidence on the relation between inside stock ownership changes and firm performance is presented in Kaplan (1989c). He examines seventy-six firms that were the subject of a management buyout (MBO). Median percentage share holdings of managers increased from 3.5% to 22.6%. He finds significant increases in operating income and operating margins in the post-buyout period, consistent with better alignment of manager and stockholder interests. Those buyouts that were subsequently sold or taken public had a mean wealth gain of 109% (median = 56%), with the wealth gain approximately equally divided between the original public shareholders and the management-buyout specialists.

Kaplan's results are consistent with the analysis of MBOs by Jensen (1986a, 1986b), who argues that the governance of these firms (and the distribution of ownership claims, inside ownership, and capital structure) is so different that they represent a new organizational form. First, in two-thirds of MBOs, management does not own all the equity and the board of directors is composed of buyout specialists who own or control an equity stake averaging 60% (see Kaplan 1989c). These specialists also act as investment bankers in the transaction. Second, these organizations are characterized by strip financing and high leverage (10 to 1 debt-equity ratios are not unusual). In strip financing, all claimants have approximately proportional holdings of each security in the complicated array of nonequity claims (excluding the most senior debt). Jensen argues that strip financing reduces conflicts of interest among classes of claimants and lowers expected bankruptcy costs. The efficiency and success of MBOs is evidenced not only by the large wealth gains found by Kaplan and DeAngelo, DeAngelo, and Rice (1984a), but also by their growth; MBOs of public corporations or divisions totaled $45 billion in 1986, compared with $1.2 billion in 1979 (Jensen and Murphy 1990b, table 10).

8.7   Poison Pills and Other Unilateral Changes in Top-Level Control Rights

Poison pills are securities issued by vote of the board of directors and, unlike some takeover defenses, do not require shareholder ratification. A basic perspective on the corporate governance problem and the importance of top-level control rights is useful in analyzing the effects of poison pills. Managers and boards of directors are the agents of shareholders, who are the principals in the contracts effected through the corporate charter. Depending on the circumstances, it can be desirable for a principal to delegate a wide range of decision rights to the agent. In no event is it sensible for the principal to delegate the ultimate control rights to the agent. Control rights are the rights to hire, fire, and set the compensation of the agent.[2] If the control rights were delegated to the agent, the agent would effectively own the decision rights (without right of sale) and use them in his or her own interests.

Poison Pills

Poison pills allow the board to unilaterally reallocate to itself some of the top-level control rights of stockholders—the right to remove the board and management in certain control transactions. These securities take a variety of forms, but all have the characteristic that they change the rights of shareholders on the occurrence of a control event—such as a tender offer, acquisition of a large block of stock or voting rights, or addition to such a block—by a party not approved by the board of directors. One common form gives target shareholders the right to buy stock of the bidder at a large discount from market value, typically

50%, as a condition for completion of the merger. Poison pills received legitimate legal status in November 1985 when the Delaware Supreme Court upheld the right of Household International to issue such a right to its shareholders. Before this decision, thirty-seven pills of various forms had been adopted, and by the end of 1986 over 380 corporations had adopted pills.[3]

Critics charge that poison pills entrench managers, and supporters argue that pills benefit shareholders by giving management and the board power to obtain favorable terms in control transactions. The most thorough studies of the effects of poison pills are Malatesta and Walkling (1983) and Ryngaert (1988). Both studies present evidence that supports the managerial entrenchment hypothesis. Malatesta and Walkling, analyzing 113 firms that adopted poison pills in the period 1982–1986, find that poison pills on average reduce shareholder wealth by a statistically significant -0.93% ($t = 4.8$) on the announcement date. The average abnormal returns are -2.3% ($t = 3.4$) for twelve firms subject to takeover bids in the two months prior to adoption of the pill. Malatesta and Walkling also find that when firms abandon plans to adopt a pill their stock price increases, and that firms adopting pills are significantly less profitable in the year prior to adoption than a control sample of firms in the same industry.

Ryngaert, in a study of 380 firms adopting pills in the period 1982–1986, finds no statistically significant effects from the pills on the entire sample. He finds, however, that for those 62 firms perceived as takeover targets, adoption of a pill reduces shareholder wealth on average by a statistically significant -1.5% ($t = 2.8$). He also finds that stock prices fall on average by 2.2% ($t = 2.8$) when a firm's pill is upheld by the courts and rise on average by 3.4% ($t = 2.2$) when it is ruled invalid, that pill defenses double the likelihood of defeating an unsolicited bid, and that such defeats are associated with large price declines. Although 51% of the firms with pills received higher offers than the initial offer, this compares unfavorably with 68% of the firms that received increased offers in a sample of seventy-six control contests with no pills in the period 1981–1984. If managers use the pills to defeat actual offers where they know they can provide more value to shareholders than the hostile offer price, the value of the firm should increase at or after defeat of the offer. Ryngaert reports no such evidence. The net-of-market returns for 21 firms in the six months after defeat of the offer average -14.4%; these results are consistent with the findings of Easterbrook and Jarrell (1984), Jarrell (1985), Bradley, Desai, and Kim (1983), and Ruback (1988b). The defeat of an offer harms, rather than benefits, shareholders.

Discriminatory Repurchases

Discriminatory repurchases are also takeover defenses not subject to shareholder ratification. In 1985 the Delaware Supreme Court approved Unocal's discriminatory tender offer for its shares, although in 1986 the Securities and Exchange Commission (SEC) amended its rules to deny the Unocal strategy to future targets. The Delaware decision provides another situation in which information about the qualitative effects of poison pills can be estimated, because discriminatory repurchases have similar characteristics. Unocal's offer to repurchase its shares at a substantial premium was available to all shareholders except Mesa Partners II, Unocal's largest shareholder, which at the time owned 13% of the firm. Jensen (1985) examines the effects of the Delaware decision on the bidder and the target. The threat of expropriation of approximately $250 million through dilution of the value of its Unocal stock holdings caused Mesa Partners to cancel its outstanding tender offer for Unocal and to sign a standstill agreement promising not to make an offer for Unocal in the future. This defeat of the Mesa offer cost Unocal shareholders an estimated $1.1 billion.

Kamma, Weintrop, and Wier (1988) estimate the effects of Delaware's approval of the discriminatory repurchase takeover defense on firms other than Unocal. If the increased availability of the defense were in shareholders' interest, the value of other firms subject to control contests should rise. Kamma, Weintrop, and Wier studied a sample of 124 firms that were the subject of 13D filings from March 16 to May 16, 1985. They find that the value of 14 Delaware firms that were hostile targets at the time fell by a statistically significant amount on the announcement of the Delaware Supreme Court decision. Their sample of 10 non-Delaware targets was unaffected by the decision, as were their samples of Delaware and non-Delaware firms that were not hostile targets but were subject to 13D filings. Total dollar losses to the Delaware target firms over the announcement period were $267 million, about 3% of their total value. Consistent with evidence from poison pills, the evidence on discriminatory repurchases from the Jensen and Kamma, Weintrop, and Wier papers indicates they are used for managerial entrenchment rather than shareholders' benefit.

8.8   Top Management Changes and Internal Control Mechanisms

Both the external takeover market and mechanisms within the corporation can encourage managers to act in shareholders' interests. Potentially important internal mechanisms include boards of directors (Fama 1980), competition among the firm's managers, and monitoring by holders of large share blocks (Shleifer and Vishny 1986). Evidence of internal monitoring of firms' managers is provided by Weisbach (1988) and Warner, Watts, and Wruck (1988). Consistent with results previously reported by Coughlan and Schmidt (1985), both papers find a statistically significant inverse relation between a firm's share performance and the likelihood of a subsequent change in its top management. This relation is predicted under the joint hypothesis that stock performance reflects information on managerial performance, and the information is used in evaluating managerial performance. Further, although it is difficult to identify management changes that are actually firings, Warner, Watts, and Wruck indicate that these results apply more strongly to management changes likely to have been forced.

Both Warner, Watts, and Wruck and Weisbach present evidence on the specific monitoring mechanisms that lead to top management changes. Weisbach finds the relation between share performance and turnover is stronger for companies whose boards are dominated by outsiders. This suggests that outside directors serve a monitoring role and rely more frequently on publicly available performance measures than do inside directors.

The inverse relation between share performance and turnover, however, cannot be attributed solely to the board of directors. Warner, Watts, and Wruck examine details of observed management changes. In addition to board monitoring, they present evidence of involvement by large blockholders and of competition among top managers leading to forced departures. Furthermore, Gilson (1989) indicates that creditors of firms with poor share performance are sometimes involved in removal of top managers. Thus several internal monitoring mechanisms appear to be responsible for top management changes.

The strength of these various internal monitoring mechanisms is examined by Warner, Watts, and Wruck. They show that unless share performance is extreme, logit specifications of the relation between share performance and turnover have no predictive ability. Moreover, if a firm falls in the lowest decile of share performance in a given year, the chance of a management change in that year is only about 14%, compared with an unconditional probability of about 11%. These figures, however, probably understate the role of internal monitoring mechanisms; as Warner, Watts, and Wruck discuss, stock performance is a noisy measure of managerial performance, and it is difficult to identify firms with the poorest performing managers. Moreover, these figures do not fully capture the effects on turnover of the interaction between internal mechanisms and external forces such as the takeover market. For example, suppose poor management triggers corporate control events, even when poor share performance is not observed. Then corporate control events should also be associated with higher management turnover. If a control event signals poor performance, the presence of well-functioning internal mechanisms implies that higher turnover should be observed even if the takeover is unsuccessful.

Turnover around Control Contests

Research on managerial turnover around corporate control events is strongly consistent with the prediction that these events are associated with higher turnover. Martin (1986) examines top management turnover following a successful takeover bid; within three years after the bid, 64% of target-firm managers holding the top three titles depart. Walsh (1988) indicates that 59% of target firms have a management change in the five years following a successful merger, compared to 33% for a control sample of nonmerged firms. Klein and Rosenfeld (1988) examine management changes following a targeted share repurchase (i.e., greenmail). In the year following payment of greenmail, the turnover rate is 27.4%, nearly triple their estimate of the unconditional turnover rate. Klein and Rosenfeld argue that board monitoring is responsible for their findings, and the higher turnover cannot easily be attributed to takeovers following greenmail. DeAngelo and DeAngelo (1989) study management turnover following proxy contests for board seats. Dissident stockholders are generally unsuccessful in capturing a majority of board seats (Dodd and Warner 1983). Nevertheless,

DeAngelo and DeAngelo find that 76% of surviving firms that had an unsuccessful proxy contest experience at least one top management change within two years following the contest. The exact mix of internal and external forces that leads to the management changes is unclear, but many such changes occur during the proxy contest itself and thus appear linked to external pressure of the dissidents' challenge. The joint impact of internal and external forces seems pronounced.

Event Studies of Top Management Changes

From the various studies of management changes following poor share performance and corporate control events, it appears that top management changes are a key variable in understanding the forces disciplining managers. An alternative way to gain insight into top management changes is to examine the stock-price effect of management change announcements. Among eight papers that do so, the results vary. Three of the eight report average price increases for their overall samples (Bonnier and Bruner 1989; Furtado and Rozeff 1987; Weisbach 1988), four find no significant average price change (Borstadt 1985; Klein, Kim, and Mahajan 1985; Reinganum 1985; Warner, Watts, and Wruck 1988), and one finds significant average price declines (Furtado and Karan 1990). The contradictory results make interpretation difficult. Moreover, Warner, Watts, and Wruck argue that a priori, economic hypotheses about internal monitoring are better tested by examining the occurrence of turnover following events such as poor stock performance than by studying the announcement effect when turnover occurs. At this point, research on the stock-price effect of management change announcements is inconclusive.

8.9 Conclusions

The major findings of the articles surveyed in this chapter are (1) patterns of stock ownership by insiders and outsiders can influence managerial behavior, corporate performance, and stockholder voting in proxy contests; (2) corporate leverage, inside stock ownership by managers, and the control market are interrelated; (3) departures from one share, one vote affect firm value and efficiency; (4) takeover resistance through defensive restructurings or poison pill provisions is associated with declines in share price; and (5) top management turnover is inversely related to share price performance.

Some Perspectives

The work surveyed here represents the expansion of financial economists' interests from financial markets and policies to research on behavior within corporations. Studies exploring the links between the firm's governance structure and the capital markets are natural for financial economists, since security prices signal the effects of various factors on organizational performance. But the current trends in financial research extend beyond this link.

The work surveyed here is associated with other research on the interaction between financial claims, organizational structure, and firm performance. For example, Alchian and Demsetz (1972) analyze the natural advantage of residual claimants in monitoring team production in organizations, while Fama and Jensen (1983a, 1983b) demonstrate how alternative organizational forms such as corporations, partnerships, and nonprofits are distinguished from each other by critical differences in the definition of their residual claims. Work by Smith and Warner (1979) analyzes the influence of bond covenants on managerial choices of investment policy and financial structures, and Brickley and Dark (1987) investigate the advantages of the franchise form of organization as a substitute for centralized monitoring of geographically dispersed operations. Since managers play a key role in determining firm behavior, there is also a link between this literature and research on compensation and managerial labor contracts (see Baker, Jensen, and Murphy 1988; Hart and Holmstrom 1987; Jensen and Zimmerman 1985; and Lazear and Rosen 1981).

The papers cited here reflect a general trend in the social sciences toward research aimed at understanding organizations—a trend observable among scholars in many fields of economics. The literature goes by various labels, including "the economics of contracting" (Holmstrom and Tirole 1987; Ross 1973), "transactions costs" (Klein, Crawford, and Alchian 1978; Williamson 1975), "property rights" (Demsetz 1982, 1983), and "corporate finance" (DeAngelo and DeAngelo 1985; Easterbrook 1984; Grossman and Hart 1982; Jensen 1986a; Myers and Majluf 1984). In labor economics, the work is progressing under the label "compensation and hierarchies" (Medoff and Abraham 1980;

Rosen 1982); in accounting, under "information and performance measurement" (Antle and Smith 1986; DeAngelo 1988; DeAngelo 1986; Healy and Kaplan 1985); and in law, under "governance and contracting" (Carney 1987; Easterbrook and Fischel 1982; Posner 1977). The intersection of efforts by scholars in these fields is creating a productive addition to the traditional study of organizations by the behavioral sciences.

Future Directions

Although it is difficult to predict the future direction of research on corporations, the work cited here signals strong growth in both theoretical and empirical research. At the same time, the breadth of empirical methods in the area has increased considerably. Much remains to be done, however, and we briefly indicate the scope in two general areas.

Ownership and voting structure. In theory, ownership structure and the allocation of voting rights are important determinants of organizational behavior and hence will be a significant focus of future research. Since firm characteristics also affect optimal ownership distribution, disentangling the direction of causality between ownership and firm behavior is a difficult task. Additional evidence on the variation of inside and outside ownership and a taxonomy are required to organize our analysis. The variation in and effects of voting rights held by a firm's insiders, external blockholders, financial institutions, and dispersed public stockholders also are not well understood. It is important to understand why and when votes are used passively and when actively—for example, why U.S. institutional money managers tend to be passive investors, seldom serving on boards of directors or directly influencing managers,[4] in contrast to LBO specialists, family funds (e.g., the Bass brothers and Pritzkers), or takeover specialists (e.g., Icahn and Pickens). This in turn leads to questions about the effectiveness of voting in monitoring managers and the relation of voting to other mechanisms such as board processes, internal managerial competition, and hostile bids. Conflicting evidence presented here on the role of blockholders and whether they serve a monitoring function is one aspect of these unsettled issues.

Capital structure, corporate behavior, and managerial discretion. The links between inside stock ownership by management, the control market, and the firm's optimal debt-equity ratio are established in theory, but the empirical importance of the relations is largely unexplored. The effects of capital structure and free cash flow/financial slack on real decisions in the organization are only beginning to be understood. In addition, work cited in this chapter on poison pills and other antitakeover defensive maneuvers highlights important questions about the optimal degree of managerial discretion. Such discretion is determined by the corporate charter, internal monitoring practices, and external factors such as the regulatory environment, statutory and administrative law, and the business judgment rule. Study of the interactions between the legal, managerial, economic, and financial implications of the business judgment rule is likely to be fruitful. For example, what are the efficiency consequences of the current judicial approach, which closely scrutinizes managerial conflicts of interest in LBOs, while virtually ignoring such conflicts when managers seize top-level control rights through poison pills?

Ownership, voting structure, capital structure, and managerial discretion interact with internal organizational forces and affect corporate behavior in important ways. Pursuit of these issues by scholars from different areas within the economics profession promises to bring exciting contributions to the development of a science of organizations.

Notes

1. U.S. Corporate Governance

1. *Barbarians at the Gate* was written by *Wall Street Journal* reporter Bryan Burrough with contributions from John Hellyar. It was published by Harper Collins in 1989.
2. The equity gains are based on the value of KKR's Borden holdings, $2.25 billion, at market close on March 14, 1995 (the last day of trading before Borden shares were delisted), and the value of RJR shares transferred to Borden to strengthen its balance sheet on two separate occasions, during February 1995 and again during March 1995, $0.392 billion and $0.640 billion, respectively. The original RJR LBO investors contributed about $3.2 billion in equity ($1.5 billion initially on February 9, 1989, and $1.7 billion in the restructuring on July 16, 1990).
3. Kaplan concludes that the poor return earned by KKR's equity investors was due to KKR's overpaying for RJR-Nabisco. Incidentally, he computes the return to the equity investors to be less than 3%. His return is slightly higher than the one we report because it is based on the average cost of KKR's investment rather than the actual cost, and apparently does not take account of the exact timing of the cash flows.
4. As revealed in *Barbarians at the Gate,* John Greeniaus, head of RJR's baking unit, told KKR that if "the earnings of this group go up 15 or 20% . . . I'd be in trouble." His charter was to spend the excess cash in his Nabisco division to limit earnings in order to produce moderate, but smoothly rising profits—a strategy that would mask the potential profitability of the business (Burrough and Hellyar 1990, pp. 370–371). Moreover, the *Wall Street Journal* reported that Greeniaus told it that the company was "looking frantically for ways to spend its tobacco cash," including a $2.8 billion plant modernization program that was expected to produce pretax returns of only 5% (Waldman 1989).
5. As reported by the Salomon Brothers High Yield Research Group (1991), as of the end of 1990, the face value of defaulted publicly placed or registered privately placed high-yield bonds in the period 1978–1990 was roughly $35 billion (about $20 billion of which entered bankruptcy). Given that recovery rates historically average about 40%, actual losses may well be below $20 billion. Not all of these bonds were used to finance control transactions, but we use the total to obtain an upper bound estimate of losses. Although the authorities have not released the totals of HLT loans and losses, bankers have told me privately that such losses are likely to be well below $10 billion.
6. A 1989 study demonstrates that, contrary to popular assertions, LBO transac-

251

tions result in increased tax revenues to the U.S. Treasury—increases that average about 60% per year on a permanent basis under the 1986 IRS code (Jensen, Kaplan, and Stiglin 1989, pp. 727–733).

Joshua Rosett (1990), analyzing over 5,000 union contracts in over 1,000 listed companies in the period 1973–1987, shows that less than 2% of the takeover premiums can be explained by reductions in union wages in the first six years after the change in control. Pushing the estimation period out to eighteen years after the change in control increases the percentage to only 5.4% of the premium. For hostile takeovers only, union wages increase by 3% and 6%, respectively, for the two time intervals.

7. Many of the most visible of these prosecutions by U.S. Attorney Giuliani were either dropped for lack of a case or reversed. The only RICO conviction, Princeton/Newport, was reversed (although other securities law violations have been upheld), and so too the GAF, Mulheren, and Chestman cases. For a brief discussion of pressures from Congress on the SEC to bring down investment bankers, arbitrageurs, and junk bonds, see Glenn Yago (1991, pp. 99–100).

2. The Modern Industrial Revolution, Exit, and the Failure of Internal Control Systems

1. In a rare finance study of exit, DeAngelo and DeAngelo (1991) analyze the retrenchment of the U.S. steel industry in the 1980s. Ghemawat and Nalebuff (1985) have an interesting paper entitled "Exit," and Anderson (1986) provides a detailed comparison of U.S. and Japanese retrenchment in the 1970s and early 1980s and their respective political and regulatory policies toward the issues. Bower (1984, 1986) analyzes the private and political responses to decline in the petrochemical industry. Harrigan (1980, 1988) conducts detailed firm and industry studies. See also Hirschman's (1970) work on exit.

2. Measured by multifactor productivity, U.S. Department of Labor (USDL) 1990, table 3. See Jensen (1991) for a summary. Multifactor productivity showed no growth between 1973 and 1980 and grew at the rate of 1.9% per year between 1950 and 1973. Manufacturing labor productivity grew at an annual rate of 2.3% in the period 1950–1981 and at 3.8% from 1981–1990 (USDL 1990, table 3). Using data recently revised by the Bureau of Economic Analysis from 1977 to 1990, the growth rate in the earlier period was 2.2% and 3.0% in the 1981–1990 period (USDL 1991, table 1). Productivity growth in the nonfarm business sector fell from 1.9% in the period 1950–1981 to 1.1% in 1981–1990 (USDL 1990, table 2). The reason for the fall apparently lies in the large growth in the service sector relative to the manufacturing sector and the low measured productivity growth in services.

There is considerable controversy over the adequacy of the measurement of productivity in the service sector. The USDL has no productivity measures for services employing nearly 70% of service workers, including, among others, health care, real estate, and securities brokerage. In addition, many believe that service sector productivity growth measures are downward biased. Service sector price measurements, for example, take no account of the improved productivity and lower prices of discount outlet clubs such as Sam's Club. The Commerce Department measures output of financial services as the value of labor used to produce it. Because labor productivity is defined as the value of total output divided by total labor inputs, it is impossible for measured productivity to grow. Between 1973 and 1987 total equity shares traded daily grew from 5.7 million to 63.8 million, while employment only doubled—implying considerably more productivity growth than the zero growth reflected in the statistics. Other factors, however, contribute to potential overestimates of productivity growth in the manufacturing sector. See Malabre and Clark (1992) and Richman (1993).

3. Nominal and real hourly compensation, *Economic Report of the President,* table B42 (1993).

4. U.S. Department of Labor (1990). Trends in U.S. productivity have been controversial issues in academic and policy circles in the last decade. One reason, I believe, is that it takes time for these complicated changes to show up in the aggregate statistics. In their book, Baumol, Blackman, and Wolff (1989, pp. ix–x) changed their formerly pessimistic position: "This book is perhaps most easily summed up as a compendium of evidence demonstrating the error of our previous ways . . . The main change that was forced upon our views by careful examination of the long-run data was abandonment of our earlier gloomy assessment of American productivity performance. It has been replaced by the guarded optimism that pervades this book. This does *not* mean that we believe retention of American leadership will be automatic or easy. Yet the statistical evidence did drive us to conclude that the many writers who have suggested that the demise of America's traditional position has already occurred or was close at hand were, like the author of Mark Twain's obituary, a bit premature . . . It should, incidentally, be acknowledged that a number of distinguished economists have also been driven to a similar evaluation."

5. As measured by the Wilshire 5,000 index of all publicly held equities.

6. Annual premiums reported by *Mergerstat Review* (1991, fig. 5) weighted by value of transaction in the year for this estimate.

7. I assume that all transactions without publicly disclosed prices have a value equal to 20% of the value of the average publicly disclosed transaction in the same year, and that they have average premiums equal to those for publicly disclosed transactions.

8. In some cases buyers overpay, perhaps because of mistakes or because of agency problems with their own shareholders. Such overpayment represents only a wealth transfer from the buying firm's claimants to those of the selling firm and not an efficiency gain.

9. Healy, Palepu, and Ruback (1992) estimate the total gains to buying- and selling-firm shareholders in the fifty largest mergers in the period 1979–1984 at 9.1%. They also find a strong positive cross-sectional relation between the value change and the cash flow changes resulting from the merger.

10. See Kaplan (1989a, 1989b, 1989c, 1992), Jensen, Kaplan, and Stiglin (1989), Pontiff, Shleifer, and Weisbach (1990), Asquith and Wizman (1990), and Rosett (1990).

11. Its high of $139.50 occurred on February 19, 1991, and it closed at $50.38 at the end of 1992.

12. Zellner (1992) discusses the difficulties traditional retailers have in meeting Wal-Mart's prices.

13. "In 1980 IBM's top-of-the-line computers provided 4.5 MIPs (millions of instructions per second) for $4.5 million. By 1990, the cost of a MIP on a personal computer had dropped to $1,000" (Keene 1991, p. 110). By 1993 the price had dropped to under $100. The technological progress in personal computers has itself been stunning. Intel's Pentium (586) chip, introduced in 1993, has a capacity of 100 MIPs—100 times the capacity of its 286 chip introduced in 1982 (Brandt 1993). In addition, the progress of storage, printing, and other related technology has also been rapid (Christensen 1993).

14. The *Journal of Financial Economics,* which I have been editing with several others since 1973, is an example. The journal is now edited by seven faculty members with offices at three universities in different states and the main editorial administrative office located in yet another state. North-Holland, the publisher, is located in Amsterdam, the printing is done in India, and mailing and billing is executed in Switzerland. This "networked organization" would have been extremely inefficient two decades ago without fax machines, high-speed modems, electronic mail, and overnight delivery services.

15. Wruck and Jensen (1994) provide an analysis of the critical organizational innovations that total quality management is bringing to the technology of management.

16. A collapse I predicted in Jensen 1989b.

17. Steel industry employment is now down to 160,000 from its peak of 600,000 in 1953 (Fader 1993).

18. I am indebted to Steven Cheung for discussions on these issues.

19. Although migration will play a role, it will be relatively small compared to the export of the labor in products and services. Swissair's 1987 transfer of part of its reservation system to Bombay and its 1991 announcement of plans to transfer 150 accounting jobs to the same city are small examples (Economist Intelligence Unit 1991).

20. Thailand and China have played a role in the world markets in the last decade, but since it has been such a small part of their potential I have left them in the potential entrant category.

21. In a recent article focusing on the prospects for textile manufacturer investment in central European countries, van Delden (1993, p. 43) reports: "When major French group Rhone Poulenc's fibres division started a discussion for a formal joint venture in 1991, they discovered an example of astonishing competitiveness. Workers—whose qualifications matched those normal in the West—cost only 8% of their West European counterparts, and yet achieved productivity rates of between 60% and 75% compared to EC level. Moreover,

energy costs of the integrated power station are 50% below West German costs, and all of this is complemented by extremely competitive raw material prices."

The textile industry illustrates the problems with chronic excess capacity brought on by a situation where the worldwide demand for textiles grows fairly constantly, but growth in the productivity of textile machinery through technological improvements is greater. Moreover, additional capacity is being created because new entrants to the global textile market must upgrade outdated (and less productive) weaving machinery with new technology to meet minimum global quality standards. This means excess capacity is likely to be a continuing problem in the industry and that adjustment will have to occur through exit of capacity in high-cost Western textile mills.

22. Total quality management programs strongly encourage managers to benchmark their firm's operations against the most successful worldwide competitors, and good cost systems and competitive benchmarking are becoming more common in well-managed firms.

23. Shleifer and Summers (1988) seem to take the position that all implicit contracts should be enforced rigidly and never be breached.

24. A partial list of references includes Chapter 3 of this book, Dann and DeAngelo (1988), Mann and Sicherman (1991), Baker and Wruck (1989), Berger and Ofek (1993), Bhide (1993), Brickley, Jarrell, and Netter (1988), Denis (1994), Donaldson (1990), DeAngelo and DeAngelo (1991), DeAngelo, DeAngelo, and Rice (1984a), Esty (1997a, 1997b), Grundfest (1990b), Holderness and Sheehan (1991), Jensen (1986a, 1986b, 1988, 1989b, 1991), Kaplan (1989a, 1989b, 1992), Lang, Poulsen, and Stulz (1995), Lang and Walkling (1991), Lewellen, Loderer, and Martin (1987), Martin and McConnell (1991), Lichtenberg (1992), Lichtenberg and Siegel (1990b), Ofek (1993), Palepu (1990), Pound (1988, 1991, 1992), Roe (1990, 1991), Smith (1990), Tedlow (1991), Sull, Tedlow, and Rosenbloom (1997), Tiemann (1990), Wruck and Stephens (1992a, 1992b), Wruck (1990, 1991, 1997), Wruck and Palepu (1992).

25. In May 1985, Uniroyal approved an LBO proposal to block hostile advances by Carl Icahn. About the same time, BF Goodrich began diversifying out of the tire business. In January 1986, Goodrich and Uniroyal independently spun off their tire divisions and together, in a 50–50 joint venture, formed the Uniroyal-Goodrich Tire Company. By December 1987, Goodrich had sold its interest in the venture to Clayton and Dubilier; Uniroyal followed soon after. Similarly, General Tire moved away from tires: the company, renamed GenCorp in 1984, sold its tire division to Continental in 1987. Other takeovers in the industry during this period include the sale of Firestone to Bridgestone and Pirelli's purchase of the Armstrong Tire Company. By 1991, Goodyear was the only remaining major American tire manufacturer. Yet it too faced challenges in the control market: in 1986, following three years of unprofitable diversifying investments, Goodyear initiated a major leveraged stock repurchase and restructuring to defend itself from a hostile takeover from Sir James Goldsmith.

Uniroyal-Goodrich was purchased by Michelin in 1990. See Tedlow (1991) and Sull, Tedlow, and Rosenbloom (1997).

26. Had this merger occurred in a stock-for-stock deal, no exit would have occurred; in other words, no reduction in investment in the oil industry would have occurred.

27. In 1992 dollars, calculated from *Mergerstat Review* (1991, pp. 100f.).

28. In 1992 dollars, *Mergerstat Review* (1991, Figs. 29 and 38).

29. Because of the sharp decline in Japanese stock prices, the Japanese firms ranked among the top thirty-five firms would have performed less well if the period since 1990 had been included.

30. Hall (1993), in a large sample free of survivorship bias, finds lower market valuation of R&D in the 1980s and hypothesizes that this is due to a higher depreciation rate for R&D capital. The Stern Stewart Performance 1000 (1992) ranks companies by a measure of the economic value added by management decisions that is an alternative to performance measures 1–3 summarized in Table 2.4. GM also ranks at the bottom of this list.

31. Changes in market expectations about the prospects for a firm (and therefore changes in its market value) obviously can affect the interpretation of the performance measures. Other than using a long period of time there is no simple way to handle this problem. The large increase in stock prices in the 1980s would indicate that expectations were generally being revised upward.

32. CEO turnover approximately doubles from 3 to 6% after two years of poor performance (stock returns more than 50% below equivalent-risk market returns (Weisbach 1988)), or increases from 8.3 to 13.9% from the highest to the lowest performing decile of firms (Warner, Watts, and Wruck 1988). See also DeAngelo (1988) and DeAngelo and DeAngelo (1989).

33. See Jensen and Murphy (1990a, 1990b) for similar estimates based on earlier data.

34. In their excellent analysis of boards, Lipton and Lorsch (1992) also criticize the functioning of traditionally configured boards, recommend limiting membership to seven or eight people, and encourage equity ownership by board members. Research supports the proposition that as groups increase in size they become less effective because the coordination and process problems overwhelm the advantages gained from having more people to draw on (see Hackman 1990; Steiner 1972).

35. Lipton and Lorsch (1992) stop short of recommending appointment of an independent chairman, recommending instead the appointment of a "lead director" whose function would be to coordinate board activities.

36. Gersick and Hackman (1990) and Hackman (1993) study a similar problem—namely, the issues associated with habitual behavior routines in groups—to understand how to create more productive environments. They apply the analysis to airline cockpit crews.

37. See Roe (1990, 1991), Black (1990), and Pound (1991).

38. See Porter (1992a, 1992b, 1992c). Hall et al. (1993) provide excellent empirical tests of the myopic capital market hypothesis on which much of debate on the functioning of U.S. capital markets rests.

39. See Kaplan (1989a, 1989b, 1989c, 1992), Smith (1990), Wruck (1990), Lichtenberg (1992), Lichtenberg and Siegel (1990b), Healy, Palepu, and Ruback (1992), and Ofek (1993).

There have now been a number of detailed clinical and case studies of these transactions that document the effects of the changes on incentives and organizational effectiveness as well as the risks of bankruptcy from over-leveraging. See Baker and Wruck (1989), Wruck (1991, 1997), Holderness and Sheehan (1988, 1991), Wruck and Keating (1992a, 1992b), Wruck and Stephens (1992a, 1992b), Jensen and Barry (1992), Jensen, Burkhardt, and Barry (1992), Jensen, Dial, and Barry (1992), Lang and Stulz (1992), Denis (1994).

40. See Jensen (1986a) and the references in n. 39.

41. Assets do change somewhat after an LBO because such firms often engage in asset sales after the transaction to pay down debt and to get rid of assets that are peripheral to the organization's core focus.

42. See Palepu (1990) for a review of research on LBOs, their governance changes, and their productivity effects. Kaplan and Stein (1993) show similar results in more recent data.

43. See references in n. 39 above. In a counterexample, Healy and Palepu (1995) argue in their study of CUC that the value increase following its recapitalization occurred not because of incentive effects of the deal, but because of the information the recapitalization provided to the capital markets about the nature of the company's business and profitability.

44. In Chapter 3 of this volume and in Jensen (1989b) I analyze the LBO association; Sahlman (1990) analyzes the venture capital funds.

45. Counterexamples are Bower (1970), Baldwin and Clark (1992), Baldwin (1982, 1988, 1991), Baldwin and Trigeorgis (1992), and Shleifer and Vishny (1989).

46. See Harris (1991), Harris and Raviv (1988b), and Stulz (1990).

47. Jensen (1989a, 1989b), Kester (1991), Sahlman (1990), Pound (1988, 1991, 1992).

48. Examples of this work include Gilson, John, and Lang (1990), Wruck (1990, 1991), Lang and Stulz (1992), Lang, Poulsen, Stulz (1995) on bankruptcy and financial distress, Warner, Watts, Wruck (1988), Weisbach (1988), Jensen and Murphy (1990a, 1990b) and Gibbons and Murphy (1990) on executive turn-over, compensation, and organizational performance, Esty (1997a, 1997b) on the effects of organizational form on thrift losses, Gilson and Kraakman (1991) on governance, Brickley and Dark (1987) on franchising, Boycko, Shleifer, and Vishny (1994), Kaplan (1989a, 1989b, 1989c, 1992), Smith (1990), Kaplan and Stein (1993), Palepu (1990), and Sahlman (1990) on lever-aged buyouts and venture capital organizations.

49. The 1989 Financial Institutions Reform, Recovery, and Enforcement Act in-creased federal authority and sanctions by shifting regulation of the savings and loan (S&L) industry from the Federal Home Loan Bank Board to the Trea-sury and insurance of the industry from the FSLIC to the FDIC. The act banned thrift investment in high-yield bonds, and raised capital ratios and insurance

premiums. The 1990 Comprehensive Thrift and Bank Fraud Prosecution and Tax Payer Recovery Act increased criminal penalties for financial institution-related crimes. The 1991 FDIC Improvement Act tightened examination and auditing standards, recapitalized the Bank Insurance Fund, and limited foreign bank powers. The Truth in Banking Act of 1992 required stricter disclosure of interest rates and fees on deposit accounts and tightened advertising guidelines. The National Association of Insurance Commissioners (NAIC) substantially restricted the ability of insurance companies to invest in high-yield debt in the period 1990–1991.

50. See Chapter 3 of this volume, Jensen (1991), Roe (1990, 1991), Grundfest (1990b), Bhide (1993), Black (1990), Pound (1988, 1991, 1992), DeAngelo, DeAngelo, and Gilson (1994).

51. Most conservatively, one could assume that the cutback in R&D and capital expenditures under the alternative strategy results in a reduction in intermediate cash flows by the amount of the net cash paid to shareholders in the form of dividends and share repurchases and a final equity value of zero.

$$V_T - V'_T = V_n + d_t(1 + r)^{n-t} - B_n \sum (K_t + R_t)(1 + i)^{n-t} \tag{4}$$

I expect this measure provides an unreasonably high estimate of the productivity of R&D and investment expenditures and therefore do not report it.

3. Active Investors, LBOs, and the Privatization of Bankruptcy

1. For the argument that takeover gains to shareholders come from wealth redistribution from other parties see Shleifer and Summers (1988). However, no evidence has yet been produced that supports this argument. For surveys of the evidence on the effects of control-related transactions, see Jensen and Ruback (1983) and Jarrell, Brickley, and Netter (1988). Lichtenberg and Siegel (1987, 1990a) analyze census data on 18,000 plants and 33,000 auxiliary establishments in the U.S. manufacturing sector in the period 1972–1981 and find that changes in ownership significantly increase productivity and reduce administrative overhead.

2. Even the most voracious maximizer of stockholder wealth must care about the other constituencies of the corporation. Value maximizing implies the corporation should expend resources (to the point where marginal costs equal marginal benefits) in the service of customers, employers, communities, and other parties who affect firm value by influencing the terms on which they contract with the organization or through the threat of restrictive regulation or decline in reputation. If this is the meaning of "stakeholder theory," there is no conflict with value maximization as the corporate objective.

3. A short explanation may help here. Consider that most takeover offers averaged a 50% premium over market prices. Assume that a company's shares were trading at $100 apiece. A 50% premium would mean that the takeover bid came in at $150 a share. The pre-LBO owners therefore had seen one-third of the value of their company destroyed or at least gone unrealized.

4. See Baker, Jensen, and Murphy (1988); Jensen and Murphy (1990b).
5. For a discussion of the waste of free cash flow, see Jensen (1986a). For less technical surveys of developments in the takeover market, see Jensen (1986b, 1988).
6. Evidence on stock price increases comes from DeAngelo, DeAngelo, and Rice (1984a). See also Lehn and Poulsen (1988).
7. The average total returns before adjustment for market returns are 235%, with pre-buyout shareholders earning 46.7% and post-buyout investors earning 128%.
8. See Kaplan (1990); see also Marais, Schipper, and Smith (1989).
9. Press reports typically estimate bondholder losses at $1 billion on RJR's $5 billion of debt outstanding prior to the buyout. While it is true that RJR's longest bond fell 20% on the announcement of the proposal, much of RJR's debt was shorter term, and the effect on the shorter-term debt was much smaller.
10. The increase in employment is statistically significant, and the difference from industry trends is insignificantly different from zero. The data cover only companies without significant divestitures in the post-buyout period.
11. These estimates are discussed in detail in Jensen, Kaplan, and Stiglin (1989).
12. I am indebted to Mark Wolfson for helping me see this point.
13. The American Law Institute has proposed a minimum tax on corporate distributions as an alternative way to accomplish "debt disqualification" (American Law Institute, 1988). This proposal would exacerbate the major free cash flow problem facing the American corporate sector by locking into place penalties for the distributions that must occur to resolve the problem. See Jensen (1986a).

4. Theory of the Firm

1. We do not use the term "capital structure" because that term usually denotes the relative quantities of bonds, equity, warrants, trade credit, and so on, that represent the liabilities of a firm. Our theory implies there is another important dimension to this problem—namely, the relative amount of ownership claims held by insiders (management) and outsiders (investors with no direct role in the management of the firm).
2. Reviews of this literature are given by Peterson (1965), Alchian (1965, 1968), Machlup (1967), Shubik (1970), Cyert and Hedrick (1972), Branch (1973), and Preston (1975).
3. See Williamson (1964, 1970, 1975), Marris (1964), Baumol (1959), Penrose (1958), and Cyert and March (1963). Thorough reviews of these and other contributions are given by Machlup (1967) and Alchian (1965).

   Simon (1955) developed a model of human choice incorporating information (search) and computational costs that also has important implications for the behavior of managers. Unfortunately, Simon's work has often been misinterpreted as a denial of maximizing behavior, and misused, especially in the marketing and behavioral science literature. His later use of the term "satisficing" (Simon 1959) has undoubtedly contributed to this confusion because it suggests rejection of maximizing behavior rather than maximization subject to costs of information and of decision making.

4. See Meckling (1976) for a discussion of the fundamental importance of the assumption of resourceful, evaluative, maximizing behavior on the part of individuals in the development of theory. Klein (1976) takes an approach similar to the one we embark on in this chapter in his review of the theory of the firm and the law.

5. See Coase (1937, 1959, 1960), Alchian (1965, 1968), Alchian and Kessel (1962), Demsetz (1967), Alchian and Demsetz (1972), Monson and Downs (1965), Silver and Auster (1969), and McManus (1975).

6. Property rights are of course human rights, that is, rights possessed by human beings. The introduction of the wholly false distinction between property rights and human rights in many policy discussions is surely one of the all-time great semantic flimflams.

7. See Berhold (1971), Ross (1973, 1974a), Wilson (1968, 1969), and Heckerman (1975).

8. Given the optimal monitoring and bonding activities by the principal and agent.

9. These contracts include implicit (informal) as well as explicit (formal) contracts.

10. As it is used in this chapter the term "monitoring" includes more than just measuring or observing the behavior of the agent. It includes efforts on the part of the principal to "control" the behavior of the agent through budget restrictions, compensation policies, operating rules, and the like.

11. As we show later, the existence of positive monitoring and bonding costs will result in the manager of a corporation possessing control over some resources that he can allocate (within certain constraints) to satisfy his own preferences. However, to the extent that he must obtain the cooperation of others in order to carry out his tasks (such as divisional vice presidents) and to the extent that he cannot control their behavior perfectly and costlessly, they will be able to appropriate some of these resources for their own ends. In short, there are agency costs generated at every level of the organization. Unfortunately, the analysis of these more general organizational issues is even more difficult than that of the "ownership and control" issue because the nature of the contractual obligations and rights of the parties are much more varied and generally not as well specified in explicit contractual arrangements. They do exist, nevertheless, and we believe that extensions of our analysis in these directions show promise of producing insights into a viable theory of organization.

12. They define the classical capitalist firm as a contractual organization of inputs in which there is "(a) joint input production, (b) several input owners, (c) one party who is common to all the contracts of the joint inputs, (d) who has rights to renegotiate any input's contract independently of contracts with other input owners, (e) who holds the residual claim, and (f) who has the right to sell his contractual residual status."

13. By "legal fiction" we mean the artificial construct under the law that allows certain organizations to be treated as individuals.

14. For example, we ordinarily think of a product as leaving the firm at the time it is sold, but implicitly or explicitly such sales generally carry with them continuing contracts between the firm and the buyer. If the product does not perform as expected, the buyer often can and does have a right to satisfaction. Explicit evidence that such implicit contracts do exist is the practice we occasionally observe of specific provision that "all sales are final."

15. This view of the firm points up the important role the legal system and the law play in social organizations, especially the organization of economic activity. Statutory laws set bounds on the kinds of contracts into which individuals and organizations may enter without risking criminal prosecution. The police powers of the state are available and used to enforce performance of contracts or to enforce the collection of damages for nonperformance. The courts adjudicate conflicts between contracting parties and establish precedents that form the body of common law. All of these government activities affect both the kinds of contracts executed and the extent to which contracting is relied upon. This in turn determines the usefulness, productivity, profitability, and viability of various forms of organization. Moreover, new laws as well as court decisions often can and do change the rights of contracting parties ex post, and they can and do serve as a vehicle for redistribution of wealth. An analysis of some of the implications of these facts is contained in Jensen and Meckling (1978); we do not pursue them here.

16. For use in consumption, for the diversification of his wealth, or more importantly, for the financing of "profitable" projects he could not otherwise finance out of his personal wealth. We deal with these issues below after having developed some of the elementary analytical tools necessary to their solution.

17. Such as office space, air conditioning, thickness of the carpets, friendliness of employee relations, and so forth.

18. And again we assume that for any given market value of these costs, F, to the firm the allocation across time and across alternative probability distributions is such that the manager's current expected utility is at a maximum.

19. At this stage when we are considering a 100% owner-managed firm, the notion of a "wage contract" with himself has no content. However, the 100% owner-managed case is only an expositional device used in passing to illustrate a number of points in the analysis, and we ask the reader to bear with us briefly while we lay out the structure for the more interesting partial ownership case where such a contract does have substance.

20. The manager's utility function is actually defined over wealth and the future time sequence of vectors of quantities of non-pecuniary benefits, X_t. Although the setting of his problem is somewhat different, Fama (1970b, 1972) analyzes the conditions under which these preferences can be represented as a derived utility function defined as a function of the money value of the expenditures (in our notation F) on these goods conditional on the prices of goods. Such a utility function incorporates the optimization going on in the background that de-

fines $\hat{X}$ discussed above for a given F. In the more general case where we allow a time series of consumption, $\hat{X}_t$, the optimization is being carried out across both time and the components of X_t for fixed F.

21. This excludes, for instance, (a) the case where the manager is allowed to expend corporate resources on anything he pleases, in which case F would be a perfect substitute for wealth, or (b) the case where he can "steal" cash (or other marketable assets) with constant returns to scale—if he could the indifference curves would be straight lines with slope determined by the fence commission.

22. Point D defines the fringe benefits in the optimal pay package since the value to the manager of the fringe benefits, F^*, is greater than the cost of providing them, as is evidenced by the fact that U_2 is steeper to the left of D than the budget constraint with slope equal to -1.

   That D is indeed the optimal pay package can easily be seen in this situation since if the conditions of the sale to a new owner specified that the manager would receive no fringe benefits after the sale, he would require a payment equal to V_3 to compensate him for the sacrifice of his claims to V^* and fringe benefits amounting to F^* (the latter with total value to him of $V_3 - V^*$). But if $F = 0$, the value of the firm is only $\overline{V}$. Therefore, if monitoring costs were zero, the sale would take place at V^* with provision for a pay package that included fringe benefits of F^* for the manager.

   This discussion seems to indicate there are two values for the "firm," V_3 and V^*. This is not the case if we realize that V^* is the value of the right to be the residual claimant on the cash flows of the firm and $V_3 - V^*$ is the value of the managerial rights, that is, the right to make the operating decisions that include access to F^*. There is at least one other right that has value but plays no formal role in the analysis as yet—the value of the control right. By "control right" we mean the right to hire and fire the manager, and we leave this issue to a future paper.

23. The distance $V^* - V'$ is a measure of what we will define as the "gross agency costs." The distance $V_3 - V_4$ is a measure of what we call "net agency costs," and it is this measure of agency costs that is minimized by the manager in the general case where we allow investment to change.

24. I^* is the value-maximizing and Pareto-optimal investment level that results from the traditional analysis of the corporate investment decision if the firm operates in perfectly competitive capital and product markets and the agency cost problems discussed here are ignored. See Debreu (1959, chap. 7), Jensen and Long (1972), Long (1972), Merton and Subrahmanyam (1974), Hirshleifer (1970, 1989), and Fama and Miller (1972).

25. Each equilibrium point such as that at E is characterized by $(\hat{\alpha}, \hat{F}, W_T)$ where W_T is the entrepreneur's post-investment financing wealth. Such an equilibrium must satisfy each of the following four conditions:

$$(1) \qquad \hat{W}_T + F = \overline{V}(I) + W - I = \overline{V}(I) - K,$$

where $K \equiv I - W$ is the amount of outside financing required to make the investment I. If this condition is not satisfied there is an uncompensated wealth transfer (in one direction or the other) between the entrepreneur and outside equity buyers.

(2) $$U_F(\hat{W}_T,\hat{F})/U_{W_T}(\hat{W}_T,\hat{F}) = \hat{\alpha},$$

where U is the entrepreneur's utility function on wealth and perquisites, U_F and U_{W_T} are marginal utilities, and $\hat{\alpha}$ is the manager's share of the firm.

(3) $$(1 - \hat{\alpha})V(I) = (1 - \hat{\alpha})[\overline{V}(I) - \hat{F}] \geq K,$$

which says the funds received from outsiders are at least equal to K, the minimum required outside financing.

(4) Among all points $(\hat{\alpha},\hat{F},\hat{W}_T)$ satisfying conditions (1)–(3), (α, F, W_T) gives the manager highest utility. This implies that $(\hat{\alpha},\hat{F}, W_T)$ satisfy condition (3) as an equality.

26. *Proof.* Note that the slope of the expansion path (or locus of equilibrium points) at any point is $(\Delta V - \Delta I)/\Delta F$ and at the optimum level of investment this must be equal to the slope of the manager's indifference curve between wealth and market value of fringe benefits, F. Furthermore, in the absence of monitoring, the slope of the indifference curve, $\Delta W/\Delta F$, at the equilibrium point, D, must be equal to $-\alpha'$. Thus,

$$(\Delta V - \Delta I)/\Delta F = -\alpha' \tag{2}$$

is the condition for the optimal scale of investment and this implies that condition (1) holds for small changes at the optimum level of investment, I'.

27. Since the manager's indifference curves are negatively sloped, we know that the optimum scale of the firm, point D, will occur in the region where the expansion path has negative slope, that is, the market value of the firm will be declining and the *gross* agency costs, A, will be increasing, and thus the manager will not minimize them in making the investment decision (even though he will minimize them for any *given* level of investment). However, we define the *net* agency cost as the dollar equivalent of the welfare loss the manager experiences because of the agency relationship evaluated at $F = 0$ (the vertical distance between the intercepts on the Y axis of the two indifference curves on which points C and D lie). The optimum solution, I', does satisfy the condition that net agency costs are minimized. But this simply amounts to a restatement of the assumption that the manager maximizes his welfare.

Finally, it is possible for the solution point D to be a corner solution, and in this case the value of the firm will not be declining. Such a corner solution can occur, for instance, if the manager's marginal rate of substitution between F and wealth falls to zero fast enough as we move up the expansion path, or if the investment projects are "sufficiently" profitable. In these cases the expansion path will have a corner that lies on the maximum value budget constraint with intercept $\overline{V}(I^*) - I^*$, and the level of investment will be equal to the idealized optimum, I^*. However, the market value of the residual claims will be less than V^* because the manager's consumption of perquisites will be larger than F^*, the zero agency cost level.

28. The careful reader will note that point C will be the equilibrium point only if the contract between the manager and outside equity holders specifies with no ambiguity that they have the right to monitor to limit his consumption of perquisites to an amount no less than F''. If any ambiguity regarding these rights exists in this contract, then another source of agency costs arises which is symmetrical to our original problem. If they could do so the outside equity holders would monitor to the point where the net value of *their* holdings, $(1 - \alpha)V - M$, was maximized, and this would occur when $(\partial V/\partial M)(1 - \alpha) - 1 = 0$, which would be at some point between points C and E in Figure 4.3. Point E denotes the point where the value of the firm net of the monitoring costs is at a maximum, that is, where $\partial V/\partial M - 1 = 0$. But the manager would be worse off than in the zero monitoring solution if the point where $(1 - \alpha)V - M$ was at a maximum were to the left of the intersection between BCE and the indifference curve U_3 passing through point B (which denotes the zero monitoring level of welfare). Thus if the manager could not eliminate enough of the ambiguity in the contract to push the equilibrium to the right of the intersection of the curve BCE with indifference curve U_3 he would not engage in any contract that allowed monitoring.

29. If we could establish the existence of a feasible set of alternative institutional arrangements that would yield net benefits from the reduction of these costs, we could legitimately conclude the agency relationship engendered by the corporation was not Pareto-optimal. However, we would then be left with the problem of explaining why these alternative institutional arrangements have not replaced the corporate form of organization.

30. The monitoring and bonding costs will differ from firm to firm depending on such factors as the inherent complexity and geographical dispersion of operations, and the attractiveness of perquisites available in the firm (consider the mint).

31. Where competitors are numerous and entry is easy, persistent departure from profit-maximizing behavior inexorably leads to extinction. Economic natural selection holds the stage. In these circumstances, the behavior of the individual units that constitute the supply side of the product market is essentially routine and uninteresting and economists can confidently predict industry behavior without being explicitly concerned with the behavior of these individual units.

    When the conditions of competition are relaxed, however, the opportunity set of the firm is expanded. In this case, the behavior of the firm as a distinct operating unit is of separate interest. Both for purposes of interpreting particular behavior within the firm and for predicting responses of the industry aggregate, it may be necessary to identify the factors that influence the firm's choices within this expanded opportunity set and embed these in a formal model (Williamson 1964, p. 2).

32. Assuming there are no special tax benefits to ownership nor utility of ownership other than that derived from the direct wealth effects of ownership, such as might be true for professional sports teams, race horse stables, firms that carry the family name, and so forth.

33. Marris (1964, pp. 7–9) is the exception, although he argues that there exists some "maximum leverage point" beyond which the chances of "insolvency" are in some undefined sense too high.

34. By "limited liability" we mean the same conditions that apply to common stock. Subordinated debt or preferred stock could be constructed that carried with it liability provisions; that is, if the corporation's assets were insufficient at some point to pay off all prior claims (such as trade credit, accrued wages, senior debt, and the like) and if the personal resources of the "equity" holders were also insufficient to cover these claims, the holders of this "debt" would be subject to assessments beyond the face value of their claim (assessments that might be limited or unlimited in amount).

35. Alchian and Demsetz (1972, p. 709) argue that one can explain the existence of both bonds and stock in the ownership structure of firms as the result of differing expectations regarding the outcomes to the firm. They argue that bonds are created and sold to "pessimists" and stocks with a residual claim with no upper bound are sold to "optimists."

   As long as capital markets are perfect with no taxes or transaction costs and individual investors can issue claims on distributions of outcomes on the same terms as firms, such actions on the part of firms cannot affect their values. The reason is simple. Suppose such "pessimists" did exist and yet the firm issues only equity claims. The demand for those equity claims would reflect the fact that the individual purchaser could on his own account issue "bonds" with a limited and prior claim on the distribution of outcomes on the equity that is exactly the same as that which the firm could issue. Similarly, investors could easily unlever any position by simply buying a proportional claim on both the bonds and stocks of a levered firm. A levered firm could therefore not sell at a different price than an unlevered firm solely because of the existence of such differential expectations. See Fama and Miller (1972, chap. 4) for an excellent exposition of these issues.

36. Corporations did use both prior to the institution of the corporate income tax in the United States, and preferred dividends have, with minor exceptions, never been tax deductible.

37. See Kraus and Litzenberger (1975) and Lloyd-Davies (1975).

38. And if there is competitive bidding for the firm from potential owner-managers, the absentee owner will capture the capitalized value of these agency costs.

39. The spectrum of claims that firms can issue is far more diverse than is suggested by our two-way classification—fixed versus residual. There are convertible bonds, equipment trust certificates, debentures, revenue bonds, warrants, and so on. Different bond issues can contain different subordination provisions with respect to assets and interest. They can be callable or non-callable. Preferred stocks can be "preferred" in a variety of dimensions and can contain a variety of subordination stipulations. In the abstract, we can imagine firms issuing claims contingent on a literally infinite variety of states of the world such as those considered in the literature on the time-state-preference models of Arrow (1964b), Debreu (1959), and Hirshleifer (1970).

40. An apt analogy is the way one would play poker on money borrowed at a fixed interest rate, with one's own liability limited to some very small stake. Fama and Miller (1972, pp. 179–180) also discuss and provide a numerical example of an investment decision that illustrates very nicely the potential inconsistency between the interests of bondholders and stockholders.

41. The portfolio diversification issues facing the owner-manager are brought into the analysis in Section 4.5.

42. See Smith (1976) for a review of this option pricing literature and its applications; see also Galai and Masulis (1976), who apply the option pricing model to mergers, and corporate investment decisions.

43. Although we used the option pricing model above to motivate the discussion and provide some intuitive understanding of the incentives facing the equity holders, the option pricing solutions of Black and Scholes (1973) do not apply when incentive effects cause V to be a function of the debt-equity ratio as it is in general and in this example. Long (1974) points out this difficulty with respect to the usefulness of the model in the context of tax subsidies on interest and bankruptcy cost. The results of Merton (1974) and Galai and Masulis (1976) must be interpreted with care since the solutions are strictly incorrect in the context of tax subsidies and agency costs.

44. The numerical example of Fama and Miller (1972, pp. 179–180) is a close representation of this case in a two-period state model. However, they go on to make the following statement on p. 180: "From a practical viewpoint, however, situations of potential conflict between bondholders and shareholders in the application of the market value rule are probably unimportant. In general, investment opportunities that increase a firm's market value by more than their cost both increase the value of the firm's shares and strengthen the firm's future ability to meet its current bond commitments." This first issue regarding the importance of the conflict of interest between bondholders and stockholders is an empirical one, and the last statement is incomplete—in some circumstances the equity holders could benefit from projects whose net effect was to reduce the total value of the firm as they and we have illustrated. The issue cannot be brushed aside so easily.

45. Myers (1977) points out another serious incentive effect on managerial decisions of the existence of debt, which does not occur in our simple single-decision world. He shows that if the firm has the option to take future investment opportunities, the existence of debt that matures after the options must be taken will cause the firm (using an equity value maximizing investment rule) to refuse to take some otherwise profitable projects because they would benefit only the bondholders and not the equity holders. This will (in the absence of tax subsidies to debt) cause the value of the firm to fall. Thus (although Myers does not use the term) these incentive effects also contribute to the agency costs of debt in a manner perfectly consistent with the examples discussed in the text.

46. Black and Scholes (1973) discuss ways in which dividend and future financing policy can redistribute wealth between classes of claimants on the firm.

47. Black, Miller, and Posner (1978) discuss many of these issues with particular reference to the government regulation of bank holding companies.

48. In other words, these costs will be taken into account in determining the yield to maturity on the issue. For an examination of the effects of such enforcement costs on the nominal interest rates in the consumer small loan market, see Benston (1977).

49. To illustrate the fact that it will sometimes pay the manager to incur "bonding" costs to guarantee the bondholders that he will not deviate from his promised behavior, let us suppose that for an expenditure of $\$b$ of the firm's resources he can guarantee that project 1 will be chosen. If he spends these resources and takes project 1, the value of the firm will be $V_1 - b$; and as long as $(V_1 - b) > V_2$, or alternatively $(V_1 - V_2) > b$, he clearly will be better off since his wealth will be equal to the value of the firm minus the required investment, I (which we assumed for simplicity to be identical for the two projects).

On the other hand, to prove that the owner-manager prefers the lowest-cost solution to the conflict, let us assume he can write a covenant into the bond issue that will allow the bondholders to prevent him from taking project 2, if they incur monitoring costs of $\$m$, where $m < b$. If he does this, his wealth will be higher by the amount $b - m$. To see this, note that if the bond market is competitive and makes unbiased estimates, potential bondholders will be indifferent between:

(i) a claim X^* with no covenant (and no guarantees from management) at a price of B_2;

(ii) a claim X^* with no covenant (and guarantees from management, through bonding expenditures by the firm of $\$b$, that project 1 will be taken) at a price of B_1; and

(iii) a claim X^* with a covenant and the opportunity to spend m on monitoring (to guarantee project 1 will be taken) at a price of $B_1 - m$.

The bondholders will realize that (i) represents in fact a claim on project 2 and that (ii) and (iii) represent a claim on project 1 and are thus indifferent between the three options at the specified prices. The owner-manager, however, will not be indifferent between incurring the bonding costs, b, directly, or including the covenant in the bond indenture and letting the bondholders spend m to guarantee that he take project 1. His wealth in the two cases will be given by the value of his equity plus the proceeds of the bond issue less the required investment, and if $m < b < V_1 - V_2$, then his post-investment-financing wealth, W, for the three options will be such that $W_i < W_{ii} < W_{iii}$. Therefore, since it would increase his wealth, he would voluntarily include the covenant in the bond issue and let the bondholders monitor.

We would like to mention, without going into the problem in detail, that similar to the case in which the outside equity holders are allowed to monitor the manager-owner, the agency relationship between the bondholders and stockholders has a symmetry if the rights of the bondholders to limit actions of the manager are not perfectly spelled out. Suppose the bondholders, by spending sufficiently large amounts of resources, could force management to take actions that would transfer wealth from the equity holders to the bondholders (by taking sufficiently less risky projects). One can easily construct situations where such actions could make the bondholders better off, hurt the equity holders, and actually lower the total value of the firm. Given the nature of the debt contract, the original owner-manager might maximize his wealth in such a situation by selling off the equity and keeping the bonds as his "owner's" interest. If the nature of the bond contract is given, this may well be an inefficient solution since the total agency costs (i.e., the sum of monitoring and value loss) could easily be higher than the alternative solution. However, if the owner-manager could strictly limit the rights of the bondholders (perhaps by inclusion of a provision that expressly reserves all rights not specifically granted to the bondholder for the equity holder), he would find it in his interest to establish the efficient contractual arrangement since by minimizing the agency costs he would be maximizing his wealth. These issues involve the fundamental nature of contracts and for now we simply assume that the rights of bondholders are strictly limited and unambiguous and that all rights not specifically granted them are reserved for the stockholders—a situation descriptive of actual institutional arrangements. This allows us to avoid the incentive effects associated with bondholders potentially exploiting stock-holders.

50. If the firm were allowed to sell assets to meet a current debt obligation, bankruptcy would occur when the total market value of the future cash flows expected to be generated by the firm is less than the value of a current payment on a debt obligation. Many bond indentures do not, however, allow for the sale of assets to meet debt obligations.

51. While this is true in principle, the actual behavior of the courts frequently involves the provision of some settlement to the common stockholders even when the assets of the company are not sufficient to cover the claims of the creditors.

52. If under bankruptcy the bondholders have the right to fire the management, the management will have some incentives to avoid taking actions that increase the probability of this event (even if it is in the best interest of the equity holders) if they (the management) are earning rents or if they have human capital specialized to this firm or if they face large adjustment costs in finding new employment. A detailed examination of this issue involves the value of the control rights (the rights to hire and fire the manager), and we leave it to a subsequent paper.

53. Kraus and Litzenberger (1975) and Lloyd-Davies (1975) demonstrate that the total value of the firm will be reduced by these costs.

54. These include only payments to all parties for legal fees, professional services, trustees' fees, and filing fees. They do not include the costs of management time or changes in cash flows due to shifts in the firm's demand or cost functions discussed later in this chapter.

55. Which, incidentally, exist only when the debt has some probability of default.

56. Our theory is capable of explaining why in the absence of the tax subsidy on in-

terest payments, we would expect to find firms using both debt and preferred stocks—a problem that has long puzzled at least one of the authors. If preferred stock has all the characteristics of debt except for the fact that its holders cannot put the firm into bankruptcy in the event of nonpayment of the preferred dividends, then the agency costs associated with the issuance of preferred stock will be lower than those associated with debt by the present value of the bankruptcy costs.

However, these lower agency costs of preferred stock exist only over some range if, as the amount of such stock rises, the incentive effects caused by their existence impose value reductions that are larger than that caused by debt (including the bankruptcy costs of debt). There are two reasons for this. First, the equity holder's claims can be eliminated by the debtholders in the event of bankruptcy, and second, the debtholders have the right to fire the management in the event of bankruptcy. Both of these will tend to become more important as an advantage to the issuance of debt as we compare situations with large amounts of preferred stock to equivalent situations with large amounts of debt because they will tend to reduce the incentive effects of large amounts of preferred stock.

57. One other condition also has to hold to justify the incurrence of the costs associated with the use of debt or outside equity in our firm. If there are other individuals in the economy who have sufficiently large amounts of personal capital to finance the entire firm, our capital-constrained owner can realize the full capital value of his current and prospective projects and avoid the agency costs by simply selling the firm (i.e., the right to take these projects) to one of these individuals. He will then avoid the wealth losses associated with the agency costs caused by the sale of debt or outside equity. If no such individuals exist, it will pay him (and society) to obtain the additional capital in the debt market. This implies, incidentally, that it is somewhat misleading to speak of the owner-manager as the individual who bears the agency costs. One could argue that it is the project that bears the costs since, if it is not sufficiently profitable to cover all the costs (including the agency costs), it will not be taken. We continue to speak of the owner-manager bearing these costs to emphasize the more correct and important point that he has the incentive to reduce them because, if he does, his wealth will be increased.

58. We continue to ignore for the moment the additional complicating factor involved with the portfolio decisions of the owner, and the implied acceptance of potentially diversifiable risk by such 100% owners in this example.

59. We continue to ignore such instruments as convertible bonds and warrants.

60. Note, however, that even when outsiders own none of the equity, the stockholder-manager still has some incentives to engage in activities that yield him non-pecuniary benefits but reduce the value of the firm by more than he personally values the benefits if there is any risky debt outstanding. Any such actions he takes that reduce the value of the firm, V, tend to reduce the value of the bonds as well as the value of the equity. Although the option pricing model does not in general apply exactly to the problem of valuing the debt and equity

of the firm, it can be useful in obtaining some qualitative insights into matters such as this. In the option pricing model, $\partial S/\partial V$ indicates the rate at which the stock value changes per dollar change in the value of the firm (and similarly for $\partial S/\partial V$). Both of these terms are less than unity (cf. Black and Scholes 1973). Therefore, any action of the manager that reduces the value of the firm, V, tends to reduce the value of both the stock and the bonds, and the larger is the total debt-equity ratio, the smaller is the impact of any given change in V on the value of the equity, and therefore the lower is the cost to him of consuming non-pecuniary benefits.

61. This occurs, of course, not at the intersection of $A_{S_o}(E)$ and $A_B(E)$, but at the point where the absolute value of the slopes of the functions are equal—that is, where $A'_{S_o}(E) + A'_B(E) = 0$.

62. On the average, however, top managers seem to have substantial holdings in absolute dollars. A recent survey by Wytmar (1974, p. 1) reported that the median value of 826 chief executive officers' stockholdings in their companies at year end 1973 was \$557,000, and it was \$1.3 million at year end 1972.

63. These diversification effects can be substantial. Evans and Archer (1968) show that, for NYSE-listed securities, on average approximately 55% of the total risk (as measured by standard deviation of portfolio returns) can be eliminated by following a naive strategy of dividing one's assets equally among forty randomly selected securities.

64. The work of Myers (1977), which views future investment opportunities as options and investigates the incentive effects of the existence of debt in such a world where a sequence of investment decisions is made, is another important step in the investigation of the multiperiod aspects of the agency problem and the theory of the firm.

65. Becker and Stigler (1974) analyze a special case of this problem involving the use of nonvested pension rights to help correct for this end game play in the law enforcement area.

66. By our colleague David Henderson.

67. This also suggests that *some* outside debtholders can protect themselves from "exploitation" by the manager by purchasing a fraction of the total equity equal to their fractional ownership of the debt. All debtholders, of course, cannot do this unless the manager does so also. In addition, such an investment rule restricts the portfolio choices of investors and therefore would impose costs if followed rigidly. Thus the agency costs will not be eliminated this way either.

68. Consider the situation in which the bondholders have the right in the event of bankruptcy to terminate his employment and therefore to terminate the future returns to any specific human capital or rents he may be receiving.

69. See Fama (1970a) for a survey of this "efficient markets" literature.

70. See Jensen (1969) for an example of this evidence and references.

71. Ignoring any pure consumption elements in the demand for security analysis.

72. Again ignoring the value of the pure consumption elements in the demand for security analysis.

5. Stockholder, Manager, and Creditor Interests

1. See, for example, Chapter 4 of this volume, Modigliani and Miller (1958), Fama and Miller (1972), Black and Cox (1976), Myers (1977), Black et al. (1978), and Smith and Warner (1979).

6. Rights and Production Functions

1. At the Conference on the Effects of Labor Participation in the Management of Business Firms in the Western World, Armen Alchian pointed out to us that a parallel problem exists in defining utility functions—that is, the utility function is conditioned on the set of rights associated with the goods that enter the function. The utility of a good depends on the uses to which the good can be put, and those uses depend on the structure of rights. Can I, for instance, make wine out of "my" grapes as well as eat them? Can I drive "my" car at speeds in excess of fifty-five miles per hour? The content of the word "my" is ultimately the question of rights, as the "owners" of domestic oil during periods of federal oil price controls can testify. Lee Marvin also comes to mind: he lost an early major "palimony" case and paid substantial alimony to a girlfriend he never married.

2. The closest thing to exceptions are professional partnerships (law, accounting, etc.) and cooperatives. The latter have never been very important and the former are limited to specialized service industries. These institutional forms are discussed in more detail below.

3. What little factual material known about the experiences with codetermination in Europe is largely due to the efforts of organizational psychologists. In addition, their work has completely dominated the reports of the various official commissions (German, English, and Swedish) responsible for studying the subject (see Batstone 1976; Biedenkopf 1970; Bulletin of the European Communities 1972, 1975; Bulletin of the Press and Information Office of the Government of the Federal Republic of Germany 1976; Davies 1976; Martin 1976). Unfortunately, their results are not very useful in attempting to assess the social consequences of codetermination. They have tended to focus on how codetermination affects decision processes rather than on how it affects human welfare; whether, for example, labor representatives end up being ineffective as agents for their constituency because they lack knowledge or because of legal sanctions; or whether the important decisions are in fact made by the supervisory boards. Their focus on organizational process leads them to rely on opinion surveys and informal discussions for evidence as to the impact of codetermination. They have shown little interest in the welfare effects of codetermination—that is, what happens to economic growth or how codetermination affects costs, the rate of innovation, and capital impact on the welfare of workers. In industries and in countries where codetermination has been prevalent there has been little effort to measure the effect (if any) on the pecuniary and nonpecuniary aspect of employment.

While it is difficult to characterize accurately the views of a group by citing a single source, the following seems to us to be a fair statement of the position taken by the organizational psychologists writing on these issues: "In sum, then, a consideration of the European experience of worker representation at board level suggests that, to be even marginally effective as a meaningful form of industrial democracy, workers require parity representation on a meaningful board, a formal recognition of their link with trade unions, and a less restricted notion of board secrecy. Without such conditions worker directors are trivial in democratic terms. Even with such conditions the European experience suggests that conventional business interests will not be endangered" (Batstone 1976, p. 43). In brief, they take industrial democracy as desirable per se, and their primary concern is whether existing laws effectively bring it about.

4. Mainly mining and steel.

5. "Parity" is used in these circles to refer to equal representation on the board of directors for both workers and stockholders.

6. Such comparisons can be found in Ward (1958), Domar (1966), Oi and Clayton (1968), Pejovich (1969), Vanek (1970, 1971, 1974), Maurice and Ferguson (1972), Meade (1972, 1974), Vanek (1972), Furubotn and Pejovich (1973), Dreze (1974, 1976), Furubotn (1976), and Steinherr and Vanek (1976). For other discussions of relevance to the labor-managed firm and the codetermination movement, see Atkinson (1973), *Economist* (1976), DeVany (1977), Henderson (1977), Ryden (1978), and Shenfield (1978).

7. This quote from Meade provides an example of how writers on this subject gloss over the fact that what really characterizes these economies is a prohibition against other kinds of firms. An accurate statement would read, "A system in which the *only kind of organization legalized* is one in which, etc." While we are critical of Meade, his work certainly represents some of the better analysis in this area that is not couched specifically in the property-rights framework.

8. An alternative model sometimes postulated is one in which all claims on producer assets are held by a central government organization "which lends out the State's capital resources at rentals which will clear the market" (Meade 1972, p. 402). There is no analysis or even a structure presented that implies that this rule would actually be used by a government agency if it were given the power to allocate producer assets. Our theory suggests that such a result is highly unlikely, and there is overwhelming evidence from the behavior of political systems around the world consistent with that theory. This perfectly functioning government organization is an excellent example of Nirvana fallacy pointed out by Coase (1964) and Demsetz (1969).

9. See Meade (1972) for a lucid summary and "proofs" of these propositions as well as others.

10. This result requires the assumption that in the short run the cost of entry is infinite. On the other hand, Proposition 1 requires that entry is costless in the long run. The multiproduct firm will in general increase the output of the product whose price has risen but will reduce the output of all other products

and will reduce the quantity of labor demanded so that on net the firm's labor force will fall.

11. To see this, recognize that at the traditional monopoly solution profits are at a maximum. Therefore, an infinitesimally small reduction in labor input will cause a small reduction in output and no change in the level of profits but will cause an increase in average labor earnings (the ratio of "profits" plus wages to number of employees). Therefore, it pays the members of the labor-managed firm to restrict output below that of the usual monopolist. (See Meade 1972, 1974.)

12. The literature on the pure-rental firm generally says little or nothing about adjustment on the capital side. What is particularly troublesome is how newly formed firms induce production of new capital to accommodate increased demand. If the demand for capital rises, capital-goods-producing firms will want to contract output rather than expand it; and it is not easy to see in this case how newly formed capital-producing firms can come into existence to save the analysis, since they, too, will have to get capital somewhere.

13. There is an alternative to 1 and 2 as a way to raise funds, namely, through a state agency that obtains the resources either through taxes or borrowing. This alternative is in fact the Yugoslav solution and we will discuss it below.

14. In principle, this problem could be solved or at least mitigated by entry of new firms made up of young workers (i.e., workers with longer horizons who would find it in their interest to take longer-run projects). For some projects (buildings, improvements to land, and so on), however, even their horizons would be too short. More importantly, there would be other real costs to such an arrangement that would make it inefficient. There is no reason to believe that the youth population would have in its midst the optimal mix of skills and expertise required to organize and operate a new firm. In fact, there is every reason to believe this would not be the case. As existing tractor manufacturing equipment wears out, for example, we would expect it to be much less costly to replace that equipment in an ongoing tractor firm (with experienced personnel, and so on) than it would be to start an entirely new firm.

15. The existence of the savings bank per se is not crucial to this discussion. Even nondemocratic Yugoslav-type governments allow some individual wealth accumulation. They usually sanction private claims on productive consumer assets like precious stones, jewelry, art, antiques, fine china, tableware, and an array of what are usually referred to as "consumer durables." These consumer assets represent nontrivial alternative investment opportunities with their own rates of return (pecuniary plus nonpecuniary) that workers weigh in deciding how much investment to make in the firm. Even these alternatives are not essential to the point at issue, however, since in their absence the relevant interest rate for comparison, i, is simply defined as the individual's own marginal rate of substitution between current and future consumption.

16. Jaroslav Vanek successfully gives the impression that he is open to many of the potential faults of the system he analyzes and advocates in his book. He also leaves the reader with the impression that he has analyzed and explained away

the potential problems, as in his comments on the horizon problem: "The more or less philosophical problem arising from the fact that in the future over which the discounting operation is performed different individuals may be employed at different times we dispose of, as before, by postulating that all members of the labor-managed firm are equals, whether in time or space" (1970, pp. 296–297). Dreze (1976) never mentions the horizon problem.

17. We have plenty of evidence on this issue in the form of pension systems for government employees.

18. This result also holds directly if the *flows C, E, C*,* and *E** are perpetuities. In the general multiperiod case with nonuniform cash flows, the present value of an individual worker's share in the cash flow generated by the new project must be large enough to reimburse him for the present value of the loss he suffers from having to share cash flows on past investments with new workers.

19. This point provides a good example of the subtle way that property-rights structures or "rules of the game" influence human behavior and thus production functions.

20. We ignore here the horizon problem introduced by the finite life of individuals.

21. See Jensen (1972) or Fama (1976) for a survey of the literature on portfolio theory, the nature of risk, and the pricing of capital assets in a stock market economy.

22. See Bailey and Jensen (1972) for an exposition of these points and how they affect the social rate of discount for governmental projects.

23. The nonnegotiability provision is required because without it voluntary exchanges by workers of their shares and the reluctance of new workers to buy shares would soon result in a structure identical to the traditional corporate form. Note also that the structure in which labor owns nonnegotiable shares is very close to the codetermined firm—the major differences being the exact definition of the voting rights and powers attached to the negotiable and nonnegotiable shares.

24. The strictly egalitarian sharing rule must be abandoned to prove optimality. Instead, workers are given "shares" in the total earnings that depend on the quality and quantity of their labor. Exactly how these shares are in fact determined is never spelled out. What Dreze argues is that in principle it is possible to set these shares such that the usual marginal productivity conditions hold and this is the presumption used in the "proof" of Proposition 1 (see Dreze 1976, p. 1127). Without establishing the incentives that cause the firm to set the shares in exactly this manner, the proof is little more than a "possibility theorem." This issue is discussed in more detail in Section 6.5.

25. This aspect of the sharing arrangement in fact amounts to forcing the entrepreneur to enter into a contract to share future earnings with future workers whose identities are unknown and for which he receives no compensation—a peculiar contract, to say the least.

26. See Meckling (1976) for an expanded discussion of these issues.

27. This is exactly equivalent to why we cannot buy a Cadillac built exactly to our

specifications at the same price as an "off-the-shelf" version. Furthermore, the additional costs that would be incurred in producing a tailored Cadillac fully explains why we are not now driving one. It isn't worth it!

28. For a discussion of how this problem is resolved among holders of different types of financial claims on the corporation, see Chapter 4 of this volume, Myers (1977), Fama (1978), and Smith and Warner (1979).

29. Furubotn (1976) solves this problem by assuming that an original majority, all of whom have identical utility functions, maintains political control and the manager maximizes their utility.

30. According to Jan Vanek (1972, p. 220), "The danger often referred to in Yugoslavia of the work collectivities 'eating up their factories' can therefore be seen not merely in its crude form of lack of maintenance and of replacement of physical assets, excess distribution and pilfering of resources forming the enterprise's circulating capital, but also in the more subtle form of greater or lesser depreciation of all assets in real terms through improper or inadequate operation of the enterprise."

31. This does not mean that the workers would find it desirable to take all of the assets out of the firm, though those approaching retirement would want to do just that.

32. Jan Vanek (1972, p. 221) provides an example: "The balance sheet capital values of the worker-managed enterprises would have become utterly meaningless in the course of time, were it not for several general revaluations of fixed assets of enterprises, imposed on the economy by Government Orders or (later) special legislative enactments (amounting to approximately 17 percent for each two year period, while a 60 percent revalorization of assets was a part of the 1965 Reform)."

33. Ward gives an example reminiscent of the voting habits of Chicagoans under the Daley Machine: "A phenomenon known as the 'dead brigades' (mrtvi brigadi) may have been an instance of this, *Ekonomska Politika* (1953, 2, 1034), Kardelj (1954, p. 487). For example the coal mining concern mentioned . . . above might hire an unskilled worker for 6000 dinars per month, which would add 8100 dinars to the calculated wage fund, i.e., to labor cost in the accounting sense. This would substantially reduce accounting profits and hence the amount of taxation under the steeply progressive profits tax law. If the firm expected to make a fairly high level of profits, this could be to the monetary advantage of the 'in-group' workers even if the newly hired worker performed no work at all. From above descriptions it seems that the dead brigades in fact had little to do. In some cases the dead brigades were in fact 'dead souls,' fictitious employees" (Ward 1958, pp. 584–585).

34. Furubotn (1976) assumes, for example, that the constraint imposed by the state on maintenance of capital is effective, and he takes the state definition of income as binding in the determination of the annual wage fund.

35. Pejovich (1969) also discusses the issues covered in this section.

36. For example, consider the U.S. post office, projects of the U.S. Army Corps of Engineers, and the English railroads.

37. Setting all prices and output centrally is such a huge task that in fact it cannot be done. See Roberts (1969) for a detailed discussion of these issues.
38. This phenomenon has been tagged with the "moral hazard" label, which carries with it some unfortunate moral connotations of no aid to positive analysis.
39. This is another example of the agency costs defined and analyzed in Chapter 4.

7. Organizational Forms and Investment Decisions

1. Wolfson (1983) documents examples of the dependence of cost functions on organizational form in various forms of oil and gas limited partnerships. In particular, he provides evidence on how the choice of organizational form affects agency costs.
2. If proprietor B both manages the corporation and owns shares in it, the corporate opportunity set $F(K;OC)$ depends on B's stock ownership fraction. Figure 7.2 portrays the polar case in which she sells off all her claims on the corporation. In Chapter 4, Jensen and Meckling analyze the intermediate cases in which the proprietor maintains both management and stock ownership interests in the corporation.
3. Reagan and Stulz (1986) analyze situations in which workers bear "too little" risk and charge less than the market price for risk bearing.
4. See Wakeman (1981) for additional analysis and evidence on the function of bond rating services.
5. John Hetherington and Fischer Black, in a personal communication, pointed out that in many cases the policyholders of mutual insurance companies and the depositors of mutual savings banks are creditors rather than residual claimants because they have no way to force payments in excess of the promised interest on the face value of their claims. Hetherington also suggests that in cases where the assets of such organizations exceed the liabilities to creditors and customers there is a pool of "unowned" assets. In an interesting response to this, Wisconsin law provides that all surplus in liquidation of a mutual insurance company goes to the state school fund. These observations do not invalidate our main point. The redeemability of the claims in mutual insurance companies and savings banks is still a powerful control device.

8. The Distribution of Power among Corporate Managers, Shareholders, and Directors

1. SEC Release No. 34–24623 (June 22, 1987), 17 CFR Part 240.
2. See Fama and Jensen (1983a, 1983b).
3. See Office of the Chief Economist of the SEC (1986); Ryngaert (1988).
4. See Waldo (1985, table 5.1), who shows that all major shareholders represent only 1.6% of *Fortune* 500 directors.

References

Alchian, Armen A. 1950. "Uncertainty, Evolution, and Economic Theory." *Journal of Political Economy* 58, no. 3 (June), pp. 211–221.

—— 1965. "The Basis of Some Recent Advances in the Theory of Management of the Firm." *Journal of Industrial Economics* (November), pp. 30–44.

—— 1968. *Corporate Management Behavior and Property Rights*. Economic Policy and the Regulation of Securities, ed. Henry Manne. Washington, D.C.: American Enterprise Institute.

—— 1974. *Some Implications of Recognition of Property Right Transaction Costs*. First Interlaken Conference on Analysis and Ideology, June 1979. Economics and Social Institute, ed. Karl Bruner. The Hague: Nyhoff.

Alchian, Armen A., and W. R. Allen. 1969. *Exchange and Production: Theory in Use*. Belmont, Calif.: Wadsworth.

Alchian, Armen A., and Harold Demsetz. 1972. "Production, Information Costs, and Economic Organization." *American Economic Review* 62, no. 5 (December), pp. 777–795.

Alchian, Armen A., and R. A. Kessel. 1962. "Competition, Monopoly, and the Pursuit of Pecuniary Gain," in H. Gregg Lewis (ed.), *Aspects of Labor Economics*, pp. 157–182. Princeton, N.J.: National Bureau of Economic Research.

American Bar Foundation. 1971. "Commentaries on Model Debenture Indenture Provisions." Chicago: American Bar Foundation.

American Law Institute. 1988. "Federal Income Tax Project." Tax Advisory Group draft no. 18, subchapter C (supplemental study), part 1, Distribution Issues.

Anderson, Douglas. 1986. "Managing Retreat: Disinvestment Policy," in Thomas K. McCraw (ed.), *America versus Japan*. Boston: Harvard Business School Press, pp. 337–372.

Antle, Rick, and Abbie Smith. 1986. "An Empirical Investigation of the Relative Performance Evaluation of Corporate Executives." *Journal of Accounting Research* 24, no. 1, pp. 1–39.

Argyris, Chris. 1990. *Overcoming Organizational Defenses*. New York: Allyn and Bacon.

Arrow, Kenneth J. 1964a. "Control in Large Organizations." *Management Science* 10 (April), pp. 397–408.

—— 1964b. "The Role of Securities in the Optimal Allocation of Risk Bearing." *Review of Economic Studies* 31, no. 86 (January), pp. 91–96.

Asquith, Paul, and E. Han Kim. 1982. "The Impact of Merger Bids on the Participating Firms' Security Holders." *Journal of Finance* 37, no. 5, pp. 1209–28.

Asquith, Paul, and Thierry A. Wizman. 1990. "Event Risk, Covenants, and Bond-holder Returns in Leveraged Buyouts." *Journal of Financial Economics* 27, no. 1, pp. 195–213.

Atkinson, A. B. 1973. "Worker Management and the Modern Industrial Enterprise." *Quarterly Journal of Economics* 87 (August), pp. 375–392.

Atkinson, T. R. 1967. "Trends in Corporate Bond Quality," in *Studies in Corporate Bond Finance 4*. New York: National Bureau of Economic Research.

Bailey, Martin J., and Michael C. Jensen. 1972. "Risk and the Discount Rate for Public Investments," in Michael C. Jensen (ed.), *Studies in the Theory of Capital Markets*. New York: Praeger.

Baker, George P., Michael C. Jensen, and Kevin J. Murphy. 1988. "Compensation and Incentives: Practice vs. Theory." *Journal of Finance* 43, no. 3, pp. 593–616. Reprinted in Michael C. Jensen, *Foundations of Organizational Strategy* (Cambridge: Harvard University Press, 1998).

Baker, George P., and Karen Wruck. 1989. "Organizational Changes and Value Creation in Leveraged Buyouts: The Case of O. M. Scott & Sons Company." *Journal of Financial Economics* 25, no. 2, pp. 163–190.

Baldwin, Carliss Y. 1982. "Optimal Sequential Investment When Capital Is Not Readily Reversible." *Journal of Finance* 37, no. 3, pp. 763–782.

——— 1988. "Time Inconsistency in Capital Budgeting." Unpublished working paper. Boston: Harvard Business School.

——— 1991. "How Capital Budgeting Deters Innovation—and What to Do About It." *Research Technology Management* 34, no. 6, pp. 39–45.

Baldwin, Carliss Y., and Kim B. Clark. 1992. "Capabilities and Capital Investment: New Perspectives on Capital Budgeting." *Journal of Applied Corporate Finance* 5, no. 2, pp. 67–82.

Baldwin, Carliss Y., and Lenos Trigeorgis. 1992. "Toward Remedying the Under-investment Problem: Competitiveness, Real Options, Capabilities and TQM." Unpublished Working Paper. Boston: Harvard Business School.

Batstone, Eric. 1976. "Industrial Democracy and Worker Representation at Board Level: A Review of the European Experience," in *Industrial Democracy: European Experience. Industrial Democracy Committee Research Report*. London: Her Majesty's Stationery Office.

Baumol, W. J. 1959. *Business Behavior, Value and Growth*. New York: Macmillan.

Baumol, William, Sue Anne Beattey Blackman, and Edward Wolff. 1989. *Productivity and American Leadership*. Cambridge: MIT Press.

Becker, Gary S. 1957. *The Economics of Discrimination*. Chicago: University of Chicago Press.

Becker, Gary S., and George J. Stigler. 1974. "Law Enforcement, Malfeasance, and Compensation of Enforcers." *Journal of Legal Studies* 3 (January), pp. 1–18.

Benston, George J. 1977. "The Impact of Maturity Regulation on High Interest Rate Lenders and Borrowers." *Journal of Financial Economics* 4, no. 1, pp. 23–49.

——— 1985. "The Self-Serving Management Hypothesis: Some Evidence." *Journal of Accounting and Economics* 7, no. 1–3, pp. 67–84.

Berger, Philip, and Eli Ofek. 1993. "Leverage and Value: The Role of Agency Costs and Taxes." Unpublished manuscript. Philadelphia: Wharton School.

Berhold, M. 1971. "A Theory of Linear Profit Sharing Incentives." *Quarterly Journal of Economics* 85 (August), pp. 460–482.

Berle, Adolf A., and Gardiner C. Means. 1932. *The Modern Corporation and Private Property.* New York: Macmillan.

Bhagat, Sanjai. 1983. "The Effect of Pre-Emptive Right Amendments on Shareholder Value." *Journal of Financial Economics* 12, no. 3, pp. 289–310.

Bhagat, Sanjai, and James A. Brickley. 1984. "Cumulative Voting: The Value of Minority Shareholder Voting Rights." *Journal of Law and Economics* 27, no. 2, pp. 339–355.

Bhattacharya, Sudipto. 1979. "Imperfect Information, Dividend Policy, and 'The Bird-in-the-Hand' Fallacy." *Bell Journal of Economics* 10, no. 1, pp. 259–270.

Bhide, Amar. 1993. "The Hidden Costs of Stock Market Liquidity." *Journal of Financial Economics* 34, no. 1, pp. 31–55.

Biedenkopf. 1970. "Mitbestimmung in Unternehmen." *Mitbestimmungs Kommission.*

Black, Bernard S. 1990. "Shareholder Passivity Reexamined." *Michigan Law Review* 89, pp. 520–608.

Black, Fischer. 1976. "The Dividend Puzzle." *Journal of Portfolio Management* 2, no. 2, pp. 5–8.

Black, Fischer, and John Cox. 1976. "Valuing Corporate Securities: Some Effects of Bond Indenture Provisions." *Journal of Finance* 31, no. 2, pp. 351–367.

Black, F., H. Merton, M. H. Miller, and R. A. Posner. 1978. "An Approach to the Regulation of Bank Holding Companies." *Journal of Business* 51, no. 3, pp. 379–412.

Black, F., and M. Scholes. 1973. "The Pricing of Options and Corporate Liabilities." *Journal of Political Economy* 81, no. 3, pp. 637–654.

Bonnier, Karl-Adam, and Robert F. Bruner. 1989. "An Analysis of the Stock Price Reaction to Management Change in Distressed Firms." *Journal of Accounting and Economics* 11, no. 1, pp. 95–106.

Borstadt, L. 1985. "Stock Price Reactions to Management Changes." Unpublished manuscript. Salt Lake City: University of Utah.

Bowen, R. E., E. W. Noreen, and J. Lacey. 1981. "Determinants of the Corporate Decision to Capitalize Interest." *Journal of Accounting and Economics* 3 (August), pp. 151–179.

Bower, Joseph L. 1970. "Planning Within the Firm." *American Economic Review* 60, no. 2, pp. 186–194.

——— 1984. "Restructuring Petrochemicals: A Comparative Study of Business and Government to Deal with a Declining Sector of the Economy," in Bruce R. Scott and George C. Lodge (eds.), *U.S. Competitiveness in the World Economy.* Boston: Harvard Business School Press.

——— 1986. *When Markets Quake.* Boston: Harvard Business School Press.

Boycko, Maxim, Andrei Shleifer, and Robert W. Vishny. 1994. "Voucher Privatization." *Journal of Financial Economics* 35, no. 2, pp. 249–266.

Bradley, Michael, Anand Desai, and E. Han Kim. 1983. "The Rationale Behind Interfirm Tender Offers: Information or Synergy?" *Journal of Financial Economics* 11, no. 1–4, pp. 183–206.

Bradley, Michael, and L. M. Wakeman. 1983. "The Wealth Effects of Targeted Share Repurchases." *Journal of Financial Economics* 11, no. 1–4, pp. 301–328.

Branch, B. 1973. "Corporate Objectives and Market Performance." *Financial Management* 2 (Summer), pp. 24–29.

Brandt, Richard. 1993. "Tiny Transistors and Gold Pizza." *Business Week,* March 29.

Brickley, James A., Sanjai Bhagat, and Ronald C. Lease. 1985a. "The Impact of Long-Range Managerial Compensation Plans on Shareholder Wealth." *Journal of Accounting and Economics* 14, no. 1–3, pp. 115–148.

—— 1985b. "The Incentive Effects of Stock Purchase Plans." *Journal of Financial Economics* 14, no. 2, pp. 195–215.

Brickley, James A., and Frederick H. Dark. 1987. "The Choice of Organizational Form: The Case of Franchising." *Journal of Financial Economics* 18, no. 2, pp. 401–420.

Brickley, James A., Gregg A. Jarrell, and Jeffrey M. Netter. 1988. "The Market for Corporate Control: The Empirical Evidence Since 1980." *Journal of Economic Perspectives* 2, pp. 49–68.

Brickley, James A., Ronald C. Lease, and Clifford W. Smith, Jr. 1988. "Ownership Structure and Voting on Antitakeover Amendments." *Journal of Financial Economics* 20, no. 1–2, pp. 267–291.

Bulletin of the European Communities. 1972. "A Statute for the European Company, the Proposal for a Fifth Directive to Coordinate the Laws of Member States as Regards the Structure of 'Societes Anonymes.'" Supplement: European Communities Commission, October.

—— 1975. "Employee Participation and Company Structure in the European Community." Supplement: European Communities Commission, August.

Bulletin of the Press and Information Office of the Government of the Federal Republic of Germany. 1976. April 6.

Burnham, James D. 1993. "Changes and Challenges: The Transformation of the U.S. Steel Industry." In *Policy Study No. 115*. St. Louis: Center for the Study of American Business, Washington University.

Burrough, Brian, and John Hellyar. 1990. *Barbarians at the Gate.* New York: Harper and Row.

Business Week. "Annual R&D Scoreboard."

Carney, William J. 1987. "The Theory of the Firm: Investor Coordination Costs, Control Premiums, and Capital Structure." *Washington University Law Quarterly* 65, pp. 1–67.

Cary, William L. 1974. "Federalism and Corporate Law: Reflections Upon Delaware." *Yale Law Journal* 83 (March), pp. 663–707.

Chandler, Alfred D., Jr. 1977. *The Visible Hand: The Managerial Revolution in American Business.* Cambridge, Mass.: Belknap Press.

—— 1990. *Scale and Scope: The Dynamics of Industrial Capitalism.* Cambridge, Mass.: Belknap Press.

—— 1992. "The Emergence of Managerial Capitalism." Revised by Thomas J. McCraw, Harvard Business School case no. 9–384–081. Boston: Harvard Business School.

Christensen, Clayton. 1993. "The Rigid Disk Drive Industry 1956–1990: A History of Commercial and Technological Turbulence." *Business History Review* 67, no. 4, pp. 531–588.

Coase, Ronald H. 1937. "The Nature of the Firm," in *Readings in Price Theory.* New series, V. Homewood, Ill.: Irwin, pp. 331–351.

—— 1959. "The Federal Communications Commission." *Journal of Law and Economics* 2 (October), pp. 1–40.

—— 1960. "The Problem of Social Cost." *Journal of Law and Economics* 3 (October), pp. 1–44.

—— 1964. "Discussion." *American Economic Review* 54, no. 3, pp. 194–197.

Comment, Robert, and G. William Schwert. 1995. "Poison or Placebo? Evidence on the Deterrent and Wealth Effects of Modern Antitakeover Measures." *Journal of Financial Economics* 39, no. 1, pp. 3–43.

Compustat Financial Database. Standard & Poor.

Coughlan, Anne T., and Ronald M. Schmidt. 1985. "Executive Compensation, Management Turnover and Firm Performance: An Empirical Investigation." *Journal of Accounting and Economics* 7, no. 1–3, pp. 43–66.

Cyert, R. M., and C. L. Hedrick. 1972. "Theory of the Firm: Past, Present and Future: An Interpretation." *Journal of Economic Literature* 10 (June), pp. 398–412.

Cyert, R. M., and J. G. March. 1963. *A Behavioral Theory of the Firm.* Englewood Cliffs, N.J.: Prentice-Hall.

Dann, Larry Y., and Harry DeAngelo. 1988. "Corporate Financial Policy and Corporate Control: A Study of Defensive Adjustments in Asset and Ownership Structure." *Journal of Financial Economics* 20, no. 1–2, pp. 87–127.

Davies, P. L. 1976. "European Experience with Worker Representation on the Board." In *Industrial Democracy: European Experience. Industrial Democracy Committee Research Report.* London: Her Majesty's Stationery Office.

Deakin, E. B. 1979. "An Analysis of Difference Between Non-Major Oil Firms Using Successful Efforts and Full Cost Methods." *Accounting Review* 54, pp. 722–734.

DeAlessi, L. 1973. "Private Property and Dispersion of Ownership in Large Corporations." *Journal of Finance* 28, no. 4, pp. 839–851.

DeAngelo, Harry. 1991. "Union Negotiations and Corporate Policy: A Study of Labor Concessions in the Domestic Steel Industry During the 1980s." *Journal of Financial Economics* 30, no. 1, pp. 3–43.

DeAngelo, Harry, and Linda DeAngelo. 1985. "Managerial Ownership of Voting

Rights: A Study of Public Corporations with Dual Classes of Common Stock." *Journal of Financial Economics* 14, no. 1, pp. 33–70.

———. 1986. "Management Buyouts of Publicly Traded Corporations," in Thomas E. Copeland (ed.), *Modern Finance and Industrial Economics: Papers in Honor of J. Fred Weston.* Oxford: Basil Blackwell.

———. 1989. "Proxy Contests and the Governance of Publicly Held Corporations." *Journal of Financial Economics* 23, no. 1, pp. 29–59.

———. 1991. "Union Negotiations and Corporate Policy: A Study of Labor Concessions in the Domestic Steel Industry during the 1980s." *Journal of Financial Economics* 30, no. 1, pp. 3–43.

DeAngelo, Harry, Linda DeAngelo, and Stuart C. Gilson. 1994. "The Collapse of First Executive Corporation: Junk Bonds, Adverse Publicity and the 'Run on the Bank' Phenomenon." *Journal of Financial Economics* 36, no. 3, pp. 287–336.

DeAngelo, Harry, Linda DeAngelo, and Edward M. Rice. 1984a. "Going Private: Minority Freezeouts and Shareholder Wealth." *Journal of Law and Economics* 27, no. 2, pp. 367–401.

———. 1984b. "Going Private: The Effects of a Change in Corporate Ownership Structure." *Midland Corporate Finance Journal* (Summer).

DeAngelo, Harry, and Edward M. Rice. 1983. "Antitakeover Charter Amendments and Stockholder Wealth." *Journal of Financial Economics* 11, no. 1–4, pp. 329–360.

DeAngelo, Linda. 1986. "Accounting Numbers as Market Valuation Substitutes: A Study of Management Buyouts of Public Stockholders." *Accounting Review* 61, pp. 400–420.

———. 1988. "Managerial Competition, Information Costs and Corporate Governance: The Use of Accounting Performance Measures in Proxy Contests." *Journal of Accounting and Economics* 10 (January), pp. 3–36.

Debreu, Gerard. 1959. *Theory of Value.* New York: John Wiley.

Demsetz, Harold. 1967. "Toward a Theory of Property Rights." *American Economic Review* 57 (May), pp. 347–359.

———. 1969. "Information and Efficiency: Another Viewpoint." *Journal of Law and Economics* 12 (April), pp. 1–22.

———. 1982. *Economic, Legal, and Political Dimensions of Competition.* Amsterdam: North-Holland.

———. 1983. "The Structure of Ownership and the Theory of the Firm." *Journal of Law and Economics* 26, pp. 375–390.

Demsetz, Harold, and Kenneth Lehn. 1985. "The Structure of Corporate Ownership: Causes and Consequences." *Journal of Political Economy* 93, pp. 1155–77.

Denis, David J. 1994. "Organizational Form and the Consequences of Highly Leveraged Transactions: Kroger's Recapitalization and Safeway's LBO." *Journal of Financial Economics* 36, no. 2, pp. 193–224.

DeVany, Arthur. 1977. "Land Reform and Agricultural Evidence in Mexico: A General Equilibrium Analysis," in Karl Brunner and Allan Meltzer (eds.), *In-*

ternational Organization, National Policies, and Economic Development. Carnegie-Rochester Conference Series on Public Policy, vol. 6. Amsterdam: North-Holland.

Dhaliwal, D. 1980. "The Effect of the Firm's Capital Structure on the Choice of Accounting Methods." *Accounting Review* 55, pp. 78–84.

Dhaliwal, Dan S., Gerald Salamon, and E. Dan Smith. 1982. "The Effect of Owner Versus Management Control on the Choice of Accounting Methods." *Journal of Accounting and Economics* 4 (July), pp. 41–53.

Diamond, P. A. 1967. "The Role of Stock Market in a General Equilibrium Model with Technological Uncertainty." *American Economic Review* 57 (September), pp. 759–776.

Dobrzynski, Judith. 1993. "Relationship Investing." *Business Week,* March 15.

Dodd, Peter, and Richard Leftwich. 1980. "The Market for Corporate Charters: 'Unhealthy Competition' versus Federal Regulation." *Journal of Business* 53 (July), pp. 259–283.

Dodd, Peter, and Jerold B. Warner. 1983. "On Corporate Governance: A Study of Proxy Contests." *Journal of Financial Economics* 11, no. 1–4, pp. 401–438.

Domar, E. 1966. "The Soviet Collective Farm as a Producer Cooperative." *American Economic Review* 56 (September), pp. 734–757.

Donaldson, Gordon. 1990. "Voluntary Restructuring: The Case of General Mills." *Journal of Financial Economics* 27, no. 1, pp. 117–141.

Dreze, Jacques H. 1974. "The Pure Theory of Labour-Managed and Participatory Economics Part I: Certainty." CORE Discussion Paper no. 7422. University Catholique de Louvain.

—— 1976. "Some Theory of Labor Management and Participation." *Econometrica* 44, no. 6, pp. 1125–39.

Easterbrook, Frank H. 1984. "Two Agency-Cost Explanations of Dividends." *American Economic Review* 74, pp. 650–659.

Easterbrook, Frank H., and Daniel R. Fischel. 1982. "Corporate Control Transactions." *Yale Law Journal* 91, pp. 698–737.

—— 1983. "Voting in Corporate Law." *Journal of Law and Economics* 26, no. 2, pp. 395–427.

Easterbrook, Frank H., and Gregg A. Jarrell. 1984. "Do Targets Gain from Defeating Tender Offers?" *New York University Law Review* 59, pp. 277–299.

Economist. 1976. "Worker-Capitalist Dragon Seed." December 11.

—— 1990. "Out of the Ivory Tower." February 3.

Economist Intelligence Unit. 1991. "Switzerland Country Report." Report no. 3.

Ekonomska Politika. 1953. [*Economic Policy*].

Esty, Benjamin C. 1997a. "A Case Study of Organizational Form and Risk Shifting in the Savings and Loan Industry." *Journal of Financial Economics* 44, no. 1, pp. 57–76.

—— 1997b. "Organizational Form and Risk Taking in the Savings and Loan Industry." *Journal of Financial Economics* 44, no. 1, pp. 25–55.

Evans, J. L., and S. H. Archer. 1968. "Diversification and the Reduction of Dispersion: An Empirical Analysis." *Journal of Finance* 23 (December), pp. 761–767.

Fader, Barnaby J. 1993. "Struggle to Survive in the Town That Steel Forgot." *New York Times,* April 27.

Fama, Eugene F. 1970a. "Efficient Capital Markets: A Review of Theory and Empirical Work." *Journal of Finance* 25, no. 2, pp. 383–417.

—— 1970b. "Multiperiod Consumption-Investment Decisions." *American Economic Review* 55 (March), pp. 163–174.

—— 1972. "Ordinal and Measurable Utility," in Michael C. Jensen (ed.), *Studies in the Theory of Capital Markets.* New York: Praeger.

—— 1976. *Foundations of Finance.* New York: Basic Books.

—— 1978. "The Effects of a Firm's Investment and Financing Decisions on the Welfare of Its Security Holders." *American Economic Review* 68, no. 2, pp. 272–284.

—— 1980. "Agency Problems and the Theory of the Firm." *Journal of Political Economy* 88, no. 2, pp. 288–307.

Fama, Eugene F., and Michael C. Jensen. 1983a. "Agency Problems and Residual Claims." *Journal of Law and Economics* 26, no. 2, pp. 327–349. Reprinted in Michael C. Jensen, *Foundations of Organizational Strategy* (Cambridge: Harvard University Press, 1998).

—— 1983b. "Separation of Ownership and Control." *Journal of Law and Economics* 26 (June), pp. 301–325. Reprinted in Michael C. Jensen, *Foundations of Organizational Strategy* (Cambridge: Harvard University Press, 1998).

Fama, Eugene F., and M. Miller. 1972. *The Theory of Finance.* New York: Holt, Rhinehart, and Winston.

Flath, David. 1980. "The Economics of Short-Term Leasing." *Economic Inquiry* 18, pp. 247–259.

Friedman, Milton. 1970. "The Social Responsibility of Business Is to Increase Its Profits." *New York Times Magazine,* September 13, pp. 32ff.

Furtado, Eugene P., and Vijay Karan. 1990. "Causes, Consequences, and Shareholder Wealth Effects of Management Turnover: A Review of the Empirical Evidence." *Financial Management* 19, no. 2, p. 60.

Furtado, E. P., and M. S. Rozeff. 1987. "The Wealth Effects of Company Initiated Management Changes." *Journal of Financial Economics* 18, no. 1, pp. 147–160.

Furubotn, Eirik G. 1976. "The Long Run Analysis of the Labor-Managed Firm: An Alternative Interpretation." *American Economic Review* 66, no. 1, pp. 104–123.

Furubotn, Eirik G., and S. Pejovich. 1972. "Property Rights and Economic Theory: A Survey of Recent Literature." *Journal of Economic Literature* 10 (December), pp. 1137–62.

—— 1973. "Property Rights, Economic Decentralization, and the Evolution of the Yugoslav Firm, 1965–1972." *Journal of Law and Economics* 16 (October), pp. 275–302.

Galai, D., and R. W. Masulis. 1976. "The Option Pricing Model and the Risk Factor of Stock." *Journal of Financial Economics* 3, no. 1–2, pp. 53–82.

Gersick, Connie J., and J. Richard Hackman. 1990. "Habitual Routines in Task-Performing Teams." *Organizational Behavior and Human Decision Processes* 47, pp. 65–97.

Ghemawat, Pankaj, and Barry Nalebuff. 1985. "Exit." *Rand Journal of Economics* 16, pp. 184–194.

Gibbons, Robert, and Kevin J. Murphy. 1990. "Relative Performance Evaluation for Chief Executive Officers." *Industrial and Labor Relations Review* 43, no. 3, pp. 30–51.

Gilson, Ronald. 1987. "Evaluating Dual Class Common Stock: The Relevance of Substitutes." *Virginia Law Review* 73, pp. 807–844.

Gilson, Ronald, and Reinier Kraakman. 1991. "Reinventing the Outside Director: An Agenda for Institutional Investors." *Stanford Law Review* 43, pp. 863–900.

Gilson, Stuart C. 1989. "Management Turnover and Financial Distress." *Journal of Financial Economics* 25 (December), pp. 241–262.

Gilson, Stuart C., Kose John, and Larry H. P. Lang. 1990. "Troubled Debt Restructurings: An Empirical Study of Private Reorganization of Firms in Default." *Journal of Financial Economics* 27, no. 2, pp. 315–353.

Green, Richard C. 1984. "Investment Incentives, Debt and Warrants." *Journal of Financial Economics* 13, no. 1, pp. 115–136.

Grossman, Sanford J., and Oliver D. Hart. 1982. "Corporate Financial Structure and Managerial Incentives," in John J. McCall (ed.), *The Economics of Information and Uncertainty.* Chicago: University of Chicago Press.

——— 1988. "One Share/One Vote and the Market for Corporate Control." *Journal of Financial Economics* 20, no. 1–2, pp. 175–202.

Grundfest, Joseph. 1990a. "Just Vote No or Just Don't Vote." Unpublished manuscript. Stanford: Stanford Law School.

——— 1990b. "Subordination of American Capital." *Journal of Financial Economics* 27, no. 1, pp. 89–117.

Hackman, J. Richard, ed. 1990. *Groups That Work.* San Francisco: Jossey-Bass.

——— 1993. "Teams, Leaders and Organizations: New Directions for Crew-Oriented Flight Training," in E. L. Weiner, B. G. Kanki, and R. L. Helmreich (eds.), *Cockpit Resource Management.* Orlando: Academic Press.

Hagerman, Robert, and Mark Zmijewski. 1981. "An Income Strategy Approach to the Positive Theory of Accounting Standard Setting/Choice." *Journal of Accounting and Economics* 3, no. 2, pp. 129–149.

Hakansson, Nils H. 1974. "Ordering Markets and the Capital Structures of Firms with Illustrations." Institute of Business and Economic Research Working Paper no. 24. Berkeley: University of California.

——— 1976. "The Purchasing Power Fund: A New Kind of Financial Intermediary." *Financial Analysts Journal* 32, no. 6, p. 49.

——— 1978. "Welfare Aspects of Options and Supershares." *Journal of Finance* 33, no. 3, pp. 759–776.

Hall, Bronwyn H. 1993. "The Stock Market's Valuation of R&D Investment During the 1980s." *American Economic Review* 83, no. 2, pp. 259–265.

Hall, Bronwyn H., Robert E. Hall, John Heaton, and N. Gregory Mankiw. 1993. "The Value and Performance of U.S. Corporations." *Brookings Papers on Economic Activity* no. 1, pp. 1–34.

Hamanda, Robert S., and Myron S. Scholes. 1985. "Taxes and Corporate Financial Management," in Edward I. Altman and Marti G. Subrahmanyam (eds.), *Recent Advances in Corporate Finance*. Homewood, Ill.: Richard D. Irwin.

Handjinicolaou, G., and Avner Kalay. 1984. "Wealth Redistributions or Changes in Firm Value: An Analysis of Returns to the Bondholders and to the Shareholders around Dividend Announcements." *Journal of Financial Economics* 13, no. 1, pp. 35–63.

Harrigan, Kathryn R. 1980. *Strategies for Declining Businesses*. Lexington, Mass.: Lexington Books.

——— 1988. *Managing Maturing Businesses: Restructuring Declining Industries and Revitalizing Troubled Operations*. Lexington, Mass.: Lexington Books.

Harris, Milton. 1991. "The Theory of Capital Structure." *Journal of Finance* 46, pp. 297–355.

Harris, Milton, and Artur Raviv. 1988a. "Corporate Control Contests and Capital Structure." *Journal of Financial Economics* 20, no. 1–2, pp. 55–86.

——— 1988b. "Corporate Governance: Voting Rights and Majority Rules." *Journal of Financial Economics* 20, no. 1–2, pp. 203–235.

Hart, Oliver D., and Bengt Holmstrom. 1987. "The Theory of Contracts," in Truman Bewley (ed.), *Advances in Economic Theory*. Cambridge: Cambridge University Press.

Healy, Paul, and Robert S. Kaplan. 1985. "The Effect of Bonus Schemes on Accounting Decisions." *Journal of Accounting and Economics* 7, no. 1–3, pp. 85–112.

Healy, Paul M., and Krishna G. Palepu. 1995. "The Challenges of Investor Communication: The Case of CUC International, Inc." *Journal of Financial Economics* 38, no. 2, pp. 111–114.

Healy, Paul M., Krishna G. Palepu, and Richard S. Ruback. 1992. "Does Corporate Performance Improve after Mergers?" *Journal of Financial Economics* 31, no. 2, pp. 135–175.

Heard, James E., and Howard D. Sherman. 1987. *Conflicts of Interest in the Proxy System*. Washington, D.C.: Investor Responsibility Research Center.

Heckerman, D. G. 1975. "Motivating Managers to Make Investment Decisions." *Journal of Financial Economics* 2, no. 3, pp. 273–292.

Henderson, David R. 1977. "Land Reform and Agricultural Evidence in Mexico: A Comment," in Karl Brunner and Allan Meltzer (eds.), *International Organization, National Policies, and Economic Development*. Carnegie-Rochester Conference Series on Public Policy, vol. 6. Amsterdam: North-Holland.

Hirschman, Albert. 1970. *Exit, Voice and Loyalty: Responses to Decline in Firms, Organizations and States*. Cambridge: Harvard University Press.

Hirshleifer, Jack. 1970. *Investment, Interest, and Capital.* Englewood Cliffs, N.J.: Prentice-Hall.

—— 1989. "On the Theory of Optimal Investment Decisions," in *Time, Uncertainty, and Information.* Oxford and New York: Blackwell.

Hite, Gailen L., and James E. Owers. 1983. "Security Price Reactions Around Corporate Spin-Off Announcements." *Journal of Financial Economics* 12, no. 4, pp. 409–435.

Ho, Thomas S. Y., and Ronald F. Singer. 1982. "Bond Indenture Provisions and the Risk of Corporate Debt." *Journal of Financial Economics* 10, no. 4, pp. 375–406.

Holderness, Clifford G., and Dennis P. Sheehan. 1988. "The Role of Majority Shareholders in Publicly-held Corporations: An Exploratory Analysis." *Journal of Financial Economics* 20, no. 1–2, pp. 317–346.

—— 1991. "Monitoring an Owner: The Case of Turner Broadcasting." *Journal of Financial Economics* 30, no. 2, pp. 325–346.

Holmstrom, Bengt, and Jean Tirole. 1987. "The Theory of the Firm," in R. Schmalensee and R. Willig (eds.), *Handbook of Industrial Organization.* New York: Elsevier Science.

Ingersoll, Jonathan. 1977. "An Examination of Corporate Call Policies on Convertible Securities." *Journal of Finance* 32, pp. 463–478.

Jarrell, Gregg A. 1985. "The Wealth Effects of Litigation by Targets: Do Interests Diverge in a Merge?" *Journal of Law and Economics* 28, no. 1, pp. 151–177.

Jarrell, Gregg A., James A. Brickley, and Jeffrey M. Netter. 1988. "The Market for Corporate Control: The Empirical Evidence Since 1980." *Journal of Economic Perspectives* 21, pp. 49–68.

Jarrell, Gregg A., and Annette B. Poulsen. 1988. "Dual-class Recapitalizations as Antitakeover Mechanisms: The Recent Evidence." *Journal of Financial Economics* 20, no. 1–2, pp. 129–152.

Jensen, Michael C. 1969. "Risk, the Pricing of Capital Assets, and the Evaluation of Investment Portfolios." *Journal of Business* 42, no. 2, pp. 167–247.

—— 1972. "Capital Markets: Theory and Evidence." *Bell Journal of Economics and Management Science* 3 (Autumn), pp. 357–398.

—— 1979. "Tests of Capital Market Theory and Implications of the Evidence," in James L. Bicksler (ed.), *Handbook of Financial Economics.* New York: North-Holland.

—— 1983. "Organization Theory and Methodology." *Accounting Review* 50 (April). Reprinted in Michael C. Jensen, *Foundations of Organizational Strategy* (Cambridge: Harvard University Press, 1998).

—— 1985. "When Unocal Won Over Pickins, Shareholders and Society Lost." *Financier* 9 (November), pp. 50–52.

—— 1986a. "Agency Costs of Free Cash Flow: Corporate Finance and Takeovers." *American Economic Review* 76 (May), pp. 323–329.

—— 1986b. "The Takeover Controversy: Analysis and Evidence." *Midland Corporate Finance Journal* 4, no. 2, pp. 6–32.

———— 1988. "Takeovers: Their Causes and Consequences." *Journal of Economic Perspectives* 2, pp. 21–48.

———— 1989a. "Active Investors, LBOs, and the Privatization of Bankruptcy." *Journal of Applied Corporate Finance* 2, no. 1, pp. 35–44.

———— 1989b. "Eclipse of the Public Corporation." *Harvard Business Review* 67, no. 5, pp. 61–74.

———— 1991. "Corporate Control and the Politics of Finance." *Journal of Applied Corporate Finance* 4, pp. 13–33.

———— 1994. "Self-Interest, Altruism, Incentives, and Agency Theory." *Journal of Applied Corporate Finance* (Summer). Reprinted in Michael C. Jensen, *Foundations of Organizational Strategy* (Cambridge: Harvard University Press, 1998).

Jensen, Michael C., and Brian K. Barry. 1992. "Gordon Cain and the Sterling Group (A) and (B)." Harvard Business School case no. 9–492–021. Boston: Harvard Business School.

Jensen, Michael C., Willy Burkhardt, and Brian K. Barry. 1992. "Wisconsin Central Ltd. Railroad and Berkshire Partners (A): Leveraged Buyouts and Financial Distress." Harvard Business School case no. 9–190–062. Boston: Harvard Business School.

Jensen, Michael C., Jay Dial, and Brian K. Barry. 1992. "Wisconsin Central Ltd. Railroad and Berkshire Partners (B): LBO Associations and Corporate Governance." Harvard Business School case no. 9–190–070. Boston: Harvard Business School.

Jensen, Michael C., Steven Kaplan, and Laura Stiglin. 1989. "Effects of LBOs on Tax Revenues of the U.S. Treasury." *Tax Notes* 42 (February 6), pp. 727–733.

Jensen, Michael C., and J. B. Long. 1972. "Corporate Investment under Uncertainty and Pareto Optimality in the Capital Markets." *Bell Journal of Economics and Management Science* 3 (Spring), pp. 151–174.

Jensen, Michael C., and William H. Meckling. 1976. "Theory of the Firm: Managerial Behavior, Agency Costs, and Ownership Structure." *Journal of Financial Economics* 3, no. 4, pp. 305–360. Reprinted in Michael C. Jensen, *Foundations of Organizational Strategy* (Cambridge: Harvard University Press, 1998).

———— 1978. "Can the Corporation Survive?" *Financial Analysts Journal* 34, no. 1, p. 31.

———— 1979. "Rights and Production Functions: An Application to Labor-managed Firms and Codetermination." *Journal of Business* 52, no. 4, pp. 469–506.

———— 1992. "Specific and General Knowledge, and Organization Structure," in Lars Werin and Hans Wijkander (eds.), *Contract Economics*. Oxford: Basil Blackwell, pp. 251–274. Reprinted in Michael C. Jensen, *Foundations of Organizational Strategy* (Cambridge: Harvard University Press, 1998), and *Journal of Applied Corporate Finance,* Fall 1995, pp. 4–18.

———— 1994. "The Nature of Man." *Journal of Applied Corporate Finance* 7, no.

2 (Summer), pp. 4–19. Reprinted in Michael C. Jensen, *Foundations of Organizational Strategy* (Cambridge: Harvard University Press, 1998).

Jensen, Michael C., and Kevin J. Murphy. 1990a. "CEO Incentives: It's Not How Much You Pay, But How." *Harvard Business Review* 68, no. 3, pp. 138–153. Reprinted in Michael C. Jensen, *Foundations of Organizational Strategy* (Cambridge: Harvard University Press, 1998).

—— 1990b. "Performance Pay and Top Management Incentives." *Journal of Political Economy* 98, no. 2, pp. 225–284. Reprinted in Michael C. Jensen, *Foundations of Organizational Strategy* (Cambridge: Harvard University Press, 1998).

Jensen, Michael C., and Richard S. Ruback. 1983. "The Market for Corporate Control: The Scientific Evidence." *Journal of Financial Economics* 11, no. 1–4, pp. 5–50.

Jensen, Michael C., and Clifford W. Smith. 1984. "The Theory of Corporate Finance: A Historical Overview," in Michael C. Jensen and Clifford W. Smith (eds.), *The Modern Theory of Corporate Finance*. New York: McGraw-Hill, pp. 2–20.

Jensen, Michael C., and Jerold L. Zimmerman. 1985. "Management Compensation and the Managerial Labor Market." *Journal of Accounting and Economics* 7, pp. 3–9.

Kalay, Avner. 1982. "Stockholder-Bondholder Conflict and Dividend Constraints." *Journal of Financial Economics* 10, no. 2, pp. 211–233.

Kamma, Sreenivas, Joseph Weintrop, and Peggy Wier. 1988. "Investor's Perceptions of the Delaware Supreme Court Decision in Unocal vs. Mesa." *Journal of Financial Economics* 20, no. 1–2, pp. 419–440.

Kaplan, Steven N. 1989a. "Campeau's Acquisition of Federated: Value Destroyed or Value Added." *Journal of Financial Economics* 25, no. 2, pp. 191–212.

—— 1989b. "The Effects of Management Buyouts on Operating Performance and Value." *Journal of Financial Economics* 24, no. 2, pp. 217–254.

—— 1989c. "Management Buyouts: Evidence on Taxes as a Source of Value." *Journal of Finance* 44, pp. 611–632.

—— 1990. "Sources of Value in Managed Buyouts," in Yakov Amihud (ed.), *Leveraged Management Buyouts*. Chicago: Dow Jones–Irwin.

—— 1992. "Campeau's Acquisition of Federated: A Post-petition Post-mortem." *Journal of Financial Economics* 35, no. 1, pp. 123–136.

—— 1995. "Taking Stock of the RJR Nabisco Buyout." *Wall Street Journal*, March 30.

Kaplan, Steven N., and Jeremy Stein. 1993. "The Evolution of Buyout Pricing and Financial Structure in the 1980s." *Quarterly Journal of Economics* 108, pp. 313–358.

Kardelj, E. 1954. "O Nekim Medostacima u Radu Komunista [Certain Shortcomings in the Work of Communists]." *Komunist* 4, pp. 154–70.

Keene, Peter G. 1991. *Every Manager's Guide to Information Technology*. Cambridge: Harvard University Press.

Kester, Carl. 1991. *Japanese Takeovers: The Global Contest for Corporate Control.* Boston: Harvard Business School Press.

Klein, April. 1983. "The Information Content of Voluntary Corporate Divestitures." Unpublished manuscript. New York: Baruch College.

Klein, April, W. Kim, and A. Mahajan. 1985. "Informational Content of Management Changes." Unpublished manuscript. New York: Baruch College.

Klein, April, and James Rosenfeld. 1988. "Targeted Share Repurchases and Top Management Changes." *Journal of Financial Economics* 20, no. 1–2, pp. 493–506.

Klein, Benjamin, Robert Crawford, and Armen A. Alchian. 1978. "Vertical Integration, Appropriate Rents, and the Competitive Contracting Process." *Journal of Law and Economics* 21, no. 2, pp. 297–396.

Klein, William A. 1976. "Legal and Economic Perspectives on the Firm." Unpublished manuscript. Los Angeles: UCLA.

Kraus, A., and R. Litzenberger. 1975. "Market Equilibrium in a Multiperiod State Preference Model with Logarithmic Utility." *Journal of Finance* 30, no. 5, p. 1213.

Lambert, Richard A., and David F. Larcker. 1985. "Golden Parachutes, Executive Decision-Making, and Shareholder Wealth." *Journal of Accounting and Economics* 7 (April), pp. 179–204.

Lamoreaux, Naomi R. 1985. *The Great Merger Movement in American Business, 1895–1904.* Cambridge: Cambridge University Press.

Lang, Larry, Annette Poulsen, and René M. Stulz. 1995. "Asset Sales, Firm Performance, and the Agency Costs of Managerial Discretion." *Journal of Financial Economics* 37, no. 1, pp. 3–37.

Lang, Larry H. P., and René M. Stulz. 1992. "Contagion and Competitive Intraindustry Effects of Bankruptcy Announcements: An Empirical Analysis." *Journal of Financial Economics* 32, no. 1, pp. 45–60.

Lang, Larry H. P., and Ralph A. Walkling. 1991. "A Test of the Free Cash Flow Hypothesis: The Case of Bidder Returns." *Journal of Financial Economics* 29, no. 2, pp. 315–335.

Larcker, David F. 1983. "The Association Between Performance Plan Adoption and Corporate Capital Investment." *Journal of Accounting and Economics* 5, pp. 3–30.

Larner, R. J. 1970. *Management Control and the Large Corporation.* New York: Dunellen.

Lazear, Edward P., and Sherwin Rosen. 1981. "Rank-Order Tournaments as Optimum Labor Contracts." *Journal of Political Economy* 89 (October), pp. 841–864.

Lease, Ronald C., John J. McConnell, and Wayne H. Mikkelson. 1983. "The Market Value of Control in Publicly-traded Corporations." *Journal of Financial Economics* 11, no. 1–4, pp. 439–471.

——— 1984. "The Market Value of Differential Voting Rights in Closely Held Corporations." *Journal of Business* 57, pp. 443–467.

Leftwich, Richard. 1981. "Evidence of the Impact of Mandatory Changes in Accounting Principles on Corporate Loan Agreements." *Journal of Accounting and Economics* 3, no. 1, pp. 3–36.

Lehn, Kenneth, and Annette Poulsen. 1988. "Leveraged Buyouts: Wealth Created or Wealth Redistributed?" in M. Wiedenbaum and K. Chilton (eds.), *Public Policy Toward Corporate Mergers.* New Brunswick, N.J.: Transition Books.

Lewellen, Wilbur G. 1971. *The Ownership Income of Management.* New York: Columbia University Press.

Lewellen, Wilbur, Claudio Loderer, and Kenneth Martin. 1987. "Executive Compensation and Executive Incentive Problems: An Empirical Analysis." *Journal of Accounting and Economics* 9, pp. 287–310.

Lichtenberg, Frank R. 1992. *Corporate Takeovers and Productivity.* Cambridge: MIT Press.

Lichtenberg, Frank R., and Donald Siegel. 1987. "Productivity and Changes in Ownership of Manufacturing Plants." *Brookings Papers on Economic Activity.*

—— 1990a. "The Effect of Ownership Changes on the Employment and Wages of Central Office and Other Personnel." *Journal of Law and Economics* 33, no. 2, pp. 383–408.

—— 1990b. "The Effects of Leveraged Buyouts on Productivity and Related Aspects of Firm Behavior." *Journal of Financial Economics* 27, no. 1, pp. 165–194.

Lilien, Steven, and Victor Pastena. 1982. "Determinants of the Intramethod Choices in the Oil and Gas Industry." *Journal of Accounting and Economics* 4, no. 3, pp. 145–170.

Linn, Scott C., and John J. McConnell. 1983. "An Empirical Investigation of the Impact of 'Antitakeover' Amendments on Common Stock Prices." *Journal of Financial Economics* 11, no. 1–4, pp. 361–399.

Lintner, John. 1965a. "Security Prices, Risk, and Maximal Gains from Diversification." *Journal of Finance* 20 (December), pp. 587–616.

—— 1965b. "The Valuation of Risk Assets and the Selection of Risky Investments in Stock Portfolios and Capital Budgets." *Review of Economics and Statistics* 47, pp. 13–37.

Lipton, Martin. 1989. *Corporate Governance: Major Issues for the 1990s.* Address to the Third Annual Corporate Finance Forum. J. Ira Harris Center for the Study of Corporate Finance, University of Michigan School of Business.

Lipton, Martin, and Jay Lorsch. 1992. "A Modest Proposal for Improved Corporate Governance." *Business Lawyer* 48, pp. 59–77.

Lloyd-Davies, Peter R. 1975. "Optimal Financial Policy in Imperfect Markets." *Journal of Financial and Quantitative Analysis* 10, no. 3, pp. 457ff.

Long, John B. 1972. "Wealth, Welfare, and the Price of Risk." *Journal of Finance* 27, no. 2, pp. 419–433.

—— 1974. "Discussion." *Journal of Finance* 39, no. 12, pp. 185–188.

Loomis, Carol J. 1993. "Dinosaurs?" *Fortune,* May 3, pp. 36–42.

Machlup, F. 1967. "Theories of the Firm: Marginalist, Behavioral, Managerial." *American Economic Review* (March), pp. 1–33.

Magnet, Myron. 1992. "Directors, Wake Up!" *Fortune,* June 15, pp. 85–92.

Malabre, Alfred L., Jr., and Lindley H. Clark. 1992. "Dubious Figures: Productivity Statistics for the Service Sector May Understate Gains." *Wall Street Journal,* August 12.

Malatesta, Paul H. 1983. "The Wealth Effect of Merger Activity and the Objective Functions of Merging Firms." *Journal of Financial Economics* 11, no. 1–4, pp. 155–181.

Malatesta, Paul H., and Ralph A. Walkling. 1988. "Poison Pill Securities: Stockholder Wealth, Profitability, and Ownership Structure." *Journal of Financial Economics* 20.

Mann, Steven V., and Neil W. Sicherman. 1991. "The Agency Costs of Free Cash Flow: Acquisition Activity and Equity Issues." *Journal of Business* 64, pp. 213–227.

Manne, H. G. 1962. "The 'Higher Criticism' of the Modern Corporation." *Columbia Law Review* 62 (March), pp. 259–284.

—— 1965. "Mergers and the Market for Corporate Control." *Journal of Political Economy* (April), pp. 110–120.

—— 1967. "Our Two Corporate Systems: Law and Economics." *Virginia Law Review* 53 (March), pp. 259–284.

—— 1972. "The Social Responsibility of Regulated Utilities." *Wisconsin Law Review* 5, no. 4, pp. 995–1009.

Marais, L., K. Schipper, and A. Smith. 1989. "Wealth Effects of Going Private for Senior Securities." *Journal of Financial Economics* 23, no. 1, pp. 155–191.

Marris, R. 1964. *The Economic Theory of Managerial Capitalism.* Glencoe, Ill.: Free Press of Glencoe.

Martin, Andreas. 1976. "From Joint Consultation to Joint Decision-Making: The Redistribution of Workplace Power in Sweden." *Viewpoint* (June).

Martin, Kenneth J. 1986. "Firm Performance and Managerial Discipline in Contests for Corporate Control." Unpublished manuscript. West Lafayette, Ind.: Purdue University.

Martin, Kenneth J., and John J. McConnell. 1991. "Corporate Performance, Corporate Takeovers, and Management Turnover." *Journal of Finance* 46, no. 2, pp. 671–687.

Mason, E. S. 1959. *The Corporation in Modern Society.* Cambridge: Harvard University Press.

Masulis, Ronald W. 1980. "The Effects of Capital Structure Change on Security Prices: A Study of Exchange Offers." *Journal of Financial Economics* 8, no. 2, pp. 139–178.

—— 1983. "The Impact of Capital Structure Change on Firm Value: Some Estimates." *Journal of Finance* 38, pp. 107–126.

Maurice, S. C., and C. E. Ferguson. 1972. "Factor Usage by Labor-Managed Firms in a Socialist Economy." *Economica* 39 (February), pp. 18–31.

Mayers, David, and Clifford W. Smith, Jr. 1981. "Contractual Provisions, Organizational Structure, and Conflict Control in Insurance Markets." *Journal of Business* 54, no. 3, pp. 407–434.

———— 1986. "Ownership Structure and Control: The Mutualization of Stock Life Insurance Companies." *Journal of Financial Economics* 16, no. 1, pp. 73–99.

———— 1990. "On the Corporate Demand for Insurance: Evidence from the Reinsurance Market." *Journal of Business* 63, no. 1, pp. 19–40.

McCraw, Thomas K. 1981. "Rethinking the Trust Question," in T. McCraw (ed.), *Regulation in Perspective.* Boston: Division of Research, Harvard University Graduate School of Business, distributed by Harvard University Press, pp. 1–55.

———— 1992. "Antitrust: The Perceptions and Reality in Coping with Big Business." Harvard Business School case no. 9–391–292. Boston: Harvard Business School.

McManus, J. C. 1975. "The Costs of Alternative Economic Organizations." *Canadian Journal of Economics* 7 (August), pp. 334–350.

McMurray, Donald L. 1929. *Coxey's Army: A Study of the Industrial Army Movement of 1894.* Boston: Little, Brown.

Meade, J. E. 1972. "The Theory of Labour-Managed Firms and of Profit Sharing." *Economic Journal* 82, pp. 402–428.

———— 1974. "Labour-Managed Firms in Conditions of Imperfect Competition." *Economic Journal* 84 (December) pp. 817–824.

Meckling, William H. 1976. "Values and the Choice of the Model of the Individual in the Social Sciences." *Schweizerische Zeitschrift für Volkswirtschaft* (December).

Medoff, James L., and Katherine G. Abraham. 1980. "Experience, Performance, and Earnings." *Quarterly Journal of Economics* 95 (December), pp. 703–736.

Mergerstat Review. 1991. Schaumburg, Ill.: Merrill Lynch.

———— 1994. Schaumburg, Ill.: Merrill Lynch.

Merton, R. C. 1973. "The Theory of Rational Option Pricing." *Bell Journal of Economics and Management Science* 4, no. 1, pp. 141–183.

———— 1974. "On the Pricing of Corporate Debt: The Risk Structure of Interest Rates." *Journal of Finance* 29, no. 2, pp. 449–470.

Merton, R. C., and M. G. Subrahmanyam. 1974. "The Optimality of a Competitive Stock Market." *Bell Journal of Economics and Management Science* (Spring), pp. 145–170.

Mikkelson, Wayne H. 1981. "Convertible Calls and the Security Returns." *Journal of Financial Economics* 9, no. 3, pp. 237–264.

Miles, J., and J. Rosenfeld. 1983. "An Empirical Analysis of the Effects of Spin-Off Announcements and Shareholder Wealth." *Journal of Finance* 38, pp. 1597–1606.

Miller, M. H., and F. Modigliani. 1966. "Some Estimates of the Cost of Capital to the Electric Utility Industry, 1954–57." *American Economic Review* 48 (June), pp. 333–391.

Modigliani, Franco, and Merton H. Miller. 1958. "The Costs of Capital, Corporate Finance, and the Theory of Investment." *American Economic Review* 48 (June), pp. 261–297.

——— 1963. "Corporate Income Taxes and the Cost of Capital: A Correction." *American Economic Review* 53 (June), pp. 433–443.

Monson, R. J., and Anthony Downs. 1965. "A Theory of Large Managerial Firms." *Journal of Political Economy* (June), pp. 221–236.

Morck, Randall, Andrei Shleifer, and Robert W. Vishny. 1988. "Management Ownership and Market Valuation: An Empirical Analysis." *Journal of Financial Economics* 20, no. 1–2, pp. 3–24.

Munro, J. Richard. 1989. "Takeovers: The Myths Behind the Mystique." *Vital Speeches,* May 15.

Murphy, Kevin J. 1985. "Corporate Performance and Managerial Remuneration: An Empirical Analysis." *Journal of Accounting and Economics* 7 (April), pp. 11–42.

——— 1992. *Executive Compensation in Corporate America, 1992.* Washington, D.C.: United Shareholders Association.

Murphy, Kevin J., and Jay Dial. 1992. "Compensation and Strategy at General Dynamics (A) and (B)." Harvard Business School case nos. 9–493–032 and 9–493–033. Boston: Harvard Business School.

——— 1995. "Incentives, Downsizing, and Value Creation at General Dynamics." *Journal of Financial Economics* 37, no. 3, pp. 261–314.

Myers, Stewart C. 1977. "Determinants of Corporate Borrowing." *Journal of Financial Economics* 5, no. 2, pp. 147–175.

Myers, Stewart C., and Nicholas S. Majluf. 1984. "Corporate Financing and Investment Decisions When Firms Have Information that Investors Do Not Have." *Journal of Financial Economics* 13, no. 2, pp. 187–221.

Neff, Robert, Larry Holyoke, Neil Gross, and Karen Lowry Miller. 1993. "Fixing Japan." *Business Week,* March 29.

Ofek, Eli. 1993. "Capital Structure and Firm Response to Poor Performance: An Empirical Analysis." *Journal of Financial Economics* 34, no. 1, pp. 3–30.

Office of the Chief Economist of the SEC. 1986. *The Economics of Poison Pills,* March 5.

Oi, Walter Y., and Elisabeth M. Clayton. 1968. "A Peasant's View of a Soviet Collective Farm." *American Economic Review* 58, no. 1, pp. 37–59.

Palepu, Krishna G. 1986. "Predicting Takeover Targets: A Methodological and Empirical Analysis." *Journal of Accounting and Economics* 8, no. 1, pp. 3–35.

——— 1990. "Consequences of Leveraged Buyouts." *Journal of Financial Economics* 27, no. 1, pp. 247–262.

Partch, M. Megan. 1987. "The Creation of a Class of Limited Voting Common Stock and Shareholder Wealth." *Journal of Financial Economics* 18, no. 2, pp. 313–339.

Pejovich, Svetoyar. 1969. "The Firm, Monetary Policy and Property Rights in a Planned Economy." *Western Economic Journal* 7, no. 3, pp. 193–200.

Penrose, E. 1958. *The Theory of the Growth of the Firm.* New York: Wiley.

Polinsky, A. Mitchell. 1989. *An Introduction to Law and Economics.* Boston: Little, Brown.

Pontiff, Jeffrey, Andrei Shleifer, and Michael S. Weisbach. 1990. "Reversions of

Excess Pension Assets after Takeovers." *Rand Journal of Economics* 21, pp. 600–613.

Porter, Michael E. 1990. *Competitive Advantage of Nations*. New York: Free Press.

—— 1992a. *Capital Choices: Changing the Way America Invests in Industry*. Washington, D.C.: The Council on Competitiveness, cosponsored by Harvard Business School.

—— 1992b. "Capital Choices: Changing the Way America Invests in Industry." *Journal of Applied Corporate Finance* 5, pp. 4–16.

—— 1992c. "Capital Disadvantage: America's Failing Capital Investment System." *Harvard Business Review* 70, no. 5, pp. 65–82.

Posner, Richard A. 1977. *Economic Analysis of Law*. Boston: Little, Brown.

Pound, John. 1988. "Proxy Contests and the Efficiency of Shareholder Oversight." *Journal of Financial Economics* 20, no. 1–2, pp. 237–265.

—— 1991. "Proxy Voting and the SEC: Investor Protection Versus Market Efficiency." *Journal of Financial Economics* 29, no. 2, pp. 241–285.

—— 1992. "Beyond Takeovers: Politics Comes to Corporate Control." *Harvard Business Review* 70, no. 2, pp. 83–93.

—— 1993. "The Rise of the Political Model of Corporate Governance and Corporate Control." Unpublished manuscript. Cambridge: Harvard University, Kennedy School of Government.

Preston, L. E. 1975. "Corporation and Society: The Search for a Paradigm." *Journal of Economic Literature* 13 (June), pp. 434–453.

Reagan, Patricia B., and Rene M. Stulz. 1986. "Risk Bearing, Labor Contracts, and Capital Markets." *Research in Finance* 6, pp. 217–232.

Reinganum, M. R. 1985. "The Effect of Executive Succession on Stockholder Wealth." *Administrative Science Quarterly* 30, pp. 46–60.

Reynolds, A. William. 1988. Testimony by chairman and CEO, GenCorp Inc., before the Subcommittee on Oversight and Investigations, U.S. House Committee on Energy and Commerce. February 8.

Richman, Louis S. 1993. "Why the Economic Data Mislead Us." *Fortune,* March 8.

Roberts, Paul Craig. 1969. "The Polycentric Soviet Economy." *Journal of Law and Economics* 12, no. 1, pp. 163–179.

Roe, Mark J. 1990. "Political and Legal Restraints on Ownership and Control of Public Companies." *Journal of Financial Economics* 27, no. 1, pp. 7–42.

—— 1991. "A Political Theory of American Corporate Finance." *Columbia Law Review* 91, pp. 10–67.

Rosen, Sherwin. 1982. "Authority, Control, and the Distribution of Earnings." *Bell Journal of Economics and Management Science* 13, pp. 311–323.

Rosett, Joshua G. 1990. "Do Union Wealth Concessions Explain Takeover Premiums?" *Journal of Financial Economics* 27, no. 1, pp. 263–282.

Ross, Steven A. 1973. "The Economic Theory of Agency: The Principal's Problems." *American Economic Review* 62 (May), pp. 134–139.

—— 1974a. "The Economic Theory of Agency and the Principle of Similarity," in M. D. Balch et al. (eds.), *Essays on Economic Behavior under Uncertainty.* Amsterdam: North-Holland.

—— 1974b. "Options and Efficiency." Rodney L. White Center for Financial Research Working Paper no. 3074. Philadelphia: University of Pennsylvania.

—— 1977. "The Determination of Financial Structure: The Incentive-Signalling Approach." *Bell Journal of Economics and Management Science* 8, pp. 23–40.

Rozeff, Michael. 1982. "Growth, Beta and Agency Costs as Determinants of Dividend Payout Ratios." *Journal of Financial Research* 5, pp. 249–259.

Ruback, Richard S. 1988a. "Coercive Dual Class Exchange Offers." *Journal of Financial Economics* 20, no. 1–2, pp. 153–173.

—— 1988b. "Do Target Shareholders Lose in Unsuccessful Control Contests?" in Alan Auerbach (ed.), *Economics Effects of Mergers and Acquisitions.* Chicago: University of Chicago Press.

Rubenstein, M. 1974. "A Discrete-Time Synthesis of Financial Theory, Parts I and II." Institute of Business and Economic Research Working Papers no. 20 and 21. Berkeley: University of California.

Ryden, Rune. 1978. "Labour Participation in the Management of Business Firms in Sweden," in Svetoyar Pejovich (ed.), *The Codetermination Movement in the West.* Lexington, Mass.: Heath.

Ryngaert, Michael. 1988. "The Effect of Poison Pill Securities on Shareholder Wealth." *Journal of Financial Economics* 20, no. 1–2, pp. 377–417.

Sahlman, William A. 1990. "The Structure and Governance of Venture-Capital Organizations." *Journal of Financial Economics* 27, no. 2, pp. 473–521.

Sahlman, William A., and Howard H. Stevenson. 1985. "Capital Market Myopia." *Journal of Business Venturing* 1, pp. 7–30.

Salomon Brothers High Yield Research Group. 1991. *Original Issue High Yield Default Study—1990 Summary.* January 28.

Saporito, Bill. 1988. "The Tough Cookie at RJR Nabisco." *Fortune,* July 18.

Schipper, Katherine, and Abbie Smith. 1983. "Effects of Recontracting on Shareholder Wealth: The Case of Voluntary Spin-Offs." *Journal of Financial Economics* 12, no. 4, pp. 434–466.

Schipper, Katherine, and Rex Thompson. 1983. "Evidence on the Capitalized Value of Merger Activity for Acquiring Firms." *Journal of Financial Economics* 11, no. 1–4, pp. 85–119.

Schumpeter, Joseph A. 1976. *Capitalism, Socialism and Democracy.* New York: Harper & Row.

Scitovsky, T. 1943. "A Note on Profit Maximisation and Its Implications." *Review of Economic Studies* 11, pp. 57–60.

Sharpe, W. F. 1964. "Capital Asset Prices: A Theory of Market Equilibrium under Conditions of Risk." *Journal of Finance* 19 (September), pp. 425–442.

Shenfield, Arthur. 1978. "Labour Participation in Great Britain," in Svetoyar Pejovich (ed.), *The Codetermination Movement in the West.* Lexington, Mass.: Heath.

Shleifer, Andrei, and Larry Summers. 1988. "Breach of Trust in Hostile Takeovers," in A. Auerbach (ed.), *Corporate Takeovers: Causes and Consequences.* Chicago: University of Chicago Press, pp. 33–56.

Shleifer, Andrei, and Robert W. Vishny. 1986. "Large Shareholders and Corporate Control." *Journal of Political Economy* 94, pp. 461–488.

———— 1989. "Management Entrenchment: The Case of Manager-Specific Investments." *Journal of Financial Economics* 25, no. 1, pp. 123–139.

Shubik, M. 1970. "A Curmudgeon's Guide to Microeconomics." *Journal of Economic Literature* 8 (June), pp. 405–434.

Silver, M., and R. Auster. 1969. "Entrepreneurship, Profit, and Limits on Firm Size." *Journal of Business* 42 (July), pp. 277–281.

Simon, Herbert A. 1955. "A Behavioral Model of Rational Choice." *Quarterly Journal of Economics* 69, pp. 99–118.

———— 1959. "Theories of Decision Making in Economics and Behavioral Science." *American Economic Review* (June), pp. 253–283.

Smith, Abbie J. 1990. "Corporate Ownership Structure and Performance: The Case of Management Buyouts." *Journal of Financial Economics* 27, no. 1, pp. 143–164.

Smith, Adam. [1776] 1937. *The Wealth of Nations.* Edited by Edwin Cannan. Reprint, New York: Modern Library.

Smith, Clifford W., Jr. 1976. "Option Pricing: A Review." *Journal of Financial Economics* 2, no. 1–2, pp. 3–52.

———— 1982. "Pricing Mortgage Originations." *Journal of the American Real Estate & Urban Economics Association* 10, no. 3, pp. 313–330.

———— 1983. "Corporate Dividend Policy: An Analysis of Dividend Reinvestment Plans." Unpublished manuscript. Rochester, N.Y.: University of Rochester.

———— 1986. "Investment Banking and the Capital Acquisition Process." *Journal of Financial Economics* 15, no. 1–2, pp. 3–29.

Smith, Clifford W., Jr., and René Stulz. 1983. "Determinants of Firms' Hedging Policies." *Journal of Financial and Quantitative Analysis* 20, no. 4, pp. 391–405.

Smith, Clifford W., Jr., L. MacDonald Wakeman, and Gregory D. Hawkins. 1985. "Determinants of Corporate Leasing Policy/Discussion." *Journal of Finance* 40, no. 3, pp. 895–910.

Smith, Clifford W., Jr., and Jerold B. Warner. 1979. "On Financial Contracting: An Analysis of Bond Covenants." *Journal of Financial Economics* 7, no. 2, pp. 117–161.

Smith, Clifford W., Jr., and Ross Watts. 1982. "Incentive and Tax Effects on Executive Compensation Plans." *Australian Journal of Management* 7, pp. 139–157.

———— 1983. "The Structure of Executive Compensation Contracts and the Control of Management." Unpublished manuscript. Rochester, N.Y.: University of Rochester.

Spence, Michael, and R. Zeckhauser. 1971. "Insurance, Information and Individual Action." *American Economic Review* 61, no. 2, pp. 380–387.

Steiner, I. D. 1972. *Group Process and Productivity.* New York: Academic Press.

Steinherr, Alfred, and Vanek Jaroslav. 1976. "Labor-Managed Firms in Conditions of Imperfect Competition: A Comment." *Economic Journal* 86 (June), pp. 339–341.

Stewart, G. Bennett. 1990. "Remaking the Corporation from Within." *Harvard Business Review* 68, no. 4, pp. 126–137.

Stiglitz, Joseph E. 1975. "Incentives, Risk, and Information: Notes Toward a Theory of Hierarchy." *Bell Journal of Economics and Management Science* 6 (Autumn), pp. 552–579.

Stulz, René M. 1988. "Managerial Control of Voting Rights." *Journal of Financial Economics* 20, no. 1–2, pp. 25–54.

––––– 1990. "Managerial Discretion and Optimal Financing Policies." *Journal of Financial Economics* 26, pp. 3–27.

Stulz, René M., and Herb Johnson. 1985. "An Analysis of Secured Debt." *Journal of Financial Economics* 14, no. 4, pp. 501–520.

Sull, Donald N., Richard S. Tedlow, and Richard S. Rosenbloom. 1997. "Managerial Commitments and Technological Change in the US Tire Industry." *Industrial & Corporate Change* 6, no. 2, pp. 461–501.

Swartz, L. Mick. 1992. "The Impact of Third Generation Antitakeover Laws on Security Value." Unpublished manuscript. University of Manitoba.

Tedlow, Richard. 1991. "Hitting the Skids: Tires and Time Horizons." Unpublished manuscript. Boston: Harvard Business School.

Tiemann, Jonathan. 1990. "The Economics of Exit and Restructuring: The Pabst Brewing Company." Unpublished manuscript. Boston: Harvard Business School.

U.S. Bureau of the Census. 1987. *Census of Manufacturing*. Washington, D.C.: U.S. Government Printing Office.

U.S. Bureau of the Census, Housing and Household Economics Statistics Division. 1991. Washington, D.C.: U.S. Government Printing Office.

U.S. Department of Labor, Bureau of Labor Statistics, Office of Productivity and Technology. 1990. *Multifactor Productivity Measures*.

U.S. Department of Labor, Bureau of Labor Statistics. 1991. *International Comparisons of Manufacturing Productivity and Unit Labor Cost Trends*.

van Delden, Hendrik H. 1993. "Czech and Slovak Republics: Lands of Opportunity." *ITS Textile Leader* (Spring), pp. 43–48.

Vanek, Jan. 1972. *The Economics of Workers' Management: A Yugoslav Case Study*. London: Allen & Unwin.

Vanek, Jaroslav. 1970. *The General Theory of Labor-Managed Market Economics*. Ithaca, N.Y.: Cornell University Press.

––––– 1971. *The Participatory Economy: An Evolutionary Hypothesis and a Strategy for Development*. Ithaca, N.Y.: Cornell University Press.

––––– 1974. "Uncertainty and the Investment Decision Under Labour-Management and the Social Efficiency Implications." Discussion paper no. 83. Ithaca, N.Y.: Cornell University.

Vietor, Richard. 1994. *Contrived Competition*. Cambridge: Harvard University Press.

Wakeman, L. Macdonald. 1981. "The Function of Bond Rating Agencies: Theory and Evidence." Unpublished manuscript. Rochester, N.Y.: University of Rochester.

Waldman, Peter. 1989. "New RJR Chief Faces a Daunting Challenge at Debt Heavy Firm." *Wall Street Journal,* March 14, p. A1.

Waldo, Charles N. 1985. *Boards of Directors: Their Changing Roles, Structure, and Information Needs.* Westport, Conn.: Quorum Books.

Walsh, James P. 1988. "Top Management Turnover Following Mergers and Acquisitions." *Strategic Management Journal* 9, no. 2, pp. 173–183.

Ward, B. 1958. "The Firm in Illyria: Market Syndicalism." *American Economic Review* 48 (September), pp. 566–589.

Warner, Jerold B. 1977. "Bankruptcy, Absolute Priority, and the Pricing of Risky Debt Claims." *Journal of Financial Economics* 4, no. 3, pp. 239–276.

Warner, Jerold B., Ross L. Watts, and Karen H. Wruck. 1988. "Stock Prices and Top Management Changes." *Journal of Financial Economics* 20, no. 1–2, pp. 461–492.

Watson, Bruce. 1993. "For a While the Luddites Had a Smashing Success." *Smithsonian* (April), pp. 140–154.

Weisbach, Michael S. 1988. "Outside Directors and CEO Turnovers." *Journal of Financial Economics* 20, no. 1–2, pp. 431–460.

Wier, Peggy. 1983. "The Costs of Antimerger Lawsuits: Evidence from the Stock Market." *Journal of Financial Economics* 11, no. 1–4, pp. 207–224.

Williamson, Oliver E. 1964. *The Economics of Discretionary Behavior: Managerial Objectives in a Theory of the Firm.* Englewood Cliffs, N.J.: Prentice-Hall.

—— 1970. *Corporate Control and Business Behavior.* Englewood Cliffs, N.J.: Prentice-Hall.

—— 1975. *Markets and Hierarchies: Analysis and Antitrust Implications.* New York: Free Press.

Wilson, R. 1968. "On the Theory of Syndicates." *Econometrica* 36 (January), pp. 119–132.

—— 1969. "La Decision: Agregation et Dynamique des Orders de Preference," in *Editions du Centre National de la Recherche Scientifique.* Paris: Centre National de la Recherche Scientifique, pp. 288–307.

Wolfson, Mark A. 1983. "Empirical Evidence of Incentive Problems and Their Mitigation in Oil and Gas Tax Shelter Programs." Unpublished manuscript. Stanford: Stanford University.

Wruck, Karen H. 1989. "Equity Ownership Concentration and Firm Value." *Journal of Financial Economics* 23, no. 1, pp. 3–30.

—— 1990. "Financial Distress, Reorganization, and Organizational Efficiency." *Journal of Financial Economics* 27, no. 2, pp. 420–444.

—— 1991. "What Really Went Wrong at Revco?" *Journal of Applied Corporate Finance* 4, pp. 79–92.

—— 1994. "Financial Policy, Internal Control, and Performance: Sealed Air Corporation's Leveraged Special Dividend." *Journal of Financial Economics* 36, no. 2, pp. 157–192.

—— 1997. "Sealed Air Corporation's Leveraged Recapitalization (A) and (B)." Harvard Business School cases no. 9–294–122 and 9–294–123. Boston: Harvard Business School.

Wruck, Karen H., and Michael C. Jensen. 1994. "Science, Specific Knowledge and Total Quality Management." *Journal of Accounting and Economics* 18, pp. 247–287. Reprinted in Michael C. Jensen, *Foundations of Organizational Strategy* (Cambridge: Harvard University Press, 1998).

Wruck, Karen H., and A. Scott Keating. 1992a. "Sterling Chemicals, Inc." Harvard Business School case no. 9–493–025. Boston: Harvard Business School.

—— 1992b. "Sterling Chemicals, Inc.: Quality and Productivity Improvement Program." Harvard Business School case no. 9–493–026. Boston: Harvard Business School.

Wruck, Karen H., and Krishna Palepu. 1992. "Consequences of Leveraged Shareholder Payouts: Defensive versus Voluntary Recapitalizations." Harvard Business School Working Paper. Boston: Harvard Business School.

Wruck, Karen H., and Steve-Anna Stephens. 1992a. "Leveraged Buyouts and Restructuring: The Case of Safeway, Inc." Harvard Business School case no. 192–095. Boston: Harvard Business School.

—— 1992b. "Leveraged Buyouts and Restructuring: The Case of Safeway, Inc.: Media Response." Harvard Business School case no. 192–094. Boston: Harvard Business School.

Wytmar. 1974. *Wall Street Journal*, August 13.

Yago, Glenn. 1991. "The Credit Crunch: A Regulatory Squeeze on Growth Capital." *Journal of Applied Corporate Finance* (Spring).

Zellner, Wendy. 1992. "Not Everybody Loves Wal-Mart's Low Prices." *Wall Street Journal*, October 12.

Zimmerman, Jerold L. 1979. "The Costs and Benefits of Cost Allocations." *The Accounting Review* (July), pp. 504–521.

Zmijewski, M., and R. Hagerman. 1981. "An Income Strategy Approach to the Positive Theory of Accounting Standard Setting/Choice." *Journal of Accounting and Economics* 3 (August), pp. 129–149.

Acknowledgments

Chapter 1: U.S. Corporate Governance: Lessons from the 1980s

This chapter draws heavily on Michael C. Jensen, "Corporate Control and the Politics of Finance," *Journal of Applied Corporate Finance* 4, no. 2 (Summer 1991).

Chapter 2: The Modern Industrial Revolution, Exit, and the Failure of Internal Control Systems

Presidential Address to the American Finance Association, January 1993, Anaheim, California. I appreciate the research assistance of Chris Allen, Brian Barry, Susan Brumfield, Karin Monsler, and particularly Donna Feinberg; the support of the Division of Research of the Harvard Business School; and the comments and discussions with George Baker, Carliss Baldwin, Joseph Bower, Alfred Chandler, Harry and Linda DeAngelo, Ben Esty, Takashi Hikino, Steve Kaplan, Nancy Koehn, Claudio Loderer, George Lodge, John Long, Kevin Murphy, Malcolm Salter, René Stulz, Richard Tedlow, and especially Richard Hackman, Robert Hall, and Karen Wruck on many of these ideas.

Chapter 3: Active Investors, LBOs, and the Privatization of Bankruptcy

General research support was received from the Harvard Business School Division of Research and a grant was awarded by Drexel Burnham Lambert to the University of Rochester.

Chapter 4: Theory of the Firm

An earlier version of this chapter was presented at the Conference on Analysis and Ideology, Interlaken, Switzerland, June 1974, sponsored by the Center for Research in Government Policy and Business at the University of Rochester, Graduate School of Management. We are indebted to Fischer Black, Eugene Fama, Roger Ibbotson, William Klein, Michael Rozeff, Roman Weil, Oliver Williamson, an anonymous referee, and to our colleagues and members of the Finance Workshop at the University of Rochester for their comments and criticisms, in particular George Benston, Michael Canes, David Henderson, Keith Leffler, John Long, Clifford Smith, Rex Thompson, Ross Watts, and Jerold Zimmerman.

Chapter 5: Stockholder, Manager, and Creditor Interests

This research was supported by the Managerial Economics Research Center at the University of Rochester Graduate School of Management and the Salomon Brothers Center for the Study of Financial Institutions, Graduate School of Business Administration, New York University. We are indebted to Edward Altman and Marti Subrahmanyam for helpful comments and suggestions and to William H. Meckling for many stimulating discussions on the material discussed here.

Chapter 6: Rights and Production Functions

Presented at the Conference on the Effects of Labor Participation in the Management of Business Firms in the Western World, Dallas, February 1977, sponsored by the Liberty Fund; and at the Fourth Annual Interlaken Seminar on Analysis and Ideology, Interlaken, June 1977, sponsored by the Center for Research in Government Policy and Business at the University of Rochester. We are indebted to David Henderson, Eugene Fama, Keith Leffler, Frank Milne, Tom Russell, Jerold Zimmerman, and the participants in the Economics Workshop at the University of Rochester Graduate School of Management for discussions on these issues, but they should not be held responsible for our refusal to accept some of their suggestions. We are also indebted to an anonymous referee and John Gould for comments, and to Armen Alchian for helping us over the years to understand more clearly the importance of rights in determining human behavior. This work has been partially supported by the Managerial Economics Research Center at the University of Rochester Graduate School of Management.

Chapter 7: Organizational Forms and Investment Decisions

Financial support for Fama's participation is from the National Science Foundation. Jensen is supported by the Managerial Economics Research Center at the University of Rochester Graduate School of Management. The comments of Armen Alchian, Fischer Black, Douglas Breeden, Harry DeAngelo, Douglas Diamond, John Hetherington, Richard Leftwich, David Mayers, Haim Mendelson, and especially John Long are gratefully acknowledged.

Chapter 8: The Distribution of Power among Corporate Managers, Shareholders, and Directors

This research is supported by the Managerial Economics Research Center at the University of Rochester Graduate School of Management; the Division of Research, Harvard Business School; and the John M. Olin Foundation. We are grateful for helpful comments from James Brickley, Harry DeAngelo, Linda DeAngelo, Oliver Hart, Clifford Holderness, John Long, Richard Ruback, G. William Schwert, Clifford Smith, Michael Weisbach, Toni Wolcott, and Karen Wruck.

Index

ABA-ALI Model Non-Profit Corporation Act, 221
Accounting policy, 147
Acquisitions, 232
Active investor(s): defined, 54, 64; importance of, 64–67
Agency costs, 3, 5, 66, 85–87, 140, 149, 154, 155, 161, 162, 165, 166, 228, 229; defined, 86, 137–138, 178; in manager-operated firms, 105–106; of alternative contractual forms, 178; of debt, 111–120; of free cash flow, 33, 55; of outside equity, 89–108; of rental arrangements, 178; outside owner and control problem, 128–129; reducing, 115–116; sources of, of equity, 91–97
Agency problem(s), 138, 142; approach to, 87; between managers and residual claimants, 140, 142; defined, 87; multiperiod aspects, 128
Agency relationship, 137
Agency theory, 5, 6, 136, 137–138, 139; defined, 57
American Law Institute, 78
Anders, William, 38
Antitakeover amendments, 36, 152, 153, 237
Antitrust laws, 17
Asset substitution, 161, 165
AT&T, 35, 44, 45, 48; breakup and deregulation of, 34

Bankers, role of, 64
Bankruptcy, 157, 165, 228, 241; as way of rewriting contracts, 34; costs of, 116–119
Barbarians at the Gate, 10, 11, 269
Bass Brothers, 66
Bell Atlantic, 48
Bell system, breakup and deregulation of, 45
BellSouth, 48
Benchmark strategy, defined, 39
Berkshire Hathaway, 54, 66

Black-Scholes model, 113, 114
Board failure, components of: CEO as chairman, 53–54; culture, 49–50; resurrecting active investors, 54
Board of directors, 2, 65, 67, 129, 144, 147, 148; and equity, 240; and poison pills, 241; and problems with internal control system(s), 49; share ownership, 229, 238; staggered election of members, 153
Bond covenants, 154, 160, 165, 247
Bondholder loss issue, 72
Bondholder-stockholder conflict: covenants of, 160–165; from financial restrictions, 155–158; sources of, 153–165; and stock repurchases, 158
Bonding costs, 137; role of, 115–116
Bonding expenditures, relation to agency costs, 178
Bonuses, 38, 147
Bonus plans, 146, 147; Soviet, 197
Book value basis, 74
Borden, 11
Bristol Myers, 48
British Gas, 48
British Telecom, 48
Bronfmans, 66
Buffett, Warren, 54, 66
Business Roundtable, 10, 67

Call options, 161
Campeau, 77
Capacity-expanding technological change, 23
Capital asset-pricing model, 58
Capital budgeting, 59
Capital markets, 35, 107, 121, 142, 148, 162, 163, 220, 224, 235, 247; and high-yield bonds, 22; history of, 34; in the 1890s, 20; in the 1980s, 16; monitoring and discipline function, 22; relative to LBO associations and venture funds, 57; role of, 31; role of, in eliminating excess